Several years ago, Allie worked as a[n] [...] is an honor to recommend her story, written with her mother, [...] Zina and Allie journeyed through the horrors of cancer, wrestled with unanswered questions when God didn't make sense, and pressed on in unshakable hope in Christ. *Called to Live a Vibrant Life* is a story of love, hope, and joy as well as loss. This is a story of a life lived beautifully for God's glory. This story—and the people in it—moved me deeply and will do the same for you.

Peter Greer
President & CEO Hope International

Written with transparent honesty and deep and abiding love, Zina Speck shares the story of her daughter Allie's five-year journey with cancer—a journey that transformed the lives of others who came to know Allie and witness her faith and determination. Much of Allie's educational career at Messiah University was punctuated by illness, physical pain, hospitalization and treatment, but it was the power of her testimony that defined her legacy for our community. In a morning chapel she inspired students and faculty when she quoted Canon T.D. Harford-Battersby: "…so long as I have trusted Him, He has kept me. He has been faithful." Being faithful in the midst of suffering even unto death is a powerful lesson. Zina and Allie Speck's example is an encouragement for all of us.

Kim S. Phipps, PhD
President of Messiah University in Mechanicsburg, PA

Called to Live a Vibrant Life: Standing Firm and Suffering Well in the Midst of Cancer is a raw and emotional retelling of a courageous health battle. I knew Allie Speck as someone whose faith gave her an unwavering emotional peace even as her young body was being physically ravaged by a dreadful disease. Reading her real, unfiltered journal entries throughout her fight, one can only be left in awe of her strength, her dedication to others and her devotion to God. In combining her own words and heartbreaking perspective with her daughter's private thoughts, author Zina Speck has given Allie a beautiful and lasting legacy of faith and fortitude…and she has given us all a blueprint for how to fight, how to serve, how to live and how to love.

Ali Lanyon
Morning News Anchor, abc27 Harrisburg, PA

CALLED TO LIVE A VIBRANT LIFE

Standing Firm and Suffering Well in the Midst of Cancer

ALLISON SPECK AND ZINA SPECK

Foreword by Jessica C. Shand, MD

Paperback ISBN 978-1-960007-04-9
eBook ISBN 978-1-960007-05-6

Published by

Mercy & Moxie

an imprint of
Orison Publishers, Inc.
PO Box 188, Grantham, PA 17027
www.OrisonPublishers.com

A NOTE TO READERS

Called to Live a Vibrant Life, the story of Allison Speck's journey of faith, is told by two people: Allison and her mother, Zina Speck. Allison's narration is presented in italics, and Zina's narration is in "regular" roman type. Other material, such as Zina's emails to Allie Speck's prayer warriors and Allison's journal entries, poetry, stories, and testimonies, are labeled as such. The sources of quoted material are listed on the References pages at the end of the book.

To Lisa & Rich.

May Allie's testimony
inspire you to live
vibrantly for Christ!

♡allie Zina

CONTENTS

FOREWORD

When I first met Allison, I was near the beginning of my journey as a pediatric oncologist. As it would turn out, I was at the very beginning of an even deeper journey in faith, of love and in the search for meaning. Allison and her incredible family had come into our care seeking answers and definitive treatments for her cancer, and, most importantly, for hope. That journey of medicine, faith and hope—woven together beautifully in this book, often in her own poignant words—would take us to the greatest heights of joy, depths of grief and every imaginable place in between. In the years that followed that fateful meeting and despite the difference in our ages, life experiences and roles we played in the physician-patient relationship, Allison and I grew up together. Only in retrospect, now in the middle of my career, can I look back and realize what a seminal moment that fateful day in January was for my journey as a physician, a person of faith, an educator and a person called deeply to ministry of the suffering.

In medical training, we are taught the importance of placing healthy boundaries—whether emotional, psychological or physical—between ourselves and our patients for the sake of professionalism and sustainability. Deeper, experiential conversations about how we define "boundaries," or even "healthy," are often lacking, as is any mention of the care of the spirit. And while self-preservation has its merit in the difficult work of healing, I knew the moment I looked into Allison's eyes and shook her weary parents' hands that this would be a therapeutic relationship like none other. I realized in that moment, and every moment since, that I was called into that place to provide all dimensions of healing—including but not limited to cutting-edge science, a respect for faith and a continually open heart. Caring for Allison helped me define, and continue to define, what holding an open heart truly means.

A common refrain I hear from my medical students, nurses and physicians-in-training—particularly when they encounter a child or young adult suffering from cancer—is that there is nothing in their education that prepares them for the reality of this particular kind of suffering. The care (and the love) of a child or young adult with cancer challenges many assumptions we might hold about how the world is supposed to work, what our life cycle is supposed to look like, what life and death are supposed to look like. It has a way of showing us everything that was possible and everything that is being taken away. While I thought I understood all of this, at least in the theoretical sense, Allison taught me what it meant to live this truth: gracefully, without remorse and with a courage that can only come from equal parts humble devotion and a tenacious will to live and serve. Allison taught us what is given back when we lean into a faith in a mysterious, all-encompassing, universal holy Love.

In the way that she lived with cancer and in the way that she died, Allison has now also taught a generation of my students and colleagues what it truly means to attend to the suffering of a person of faith, with faith. In the later stages of Allison's illness, I completed my oncology training and moved back home to begin my professional career as an oncologist and medical educator. Our conversations continued, regarding a meaningful life and a dignified death. We giggled over her honeymoon photos while working through some tough theological questions about keeping faith in God's plan even if it meant that plan would take away everything that made sense and was held dear. I kept in touch with Allison's oncology team, who continued to work with her to balance treatment options with her goals of living fully in love and faith. During those conversations, I could feel my soul and spirit shift, and it became almost blindingly clear that Allison's journey was guiding me toward a less-trodden path in medicine, in which to better understand and to create more change in the healthcare system at that holy intersection of body and spirit.

I often teach my students that, to really attend to suffering, we must be willing to hold contradicting truths in the same space. I learned this from Allison as she navigated progressive cancer and hope for her future at the same time as a young woman in her 20s. She studied fearlessly, she traveled fearlessly, she LOVED fearlessly—and I really cannot overemphasize this fact—in a way that was informed but also unencumbered by the cancer that slowly destroyed her physical body. She made the two most courageous choices that I have ever witnessed and am ever likely to witness: to choose unconditional love and to choose to stop, for a time, temporizing treatments that would not cure her and left her less able to participate fully in the life she was creating.

Allison reminded us, just as any faith in a higher power reminds us, that how the world is supposed to work is neither up to us nor a product of our own limited design. Allison was steadfast in her belief in a God not only of mercy but also of mystery. As her cancer journey brought her deeper into suffering, Allison often told me, "There is a fine line between faith and denial. I'm not in denial." Allison faced death with as much hope and ferocity as she faced her life. When my phone rang with the news of her death in the early hours of my tradition of Ash Wednesday, it was Allison's voice that reminded me that though we are made of dust and shall return to dust, everything in between was for us to manifest with love, and the greatest medicine of all is to understand all the dimensions of what that love means.

Almost a year to the day after Allison's death—and I would like to think she would have been proud of this—I enrolled in a theological seminary. Caring for Allison moved me out of the intellectual comfort zone of traditional medical training and helped me realize that if we are to fully attend to suffering, then regardless of our profession or relationship to the sufferer, we need to explore and understand all dimensions of it. I'd like to think that Allison would have gotten a kick out of my staying up late writing papers as she often did during long chemotherapy infusions sessions—and probably with entirely more skill and patience! I hope she would be proud that her story, and her testimony, continue to educate students preparing for careers not only in medicine, but also in chaplaincy and pastoral care. Allison's legacy is one of love, inspiration and holding suffering and hope in the same blessed space. I hope her story reaches deep into your soul, just as it did mine.

Jessica C. Shand, MD
February 3, 2023

CHAPTER ONE
DID HE GET IT?

The room was quiet.

I opened my eyes, and light flooded into my world. Everything was foggy and distant, like I was submerged in water. The next instant my head seemed to surface and sound invaded my ears, crashing into me like an unexpected wave. I was not confused; I was not unaware; I was awake. I tried desperately to find a face, but everything was a white and green blur of lights and scrub uniforms. I opened my mouth, and words slurred out of the corners.

"Did he get it?"

"Did he get it?" It was more of a groan than a question. I could feel myself being moved and positioned. Things were detached and reattached all over my body. I felt dozens of hands and heard dozens of distant voices.

"Shhh. Just go back to sleep. The surgery is over," a woman's voice said. She was somewhere above my head. I tried to arch my back or turn my head, but I couldn't move. I could smell her rubber gloves.

"Wait, wait..." Tears started to form in the corners of my eyes while tightness formed in my chest. "I need to know if he got it." Words became a little easier as I concentrated on forming my mouth around one of the hardest questions of my life. "Did he get it?"

"It's okay. The doctor will talk to you in a little while, just go back to sleep. Okay?"

My arm suddenly found life, and I groped across the operating table. I found something that felt like an arm and held fast.

"No," I said a little louder. "I need you to tell me if he got it! I need to know!" Suddenly I felt something pulling at me, and the bright lights started to fade. The last thing I remember was a small voice that seemed to almost start outside and then finish inside my head. I couldn't tell if it was my voice or someone else's that whispered, "He didn't get it."

The next time my eyes opened, I could hear my mother. It was a different room, a darker room.

"Mom." She was to my right; I could feel her there on the other side of the bed rail.

"Mom…" I paused my voice, unable to finish. "Mom, he didn't get it?" I wanted her to say, "Yes, of course he got it!" I wanted everything to be okay. I wanted everything from before to be a bad dream. I held onto the bed rail and felt her hand on mine.

"No, honey…he didn't get it."

From somewhere deep inside of me, a place I could never find again if I tried, something cracked open and shook loose a sound that came from both inside and outside my body. I could feel the movement of noise in my throat and the vibration in my ears, but I could not hear it. I was far away, and my world was silent and unresponsive until my mother's voice seemed to push through my ears.

"Shhh, shhh, it's okay. Listen," she pleaded over the noise.

The sound was me, and I was screaming.

"No!" I shrieked at the top of my lungs. "No!" I screamed and sobbed the words. Although my brain still could not wrap itself completely around the magnitude of my devastation, it seemed my voice understood.

It was a death sentence…

CHAPTER TWO
CALLED

Allison Margaret Speck was born on December 28, 1990, during a snow-storm. She entered the world two weeks late and thus began her notorious ability to be late for everything. She was a healthy, robust baby, weighing nine pounds and six ounces. She created drama from the very beginning of her life, as her heart rate plummeted with each contraction, causing her to be delivered via emergency C-section.

We nicknamed her Allie. She was a sweet baby who traveled well and loved adventure! We took her everywhere. She grew up in my parents' motor home and at her dad's softball games. She began walking at nine months, and there was no turning back.

She had a normal suburban childhood filled with watching tractors make hay, riding bikes and spending lots of time outside. Allison loved her Pop Pop and Nanny, who lived next door. She was their first grandchild, and she basked in the attention.

At the age of five, she became a big sister. At first she was disappointed that her brother, Andy, was a boy and not a girl, but she changed her mind as soon as she held him. Even though they were five years apart, they became very close and spent lots of time together. Allison was creative from a young age. She wrote plays and created wardrobes for her brother, telling him how to stand and what to say. Together they created a stage with sheets and used stuffed animals as characters, entertaining us with their detailed productions.

As Allie grew older, she began to demonstrate a love of storytelling, drawing and writing. We took a coffee table and turned it into her "desk." She had a play typewriter, markers, crayons and lots of paper. She would sit at her "desk" for hours, writing wonderful stories with pictures. She had an amazing gift for imitating actors and actresses from TV, repeating their lines with exact tone and voice. She loved to sit in the bathtub and always asked me to read books. One night when I could not remember where we had stopped reading, Allison said she remembered. Without any hesitation, she repeated word-for-word the exact sentence where I had stopped reading the night before. I was amazed!

I loved it all: reading, writing, connecting with authors and characters. I understood the books I read—deeply. Sometimes I connected more with them than with other kids. Nobody else understood the fantastic, amazing places my mind had been, the way my brain never stopped working, the deep way I felt everything. No one really understood that because they hadn't experienced it. I was okay with that. It never really bothered me. I could still be a kid with my friends. I never saw myself as out of the ordinary, even though I knew something in my mind and my spirit was different. I don't know how else to explain it other than I felt the world. I felt it all.

As a child, Allie had a tender heart and an extraordinary concern for other people. She wrote letters to Santa asking him to send shoes to the orphans in Russia. She begged to sponsor a Compassion child from the time she was old enough to understand that you could send money to children in other countries to make their lives better.

At the age of ten, Allison wrote the poem below. She demonstrated an amazing grasp of God's love and sacrifice at a young age. Her faith was strong, and she trusted God to love her unconditionally.

> Pretty flowers, golden lockets,
> Angels as sweet as He.
> He who died, as I stand at His side
> Speechless for He died for me.
>
> For I know I am just a sinner,
> And I'm way below a beginner.
> But He will still love me,
> Just wait and see.
> Someday I will be with Him
> And live eternally.

I had lived my whole life in a Christian home. I had a normal childhood, a wonderful childhood, full of large open spaces and sunlight through open windows and brightly colored toys and love and laughter and tickle fights. I grew up in a small town where church was a place that felt like a big house with all my friends in it. I memorized Bible verses and loved hearing Bible stories. I loved the story of Joseph the best. My Sunday school teacher would say to my parents, "She really understands those Bible stories. She knows them all by heart."

When it came time to go to school, I excelled there too. My mom always tells the story of one of their first parent-teacher conferences when I was in second grade. The teacher sat them down and said, "Mr. and Mrs. Speck, I have something I need to show you."

My parents sat anxiously, wondering what the teacher was referring to. What did she have to show them? Then my teacher reached behind her desk and pulled out a large stack of journals and said, "Every day I ask the students to write at the beginning of class. It is to help them practice their creative writing and learn how to make sentences. Most students write about one or two sentences a day and go through a journal a month...your daughter goes through a journal every two or three days. These here," she patted the top of the stack, "are her journals for this month alone."

I thrived in school. I always seemed to get A's without needing to try extremely hard. By third grade I was in the Accelerated Reader program for gifted students. I had many friends. I played sports. I enjoyed school. Life just came easily to me, and I enjoyed every moment of it. Of course, there was middle school and mean girls and typical body image issues and growing pains with parents, but all in all, my life was above average.

I found one of Allison's diaries from 2003, which means she would have been 13 years old. She shared her reflections of the Bible verse Romans 8:28, "And we know that in all things God works for the good of those who love him, who have been called according to his purpose," and the story of Job, a biblical figure who was attacked by the devil and lost everything yet continued to worship the Lord.

Once again, I was struck by the maturity of Allison's thoughts and the way in which I believe God was preparing her spirit for her faith journey. She wrote, *"Why does God let bad stuff happen to Christians? To make us strong because maybe He has something else planned in the future that He is preparing us for. An example would be September 11th, which turned the whole nation toward Him and made us stronger. What would you say to someone like Job? That everything that happens to us, God already knew it was going to happen, and it all happens for a reason. All they need to do is to trust God."* She then wrote out part of the Bible verse 1 John 4:18: "There is no fear in love. But perfect love drives out all fear." I needed to remind myself that she was 13 when she wrote these deep perspectives.

Once during a mission trip with our church, when Allie was about 14, she looked at the leftover food after their evening meal and asked if the people they had helped that day had enough to eat. Allie encouraged the adult leaders to box up the leftovers and deliver them to the homes of the people they had been helping. The leaders were impressed by the depth of Allie's compassion and did as she suggested. The food was delivered and touched the hearts of the people in need. Allison demonstrated great compassion for people, especially those less fortunate.

Allie's reflections on the youth mission trip

> For many Christians, there is a profound moment in their life upon which they can reflect and know that they were being led by the Lord. It is what most people call their "testimony." My "moment" of redemption, however, is not contained within a single moment in time. It spans across my lifetime, resulting in a continual construction of my faith. I have often referred to my walk with Christ as "a work in progress." He has not spoken to me on one specific encounter; rather, He continually leads me in my walk with Him. One of the times that I have had to lean heavily on my walk with Christ was during a mission trip to South Carolina. I went with my church's youth group to one of the poorest sections of the South: McCaw, South Carolina. I could not believe how little these people had. God spoke to me through many people there and really opened my eyes to the suffering of the world. I know that no matter where I go in life, I want to incorporate missions work into my future. Though it may not be my profession, I still want to participate in helping and serving the needy.

This poem, written while she was in high school, is another example of Allie's ability to perceive the suffering of others and her belief in a God who delivers those who suffer from the trials of this world.

A poem written by Allison, entitled "Rich"

> Outside the wind howls
> and bends the trees with its fury.
> People on the streets pull their coats tight around
> themselves to keep out the cold.
> A cloud covers the moon
> and darkness falls, there she sits.
> Her feet wrapped in plastic;

her body covered in rags.
Rain begins to fall
and those still on the street scatter.
They run for shelter from the storm. Still she sits.
The empty cup she holds falls to the ground
and clatters on the sidewalk.
A crack of lightning lights up her face,
once so young and fair
now twisted by time and heartache.
Where did she come from?
Why was she here?
No one knew and no one really cared.
They would look down
and scowl at her as she held out her cup.
"Poor woman," some would say,
but still they walked away.
Some pointed and laughed at her,
though they did not know her.
But soon she would be richer than all of them.
Knowing this, she waited.
Silently and patiently,
as the storm raged around her.
She closed her eyes
and did not notice Him coming toward her.
He gently touched her shoulder.
At the touch of His hand, she felt healed
and young again.
Slowly she opened her eyes
to see His sweet face.
The face of someone who loved her.
"Come, My good and faithful servant,"
He whispered.
"It is time to come home."

When Allie became old enough to drive, she was known to pick up hitchhikers. She always wanted to provide them with shelter, clothes and food. She called home two times in the same week asking if we could pay for a room to get some travelers out of the cold. We charged a room to our credit card so that they had a warm place to sleep. Allison made sure the hotel offered breakfast. At a time when most teenagers became self-centered and withdrawn, she demonstrated a strong desire to help others, especially strangers.

Allison's Journal, August 2008

The world does not need another rock star thanking
God on the back of their CD.
   The world doesn't need another professional athlete
pointing to the sky.
   The world doesn't need another millionaire to tithe 10%.
   The world NEEDS devoted, selfless and fearless Christians.
   Christians who LIVE for Him.
   Christians who LOVE Him with their lives.
   Not Christians who wear gold crosses; Christians who
are willing to bear their cross daily.
   Not Christians who carry Bibles; Christians who study
the Bible and live by it.
   Not Christians with crosses tattooed on their arms;
Christians who have His word
written on their hearts.
   The world needs Jesus, and we are His hands.
   Why aren't we reaching out?
   The world is desperate
and crying out for something to believe in.
   We can give the world that something...will you?

♥Allie

I remember preparing Allison's high school graduation announcements. Allie approached me and said, "I want the scripture Jeremiah 29:11 on the front of my graduation announcements." I have to admit, at that point in my Christian walk I was not as familiar with my Bible verses as I should have been, so I located the passage in Jeremiah. It read, "'For I know the plans I have for you,' declares the Lord, 'plans to prosper you and not to harm you, plans to give you hope and a future.'" I was amazed at the depth of this scripture choice as she looked toward her future. I had no idea the impact that scripture would have on Allie's future, her testimony and our lives. That same scripture is on her headstone as a witness to those who never had the opportunity to meet Allie or hear her testimony of faith. God certainly had a plan for Allison that was not our plan. Allie's life would be lived to glorify the Lord, something she seemed to know in her spirit from a young age.

Allison's Journal, August 2008

Dear God,
   Sometimes it is hard to find my way in this world. Some-

times I just wish I could sit and talk with You because I cannot find anyone else who really understands. I am having trouble finding the words to tell You how I feel, but that is pointless because You already know. There is SO MUCH I can and want to do with my life, and I can't do it all. I feel that I can serve You in SO MANY ways, but I don't have enough years in my life. I want to do great things for You, but I don't know which path I should choose. I am praying that somehow You will show me. I am crying out for a calling. Yes, I know what I am in for by asking that question. Show me my service, my mission. I don't want to put any conditions on my request to You, Lord. Please open my eyes, my mind, my heart and my soul to see the calling I am to follow.

♥Allie

The pictures taken on my high school graduation night show me smiling—no worry or fear—with a steady boyfriend of two years under my right arm and my best friend since middle school under my left arm, and I know there is a proud, loving family standing behind the camera watching me smile. At the time these pictures were taken, I had grown into the type of person that you would expect to come out of a life of love and encouragement. I had traveled all over Europe and Australia and driven across the US; I wrote my own poetry and music; and I was homecoming queen, served on student council and had the lead in our school musical my senior year. I followed God. I never smoked or drank alcohol. I never went to parties or disobeyed my parents. I was active in my church's youth group, going on youth retreats and mission trips. I was happy, healthy and loved.

My life would make many people roll their eyes because it just seemed too perfect. Of course, there were dark times. I struggled with body image and eating habits. We had lost grandfathers, and my grandmother battled breast cancer as well as depression. But in all of these struggles, it seemed we always came out on the other side unscathed. There was always a solution. God was good. We were blessed.

When it came time to pick a college, I knew I wanted to go to a Christian college. Originally, being a natural-born adventurer, I wanted to go far from home. But to my disappointment, God led me to Messiah College [now Messiah University] which was only 30 minutes from my home. Still, I was excited to go to a Christian college. I had loved God my whole life, and I wanted to draw closer to Him than ever before. Ever since I was young, I have had a feeling in me that was hard to explain. Somewhere in me there was a knowing that God had something planned for my life that wasn't normal. Sometimes I was afraid that maybe it was only pride that spoke the words, that it was just a result of a lifetime full of teachers and parents telling me how good I am at things. But in my heart, I knew it went deeper than that. I also had a strange feeling that the big plan God had for my life would involve great sacrifice.

I interpreted this call to serve God as mission work. I was supposed to be a missionary. It made sense. I had a huge heart for the hurting and those who lived in poverty. It seemed I wanted to help the whole world; I needed to help the whole world. Sometimes it felt like a burden to me, and I would be overwhelmed by this deep love and empathy I felt for others. My family often chastised me for caring too much when I would bring hitchhikers home for a place to stay or fill the trunk of my car with stray cats or give money away to anyone who seemed like they needed it. The truth was, I had to do those things. My heart broke for those the world ignored. If I didn't do something, who would? So, what better way to serve God and cure my own bleeding heart than to be a missionary?

I threw myself into college life. I enjoyed meeting new people and drawing closer to God. I sang in the women's choir, played sports and joined clubs. But there was something holding me back. Something wasn't quite right.

Little did Allie know that this was the start of a faith journey like no other. She wrote a devotion during Lent for our church in March of 2009. She was a senior in high school at the time. She chose the scripture Matthew 10:38–39 (NKJV): "And he who does not take his cross and follow after Me is not worthy of Me. He who finds his life will lose it, and he who loses his life for My sake will find it."

A devotion written by Allison

> This message is so important that Jesus reiterates it again in Matthew 16:24–25. So, what does it mean? Of course, we are not called to literally pick up a cross and carry it. So, what is our cross? For me, it is my commitment to Christ. It is what sets me apart. Taking up your cross and following Jesus means living your life in such a way that others see Jesus in you. You take up your cross or your calling and carry it so it glorifies Him.
>
> This verse brought to mind a quote by Michael Tait: "While we may not be called to martyr our lives, we must martyr our way of life. We must put our selfish ways to death and march to a different beat. Then the world will see Jesus."

Chances are we will never be called upon to literally lose our lives for Christ. However, by choosing to follow Jesus, you are putting your old life to death and putting on a new life in Christ. If we live our lives solely for our-selves, we will lose them. If we take up our cross and live EVERY DAY for Jesus, it is then that we find true life. Jesus took up His cross and died for us; the least we can do is to take up our cross and live for Him.

Looking back on this devotion, I see the maturity of Allie's faith and what it meant for her to live for Jesus. She was 18 years old, looking forward to college and a bright future serving the Lord. She had no idea of the trials she would face in the coming months and years or that her faith and trust in the Lord would become a testimony to thousands of people. She bore her cross with an honor and grace that still amazes me. She lived her life fast-paced and filled with adventure. She traveled the world and had a voracious need to share God's love. She accomplished things that most people never dream of doing in 70 or 80 years. She did it all in 23 years.

CHAPTER THREE
THE JOURNEY BEGINS

During the end of my senior year in high school, I had started to feel...
different. I wasn't as energetic as I used to be. I just felt off. The summer
before I left for college, vague symptoms began to appear. I was tired all the
time and developed dizzy spells. Doctors said I was nervous about college.
I began running fevers every day. I was someone who barely ever got sick,
but now I felt sick all the time. My doctors tested me for different things, but
felt I was overreacting. I knew my body; I wasn't making this up. Something
was wrong. But they were doctors. They knew what they were talking about.
Didn't they?

Throughout my first semester at college, symptoms worsened, and I add-
ed more to the list: shortness of breath, loss of appetite and weight loss.
The symptoms kept getting worse. I saw an ear, nose and throat doctor,
an infectious disease doctor and a kidney specialist. After a brain MRI
and multiple blood tests, they said there was nothing wrong with me. They
assured me that whatever it was, it would resolve itself. I was supposed to
enjoy my first semester at college and not worry so much. I was young. I
was healthy. I was fine.

It was during Thanksgiving break that Allison told me she needed new
jeans. We went shopping, and it was then I realized she went down two
pants sizes from August to November, during her first semester of college.
Normally students gain what everyone calls the "freshman 15," but not Allie.
I was mildly concerned, but I knew that she was an avid exerciser and very
aware of her weight. She was eating healthy and going to the gym with a
heavy class load, and I believed it was the adjustment of being a new college
student. I bought her new jeans and decided to keep an eye on her weight
loss. I never dreamed that this could be anything serious...until the day in

December when she called me from college telling me she was having a lot of belly pain and had noticed a lump in her upper abdomen. We were headed to Messiah to hear Allie sing in the women's choir for Christmas, so I told her I would come early to evaluate this "lump."

When I entered her dorm room, she was changing, and I was shocked at the size of the lump I saw. I did not want her to see my concern, so I asked her to lie down on the couch so I could feel it. As soon as I touched it and felt the firmness and size, I knew she needed to see a doctor... ASAP. I moved up her appointment with a new family doctor. I had no idea the journey we would embark upon the day my husband took her to see the new doctor.

During the first week of December 2009 at college, I awoke with a piercing pain in my upper abdomen. I couldn't even stand up straight. I thought I pulled a muscle at the gym, so I slid out of bed and lay on the floor and tried to stretch. More pain shot through my abdomen and around to my back. I let out a small cry, surprised at how severe the pain was from such a small movement. Something was wrong. I got onto my hands and knees. Every move caused shocks of pain around my midsection. It was like there was a circle of daggers around my abdomen. With great effort I stood and made my way—slowly, doubled over, breathless with pain—to the mirror on the back of our dorm room door. Slowly I straightened my body as best I could and gingerly lifted up the front of my nightshirt. I squinted hard into the mirror. Something was strange. My upper abdomen was bulging out further than I had ever noticed it. It was like someone had shoved half of a cantaloupe under my rib cage. I didn't know what to make of it, so I took a large amount of Advil and went—very painfully—to my classes. That evening, while studying in my room, the pain was just as bad as it had been when I woke up, so I thought I should ask my roommates what they thought.

"Whoa. That's pretty freaky looking." My roommate looked concerned.

I laughed.

"Yeah, I guess. What do you think it is?" I said, looking down over my stomach. "You're both nursing majors," I said jokingly.

"Let me pull up WebMD®!" My other roommate rushed for her laptop. After typing in my symptoms, we hit search. Hepatitis and stomach cancer were two of the top results.

"That is not what I have," I said, shaking my head.

"I think you should call your mom and tell her what's going on."

The three of us had gotten to know each other pretty well since we started college, and I considered them to be two of my closest friends. I knew that if they were concerned, I should do something.

So, I called my mom and told her what was going on. She was coming up to see me sing in the college's Choral Christmas concert. I had a solo, and the whole family was coming to see me.

The day of the Christmas concert I was tired. Singing in the concert was difficult, but by then everything was difficult for me. I had just gotten used to it.

After the concert I was changing in my room to go to dinner with my family. My mom came up to the room and walked in as I was changing. I heard the door open as I pulled my sweater over my head.

"Oh my gosh!" her voice was muffled by the sound of my sweater brushing past my ears. "What is wrong with your stomach?"

"I told you it was swollen," I replied.

She told me to lie on the sofa. She began to press on my stomach, sizing and evaluating the bulge that now seemed even bigger. I winced in pain with each touch. She looked worried.

"What's wrong?" I watched her face.

"It's hard," she said, and her eyebrows came together slightly. "It shouldn't be hard like that."

"What do you think it is?" I asked her. She is a nurse so I knew she probably had some idea of what it might be.

"I don't know," she said. "It feels like your liver might be enlarged."

"What causes that?"

"I don't know. I think we should move up your doctor's appointment."

She then continued to talk with my roommates about it, and they both indicated that they thought it was concerning too. She tried to crack little jokes about the situation, and I watched the corners of her mouth twitch up into small glints of a smile, but it wasn't a real smile. It was the kind of smile I had seen a few times before, and it was a smile I would get to know very well over the next few months. It meant, "See, I'm not worried. Don't be scared." But she only smiled like that when she was worried, which meant something was wrong, which left an odd feeling in the bottom of my stomach that I didn't like.

Allison's Journal, December 10, 2009

Lord God,
   Thank You for the beautiful snow that has been falling! Thank You for helping me to get all of my work done. Please help me through this day with my doctor's appointment. Let it go well and let them find out what is wrong with me. Thank You for doctors! I pray You grant me the desire to seek You in all that I do! Praise that today I finished the 21-day challenge of reading

through the book of John! Now onto the next book! Be with me and my family this holiday season.

♥Allie

I don't remember much about the days I spent waiting for my doctor appointment. My last memory is lying on the sofa and watching my mom's face; and the next memory is sitting in a small, white examination room with my dad on December 10th, waiting for the doctor to come in. All memories in between are whitewashed over and irretrievable.

However, the fragmented memories I do have left of this time are crystal clear. I can play them back in my mind—watch them unfold through my eyes—like short movie clips.

I survey the layout of the room, the way the doctor comes in and shuts the door. I can remember exactly how she looked as she asked me the typical doctor-to-patient questions. Then, I mention the lump in my stomach. She motions to the examination table.

I lie flat. White drop ceiling and harsh lights. Her hands are on my stomach. She apologizes for her cold hands.

She makes a noise. A small humming sound. I look at her face, and it scares me. She is concerned. Very concerned. Not the wondering, motherly concern I saw on my mom's face. It is more frightening. Closer to fear than worry.

"Have you had this examined before?"

"No."

"None of the doctors you visited noticed it?"

"No."

"They didn't run any tests?"

"No. It didn't look like this when I saw them."

"How long has it been this way?"

"Um...it's hard to tell. A week? A few weeks?"

"This is not normal."

She continued to press on it. Size it up. Tap on it with her fingers. "There is something wrong here."

The memory gets hazy after this. All I remember is the fear on her face, the motion of her hand as she wrote an order for a scan at the hospital's earliest open time slot, and the first mention of the word mass.

We got home in time to receive a phone call that my CT scan would be at 6:30 that evening. We arrive at the hospital, and I sit in the waiting area with my mom. We are joking about the mocha-flavored barium contrast being disgusting! It is a lovely, thick slime that tastes like old chocolate. I have to drink two large bottles before I can get my scan.

We pretend to complain to each other. I am already in a semi-constant state of nausea and have not had an appetite for months, and they expect me to chug the contrast like water?! I threaten—half joking—that if they make me drink another sip, I will throw it up. I actually do throw up, and they bring me a new bottle. By then I begin to whine like a three-year-old who does not want to take her medicine, and my mom and I are laughing at the ridiculousness of the situation. Maybe we laughed because it was funny. Maybe we laughed because we were terrified. I still don't know.

Finally, they take me back for my scan, which I don't remember much of: lying flat, arms over my head and a lot of white plastic.

The next mental movie clip is sitting in a restaurant with my mom. Her phone rings. It is the doctor. I watch my mom's face, waiting to see if I should let my heart drop. She gives me the phone.

"Mass on the liver."

"You will need surgery."

My mom now watches my face. It is a never-ending trade-off of watching each other, wondering, are we okay?

I can only remember saying, "Okay." Then the memory is blank, and I remember nothing else.

I was scared; actually, I was petrified. The doctor stressed that the "mass" on Allison's liver was extremely large. I would get a copy of the report and, being a nurse, looked up the exact dimensions of the large mass. The numbers were underlined by the doctor, as if that indicated the significance of the size… 12 x 16 x 17 centimeters. In nonmedical language, it was 4.5 x 6 x 6.5 inches!

How could a mass of this size have been overlooked for so long? I wanted to be angry at the doctors who had dismissed her symptoms. I wanted to cry and hold her and tell her everything was going to be okay. I wanted to ask God to give me the mass and take it from my daughter. My mind was spinning! When my random thoughts slowed, my first thought was to get people praying about this situation. I was not in control, and I needed strong prayer warriors. Below is a portion of the first email I sent to eight of our strongest prayer warriors. Little did I know that this small group would grow to include thousands of people whose faith would be changed by Allie's journey.

12/15/2009 Email to Allie Speck's Prayer Warriors
I wanted to send a quick note to each of you so you can pray for Allison. Allison has not felt well since May. Last Thursday I got her an emergency appointment with a new doctor. She was in the doctor's office at 3:00 p.m., CT scan at 6:00 p.m., and by 9:30 p.m. we were told she has a mass on her liver measuring

seven to nine inches. She has been referred to a specialist. Pray for peace and healing for her. She will be taking her finals and then starting Christmas break. We hope we can resolve this issue over the holiday.

The only memories I have of meeting the specialist are these: We were waiting in a room full of old, broken down people. Wheelchairs; oxygen tanks; medical masks; body parts amputated; frail, scared faces.

After waiting a long time, we were taken back a hallway to an examination room. I was sitting at the end of an examination table facing the door, waiting for the doctor to come in. The doctor came in very abruptly. He seemed preoccupied and in a hurry. He made me nervous.

At some point he was sitting at the computer scrolling through my scans. I had never seen them. The whole time I tried peeking over his shoulder, trying to catch a glimpse of my scans. Finally, someone asked if we could see the scans. He obliged—pointing out the tumor. It took up my whole abdomen.

He said things like "cancer," "rare," "advanced," "transplant," "impossible," "radiation," "surgery," "complicated," "fatal," "untreatable." And all of them made me want everyone to leave so I didn't have to keep choking back the tears behind my eyes and the sob of fear in my throat. I remember being terrified and praying no one could tell.

He left. We were silent. He came back. He began writing things on slips of paper. Talking quickly. He had to discuss my case with other doctors. Did I need an appointment with the transplant doctor? Then it is all blank again, and I am glad. The small moments I do remember have enough fear in them to make me anxious as I recall them. I would rather not carry all those days in my mind.

12/18/2009 Email to Allie Speck's Prayer Warriors
We spent the day at the hospital. Allie had an MRI at 9:00 a.m. and an appointment with the specialist at 11:00 a.m. We sat in the waiting room until 2:30 p.m. before we saw the doctor.

After reviewing the MRI, we were told there is one very large tumor and two smaller tumors within the liver. The doctor made it clear that if Allie had surgery, it would be very difficult.

He told us the tumor could be benign or it could be malignant. He believes it is malignant, but we cannot know that without a biopsy. He is taking her case to his colleagues for review. We are emotionally drained and overwhelmed. Allison demonstrated her usual stoic behavior, but we are all concerned.

If she has surgery, it cannot be scheduled until after Christmas. Please pray that the tumor is benign and can be safely removed soon.

Allison's Journal, December 22, 2009

God,

I don't know what to say...or how to feel. I feel upset. I feel far away. I feel like I've been cast out and forgotten. I don't know what I'm supposed to do or how I'm supposed to act.

I have tried so hard for so long and I can't get up this hill of doubt. It's my fault, isn't it? But I don't know how to fix it. I can't feel You. I understand faith is not a feeling, but, God, a little miracle would be nice. I'm taking for granted all that You've already done for me. I want to help others. But, how? Where? Have I wasted too much time? Have I made too many mistakes? And now I'm sick.

The thought of death scares me. Should it? The idea of living with You is the most amazing thing I can think of; words cannot describe it. But still, sometimes when I lose sight of You, death becomes a very depressing thing. I'm scared of surgery. I'm scared of disappointing You.

I do like bringing joy to people. I am going to play my Christmas song in church. I thought about backing out, but I'm going to do it. Help me to do well and let people like it. Let them see You and feel Your love in the song.

Thank You for all who are praying for me. Bless them somehow this day. Help me and my family. Heal my body and let the doctors fix it and see all they should. Bless those in my extended family who need to know Christ and those who are lonely this holiday. Show me what to do for them.

In Jesus's name,

♥Allie

12/23/2009 Email to Allie Speck's Prayer Warriors
On a positive note, Allison received her grades from college today and got all A's. We are so proud. Also, the college selected one of Allison's poems to be included

in their spring publication. Being a freshman, it is a
great honor that her work has been chosen.

The specialist called today with news we were not
expecting. Allison has been scheduled to meet with
a liver transplant surgeon on her 19th birthday. He
again stated that the committee believes the tumors
are malignant. We know that Allison and this situation are being covered by your prayers and believe
it will make a difference in the outcome. Do not grow
weary in this task. We wish you a Merry Christmas!

*My only memory during the whole Christmas season is playing the song
I wrote during the Christmas Eve service at my church. I sat at the piano
and struggled to sing. The tumor was pushing up against my lungs at this
point and made it hard for me to sing. My microphone wasn't working, and
I remember being angry that no one could hear the first half of my song, but
I don't know if that was actually why I was angry.*

CHAPTER FOUR
FAITH THAT MOVES MOUNTAINS

I was sitting on my living room floor on Christmas Eve, wrapping presents and praying that God would show me how to help Allison. My mind was overwhelmed. My heart was hurting and confused. As a parent, I wanted the best for my child. I asked God to show me how to help Allie. I cried because I felt scared, lost and alone.

At that moment our phone rang. It was my friend whose boys had played soccer with Allie during high school. She told me that her brother had connections at Johns Hopkins and that he might be able to get Allie an appointment for a second opinion. She said she would have her brother call me. I remember believing that God had heard my broken heart and opened a door.

Within 15 minutes, I was on the phone with a doctor from Hopkins. He asked me to fax Allie's reports to his office…it was Christmas Eve at 4:30 p.m.! I had all the reports except the most recent MRI. I called the MRI department and held my breath as the phone rang repeatedly. I told myself that no one would be there at almost 5:00 p.m. on Christmas Eve, when suddenly a lady answered the phone. She told me she had her coat on and was walking out the door when the phone started to ring. She could not explain why she returned to answer the phone…but I knew the reason. God heard my plea and answered my prayer. She listened to my request and stayed late to send me Allison's MRI report. Within minutes, I was forwarding all of Allie's reports to the doctor at Hopkins.

Around 6:00 p.m., I received a call from the liver surgeon at Hopkins, telling me he wanted to see Allie first thing Monday. It was a Christmas miracle! God had heard my cry. In a three-hour span, I went from praying for guidance to having an appointment with a renowned liver surgeon in five days!

12/28/2009 Email to Allie Speck's Prayer Warriors
Today was Allison's 19th birthday! After a very long day at the hospital, we went for dinner and to paint pottery. It was an enjoyable end to another difficult day.

We met with the transplant doctor who wants to schedule surgery and stressed that it would be difficult and possibly even life-threatening. They are sure it is malignant and don't feel a biopsy is necessary. Watching Allison's face as the doctor discussed the seriousness of the surgery was one of the hardest things I have yet done as her mother. They need to know our decision.

However, through a miraculous opportunity, we were able to get a second opinion at Johns Hopkins. The surgeon reviewed Allison's reports on Christmas Eve, and we are seeing him tomorrow. Pray for God to give us clear direction. Allison wants the tumors removed, and I want them removed by the best surgeon. Pray for peace for Allison and for her not to be overcome by fear in the face of the unknown.

I cannot thank you enough for the outpouring of love we have witnessed on Allison's behalf. God surely has a wonderful plan we don't understand.

12/29/2009 Email to Allie Speck's Prayer Warriors
What a difference a day makes! We went to Johns Hopkins today and met the surgeon. What an amazing man! He used words we understood, and Allison said it was the first time she didn't feel like throwing up after talking to a doctor. The tumor is cantaloupe-sized, and, while very difficult, he feels it is removable. He also believes it could be cancer and is recommending surgery.

Based on his review, Allison felt comfortable to sign a consent form for surgery. The tentative surgery date is January 13th, my birthday. We feel Hopkins is where we belong.

I remember the first meeting with the surgeon at Hopkins so clearly. Allison was nervous after the other surgeon was so abrupt. This man was the complete opposite. He gave us reassurance while still making us aware of the seriousness of the situation. But what I remember best is Allison saying, "I would like to ask him if he is a believer in Jesus." I encouraged her to ask. My role as her parent had changed to being her advocate, to teaching her to ask important questions before making hard decisions. While most parents were giving their kids wings to fly and begin a new adventure at college or work, I was teaching my daughter to navigate the world of medicine and helping her understand her rights as a patient. This realization made me rely on God even more to understand His plan for Allison's life.

When the surgeon came back in the room to confirm the surgery date, Allison stated, "I need to know if you believe in Jesus. I need the person putting their hands inside of my body to believe in Jesus." I can still see his smile as he sat down on the stool, put his hand on Allie's knee, and said, "I most certainly do." He asked if she had any other questions before signing the surgery consent. She simply stated, "Nope…that was the most important one." And for the first time in a long time, Allie smiled a genuine smile. My mind held a million emotions at once…relief, hope, fear, sadness, love. My daughter's faith helped me to be strong.

As we were leaving the office, the nurse asked if we had visited the original Johns Hopkins Hospital. She heard Allie ask the surgeon about his faith and she told us that in the rotunda of the old building, there is a two-story statue of Jesus. I took that as God's confirmation of our decision.

01/03/2010 Email to Allie Speck's Prayer Warriors
Allison began to have severe abdominal pain and was transported to Hopkins by ambulance. I was able to ride with her, and they are doing tests to determine the next step. Pray for her comfort, as she is in so much pain. Please pray for her brother, Andy, who is at home with my husband. This is hard for all of us. I will update you as soon as we know what is happening.

01/04/2010 Email to Allie Speck's Prayer Warriors
Allison's pain is under control. The doctors feel the pain is from pressure caused by the tumor. The surgeon wants her pain controlled before surgery. Allison is receiving blood and pain medication, and then we will go home with the same surgery date, January 13th.

Allison learned that her blood type is A+. Her witty comment was, "I always knew my blood was the best." Despite the situation, she made me laugh.

We have canceled Allie's college classes for January, but we are keeping her spring schedule with hopes that she can return.

We are thankful for your support. A Facebook page entitled "Pray for Allie Speck" has been created and already has over 700 followers. We are blessed.

01/05/2010 Email to Allie Speck's Prayer Warriors
I awoke this morning with Allie on my mind and a feeling that her surgeon needs to know how many people are praying for her healing. If this email touches your heart, I am asking you to send a card to the surgeon's office. God will be working through his hands.

01/08/2010 Email to Allie Speck's Prayer Warriors
Allison's pain is under control with medication, and her surgeon feels she is ready. Surgery is scheduled for 7:30 a.m. on January 13th. The next update should be the day of surgery. Allie's Facebook page now has over 1,000 members. Her faith is already a testimony.

Allison's Journal, January 12, 2010

Dear God,
   Thank You for how You have provided for my family. I am in much better shape than my last entry. I will have my surgery tomorrow. I am ready to be better! Thank You for revealing my illness and providing doctors and a hospital that will help me be well again. You have used what most people would view as an ugly situation and made something so incredibly beautiful. I am in awe of Your works. I praise You for all You are doing and will continue to do.
   You know me, Lord. You have known me since before I was born. You are the Great Physician. Guide the doctor with Your knowledge and let him remove all of my tumors successfully and with no complica-

tions. I believe You have been working inside of me to prepare me for this surgery and to make the surgery easy for him. Lord, give me strength and courage. Do not let me miss an opportunity to spread Your love. Bless my family. Give them Your peace and joy in Jesus's name.

♥ Allie

(There was a four-leaf clover pressed inside the page with this entry.)

Allison's Journal, January 13, 2010

"But the angel said to them, 'Do not be afraid! Listen carefully, for I proclaim to you good news that brings great joy to all people: Today your Savior is born in the city of David. He is Christ the Lord'" (Luke 2:10–11 NET).

♥ Allie

Allison woke up early the morning of her surgery and wrote this entry in her journal before we headed to Johns Hopkins. I have to remind myself that she was 19 years old. I cannot help but be in awe of her faith and strength in the face of the biggest challenge of her life. Her scripture choice reminded me not to be afraid, for Christ is our Lord and Savior.

January 13th is my birthday. My only birthday wish that year was for God to restore my daughter's health. Allie strengthened my faith and kept my eyes on God when I wanted to doubt, place blame and be angry. We walked into Johns Hopkins with our armor on, ready for battle.

CHAPTER FIVE

ARE YOU THERE, GOD?

"Mom..." I paused my voice, unable to finish. "Mom, he didn't get it?" I wanted her to say, "Yes, of course he got it!" I wanted everything to be okay. I wanted everything from before to be a bad dream. I held onto the bed rail and felt her hand on mine.

"No, honey...he didn't get it."

From somewhere deep inside of me, a place I could never find again if I tried, something cracked open and shook loose a sound that came from both inside and outside my body. I could feel the movement of noise in my throat and the vibration in my ears, but I could not hear it. I was far away, and my world was silent and unresponsive until my mother's voice seemed to push through my ears.

"Shhh, shhh, it's okay. Listen," she pleaded over the noise.

The sound was me, and I was screaming.

"No!" I shrieked at the top of my lungs. "No!" I screamed and sobbed the words. Although my brain still could not wrap itself completely around the magnitude of my devastation, it seemed my voice understood.

It was a death sentence...

01/13/2010 Email to Allie Speck's Prayer Warriors
The news is not what we hoped. We were told the large mass is not removable and that there are other masses within the liver that were not seen on scans. It is cancer, and a biopsy was taken to confirm the type.

We need prayer for our entire family, but specifically for Allison's spirit as she absorbs the outcome of the surgery.

I will never forget the look on the surgeon's face when he walked into the conference room. The lady who took us to the room must have seen the fear in my eyes. She patted my shoulder and said, "Don't worry! The doctor talks to all of his families in the conference room. It does not mean anything bad; I promise." I wish I could have held her to that promise.

The surgeon entered with tears in his eyes. His first words were, "I could not remove the tumor. It is very large." The rest of the information was muffled by fear as we heard the word CANCER for the first time. How could my 19-year-old daughter, who was healthy and God-fearing, have a cancerous tumor so large it may take her life? Why? What did we do wrong? How can I possibly help her face the struggles ahead? What happens next? How soon can I see her? Does she know? These were the thoughts that screamed through my brain while he talked and gave specific tumor information and expected outcomes.

The next horrible step in this journey required me to enter the ICU and tell Allie that the surgeon did not remove the tumor and that it was cancer. The steps I walked into the ICU must be what death-row inmates feel when they walk their last steps of freedom. I was crossing into a world that was forever changed and would require more strength and courage than I felt I had to offer.

Seeing Allie in the ICU made it even worse. She was connected to multiple machines with tubes in both arms and a needle in her neck. She was groggy but alert enough to know I was there. I put on my bravest face as she asked, "Mom, he didn't get it?" I answered, "No, honey, he didn't get it." The words were no sooner out than Allie began to scream with a depth of pain I have never heard and hope to never hear again. The entire ICU stopped to listen. She paused only to take a breath and then repeated that horrific sound again and again. I tried to comfort

her, but what could I say to make the news easier?
I was at a loss for words. I kept telling her it would
be okay and I loved her and I was not going to leave
her side. We were in this battle together. I wanted
to pick her up out of that bed of tangled wires and
tubes and hold her close, but I could not. So, I simply
laid my head on the pillow next to hers and allowed
her screaming to drown out my tears as they mixed
with hers on the pillow. I did not leave her side for
the next 48 hours. Eating, showering, drinking—all
seemed unimportant. I did not want her to open her
eyes and not find me there.

As I sat there looking at my child, I had a lot of questions for God. Where are You? What happened to Your
plan for her? Why didn't You answer our prayers?
Why does Allie have to suffer? Where is the miracle
we know You can provide? Are You listening?

01/16/2010 Email to Allie Speck's Prayer Warriors
The cancer doctor came to talk to Allison about
treatment. Allison wants to start treatments as soon
as possible. It was a lot of information to absorb.
Allie has had many visitors and is emotionally overwhelmed. Pray for peace.

I remember the days after Allie's surgery as she was recovering. So many
people drove to Baltimore to visit, and the room was constantly full. At one
point, Allison said she wanted everyone to leave. I sent everyone to our rented
townhouse. It was then I realized how overwhelmed Allison was as she dealt
with her cancer diagnosis, faced the possibility of chemo, and had so many
visitors. She told me she hated how everyone sat around her bed staring at her
as if she were on display. It was true. I was devastated that I did not recognize
her need for privacy and allow her time to deal with the situation. I apologized
to her and promised to take control of her visitors. She was scared, tired, hurting, uncomfortable and confused. Expecting her to be a hostess to multiple
guests was too much. I failed in my first job as her advocate. I would not let
that happen again. I held her and allowed her to express her frustration and
anger at not only the overwhelming lack of privacy, but also the fact that her
friends had the freedom to leave and continue their normal lives outside of her
hospital room. She wanted that too. Her confession broke my heart. All the
love in the world could not give her back the life she had before cancer.

01/18/2010 Email to Allie Speck's Prayer Warriors
Allison was discharged four days after surgery.
Recovery has been hard, watching her battle pain
and anxiety. As she cries, all I can do is pray.

Thank you to the 150 people who attended the
prayer vigil for Allie at our church. She continues to
demonstrate a lot of strength and trust in her Lord,
despite the circumstances.

Allison's Journal, January 19, 2010

Dear God,
  I know there is a reason the surgery didn't work. I pray
this is a blessing in disguise. I have faith that it is. I cry out to
You for healing just as the many people cried out in the
Bible. I know You are a loving God and do not wish for
Your children to suffer. I am suffering, Lord, physically and
emotionally. I hold fast to You, and Your promise to deliver
me from evil. Fulfill Your promise, Lord. I have dedicated
my life to You, and I am going to live and serve You all of
my days. Please heal me of this cancer and grant me a
long, healthy life of happiness and serving You. Lord, heal
me. Reach down and make my cancer disappear. Heal
me, Lord. I know You have the power. Give me strength
and a good attitude. Help me to share You with anyone I
can through this. In Jesus's name, AMEN!
                                                    ♥Allie

01/20/2010 Email to Allie Speck's Prayer Warriors
Tomorrow Allie has a CT scan and an appointment
with the cancer doctors. She is "tired of being
sick." Unfortunately, there is a tough journey
ahead. She is reading through the book of Luke,
which contains several encouraging stories of
miraculous healings.

We listened to Christian radio and reflected on the
Bible story that involves three men thrown into a
fiery furnace because of their faith. Once in the fire,
the soldiers saw four men...because God was there
protecting them. The three men emerged from the

furnace alive. Read the story in Daniel chapter 3. It was our reminder that we are not alone.

01/22/2010 Email to Allie Speck's Prayer Warriors
Today was Allison's first appointment with the doctors who will treat her cancer. They talked about goals and dreams; they offered hope and talked about life after cancer.

I remember Dr. Loeb walking into the exam room wearing jeans and Keds® sneakers. When he entered the room, he hopped up on the table and sat next to Allie. That day we also met his associate, who had just returned from maternity leave. We had no idea what a strong prayer warrior she would become or that we would watch her new baby become a toddler. Allie laughed and smiled and got to know these doctors, who would literally have her life in their hands. I felt a mixture of relief and fear as we developed a plan to fight cancer. If Allison had doubts or fears, it did not show. I watched her face and saw determination, trust and hope. Our lives were about to change drastically, and we really could not comprehend the trials that lay ahead.

01/26/2010 Email to Allie Speck's Prayer Warriors
Today Allie endured a bone scan, a heart study and an appointment to discuss the possibility of radiation. It was a grueling ten-hour day. We are in for a long, hard journey, and we don't understand, so we are leaning on the Lord.

One of the hardest jobs as Allie's mom was driving her to the hospital, especially when she was sick and did not want to go. I heard parents talk about the stress of sending their kids back to school or off to college. Meanwhile, I am wondering if any parent could comprehend the sense of anxiety and fear I was feeling as I made my daughter go to the hospital for appointments, tests and, eventually, chemo. I reminded myself that this was our new reality and that before December 10th I could not have comprehended this situation either. I pushed down my anger as I heard parents worry about healthy kids who would return home at the end of the day. Father, forgive them for they do not understand…and I prayed they never would.

A story written by Allison entitled "Graffiti"

We had traveled this segment of I-83 between Harrisburg and Baltimore so many times that we could probably do it with our eyes closed. In fact, I'm pretty sure my mom literally has driven with her eyes closed at least once. The ride is never enjoyable. When we are headed down, it is usually toward another chemo treatment or new surgery, and when we are coming back, I am often consequently sick or in pain.

Driving down, I think: The worst part is the dread. Driving back, I think: The worst part is the discomfort. In the winter, I insist: The worst part is the boredom. (This often comes with a hundred miles of drab scenery and traffic.) In the summer, I decide: The worst part is the scenery. It's right there out my window, green and beautiful, and I only get to drive through it on the way to the big, sterile building of concrete and glass or to a home where my bed and a basin wait eagerly for my return.

It is a miserable ride any way you look at it, and the worst part is, even when it is over, you know you must drive it again...and again...and again.

After frequenting the same stretch of road so many times, I soon had it marked out with obscure landmarks to mark our progress. They go something like this: home, exit where you choose to go left to Hershey Park or right to Hopkins (unfortunately it is always the latter), big spinning statue of a man squatting a barbell, free concrete barriers advertised, truck stop, lake, Maryland border, the last Wendy's, big Pepsi sign, hospital.

On the way back the landmarks are different: hospital, billboard advertising what production is at the local theater, a stretch of winding road that makes me feel nauseous like I am in the movie *Fast and Furious*, a farmhouse/fireworks store, bridge with a pink monster spray-painted on it with the words *what is love*, rumble strips, river, home.

I traveled it for days, weeks, months and finally years. Cancer dragged me back and forth between two points, home and hospital, until they blurred together and one was barely distinguishable from the other. I grew tired of the journey and became familiar enough with the trip to sleep through most of it.

Then one day my order of usual landmarks was disrupted suddenly by a bridge. It came on the way home,

just between the fireworks barn and the pink monster. I
don't doubt the bridge had been there before and that
we had driven under it a hundred times, but it had never
existed for me until someone spray painted across the
arch of the bridge "DON'T GIVE UP!"

"Hmm." The noise escaped my throat before I realized
I was making it out loud and not in my head.

"What?" my mom said, peeling her eyes off the
bumper of the car ahead of us and glancing in my
direction.

"That bridge we just went under...did you see it?"

"No."

"Oh. Never mind."

Then while I was still thinking about the first bridge, we
passed under a second bridge that had in the same
black letters, "IT GETS BETTER!" I glanced at my mom.
She had not noticed.

Don't give up. It gets better.

I repeated the words in my mind over and over. Their
meaning caught somewhere inside me and stuck. I
immediately added the two bridges to my mental map.
From then on, it was almost a relief to see those words
each time we passed under them.

Two months later I was dozing in the passenger's
seat as we approached the bridge. My mom suddenly
snapped from her zombie driving state and pointed, her
eyes suddenly alive.

"Look! Look at that! 'DON'T GIVE UP!' That's for you,
Allie!" She smiled at me, proud to have been the one to
receive the divine sign sent from some heavenly spray-
paint can.

"Yeah, I see," I said, smiling weakly. It had been a long
hospital stay this time.

"And look at the next one! 'IT GETS BETTER!'"

We both smiled again, and from then on, an unspo-
ken acknowledgment passed between us each time we
saw that graffiti: mutual trust that it would prove true.

I was never so thankful for vandalism.

01/27/2010 Email to Allie Speck's Prayer Warriors
Praise the Lord, Allison's bone scan shows no signs
of cancer! We made a tough decision to withdraw

Allison from college for the spring semester so she can focus on treatment.

Before Allie's cancer, she chose Jeremiah 29:11 for her high school graduation announcements. That scripture has new meaning as we seek God's plan for Allie.

Allison's Journal, January 29, 2010

"They are like a man building a house, who dug down deep and laid the foundation on rock. When a flood came, the torrent struck the house but could not shake it because it was well built" (Luke 6:48).

♥Allie

01/29/2010 Email to Allie Speck's Prayer Warriors
Allie needs a PET scan to see if the cancer has spread. The testing and decisions are physically and spiritually exhausting! God is sustaining Allie.

02/03/2010 Email to Allie Speck's Prayer Warriors
We received Allie's PET scan results, and thank God there is no sign of cancer in her body except for the liver tumors. Tomorrow she will have surgery to insert a port in her chest and a procedure that will inject chemo directly into the biggest liver tumor.

This evening, two pastors visited our home and anointed Allison with oil. We felt God's presence.

Our lives have drastically changed in the last two months. Putting God first is a choice as we learn to let Him lead. We are instructed to be doers of the Word, not hearers only (James 1:22). We must act out our faith.

02/05/2010 Email to Allie Speck's Prayer Warriors
Both the port placement and the chemo injection went well, although Allie is very sore. There will be a scan in three weeks to check the size of the tumor.

Allie signed forms today to start chemo on Monday.
We are one step further on our journey.

I remember the consent forms and the fact that Allison was 19 years old and did not need my permission to sign for chemotherapy treatment. I cried without her seeing, as I realized the full impact of the difficult decisions she was being asked to make. Being a spectator to the multiple discussions and recommendations was overwhelming as a parent; I can only imagine how Allie felt.

02/07/2010 Email to Allie Speck's Prayer Warriors
Due to fever and nausea, Allison ended up in the local ER. Despite the negative circumstance, God showed up to let us know we are not alone. It started with the girl who registered Allison and six more people throughout the Emergency Room, who stopped to tell her they were her prayer warriors. As Romans 8:31 says, if God is with us, who can be against us?

CHAPTER SIX

ONE DAY AT A TIME

02/09/2010 Email to Allie Speck's Prayer Warriors
We have arrived to begin the first round of chemo. In
the clinic, Allie gave her doctor a "God is bigger than
Carl" bracelet. Allie named her biggest tumor Carl after
the grumpy character from the Disney movie *UP*. Her
doctor took the bracelet and promised to pray for Allie.

Allie felt well enough to chat online with her brother.
The snow is falling outside as we feel God continue to
work things out in His timing.

Today in the clinic we heard a group of nurses sing
"Happy end of chemo to you" to the tune of Happy
Birthday. They were singing to a child who no longer needs chemo. We are praying that someday soon
they will sing to Allie.

Thank you for your prayers that have carried us this
far in our journey. I sit here in Allie's room and watch
all the bald children pushing IV pumps in the hallway.
If they can endure this, so can we! Pray for all families
dealing with cancer, but especially for the children.

The first chemo drug has started. While Allie sleeps,
I am praying for her. It would be easy to become
depressed in this unit, except for the fact that these
children have such beautiful spirits. This is a whole

different world than the one you live in...I pray you never experience it.

02/11/2010 Email to Allie Speck's Prayer Warriors
Allison is receiving her second dose of chemo. About midnight she began hallucinating. It was scary, but evidently it can be a side effect of chemo.

This morning as her confusion cleared, I read to her from the Bible. Allie was fearful to receive more chemo because of the hallucinations. But the Lord spoke to us in the following scripture, Luke 12:22–26: "Then Jesus said to his disciples: 'Therefore I tell you, do not worry about your life, what you will eat; or about your body, what you will wear. For life is more than food, and the body more than clothes. Consider the ravens: They do not sow or reap; they have no storeroom or barn; yet God feeds them. And how much more valuable you are than birds! Who of you by worrying can add a single hour to your life? Since you cannot do this very little thing, why do you worry about the rest?'"

Urgent Prayer Request
Prayer warriors, we need you! Last night was exhausting and terrifying. Allison had night terrors. She appeared to be asleep, but she would scream out as if she were being tortured. I could hardly watch, yet I could not leave her side. The nurses believe it is a side effect from the chemo. I felt so helpless as I spent the night in tears, praying and reading scriptures while trying to hold her. It was one of the worst nights of my life. The nurses tell me they have seen these hallucinations with chemo, but nothing as severe as what Allison experienced. I am scared and don't know what to do except pray and ask you to pray.

This was one of many long nights spent at Allison's bedside questioning how to pray and what to do to help her. Her screams were primal, deep and terrifying. I tried to hold her, but she was inconsolable. The next morning a nurse stayed with Allie so I could go to the family kitchen for a much-needed cup of coffee. While making my coffee, another parent walked in and asked if I had heard the horrible screaming during the night. When I told that parent it was my child who was screaming, she walked over and gave me a much-needed hug while I sobbed on her shoulder. We were strangers who connected for a brief moment, mourning the loss of our "normal" lives to the evils of cancer and cancer treatment.

02/12/2010 Email to Allie Speck's Prayer Warriors
Allison is better this evening. Thank you for your prayers.

The cancer doctor visited Allie and confirmed her hallucinations are related to the chemo. It is one of the most severe reactions he has ever seen. The good news is that Allison's memory of the experience is limited. She is tired and has been very emotional throughout the day. The doctors have decided there will be no more chemo at this time. We are heading home when Allie feels ready to travel.

We will return for an MRI. I pray the chemo has been as toxic to the tumor as it has been to Allie's mind.

Allison's Journal, February 14, 2010

Dear God,
   It has been a long time. I pray that You would come and fellowship with me this morning, although I have been unable or unwilling to meet with You. I pray You reignite my passion for You.
   Luke 9:23–25 (NKJV): "…Take up [your] cross daily, and follow Me…For what profit is it to a man if he gains the whole world, and is himself destroyed or lost?" I do not want to gain the whole world and lose my soul.
                                                    ♥Allie

02/14/2010 Email to Allie Speck's Prayer Warriors
Today is a better day. We were home and slept in our beds.

This morning we attended church. This afternoon we had a visit from a friend who is a cancer survivor. He came to encourage Allie. God has brought so many amazing people into our lives on this journey.

We are so proud of Allison. The local paper wrote an article entitled "Speck's strength, faith in cancer fight inspires others." What an accurate choice of words as we watch her remain faithful, inspiring us and others.

02/17/2010 Email to Allie Speck's Prayer Warriors
Allison has had several bad days. It is so hard to watch a girl who never slowed down become a girl who needs help to walk up the steps.

Please pray for the tumor to be smaller and for less pain, a desire to eat, relief from nausea and more energy.

We have received emails from people all over the world telling us how this journey has influenced their walk with God. Tonight, Tom and Andy went to Ash Wednesday service, where Andy was the worship leader. We are so proud of him and his faith. Pray for him as he watches his sister's battle and learns how to walk his own faith journey.

02/18/2010 Email to Allie Speck's Prayer Warriors
Allison has extreme pain in her throat and chest. We went to the ER and discovered her white blood cell count is dangerously low and causing sores in her mouth and throat.

She will be in the hospital until her blood counts increase. This afternoon she asked me, "Will I always feel this bad?" My answer was, "I hope and pray not." It breaks my heart to see her so sick!

02/19/2010 Email to Allie Speck's Prayer Warriors
Last night Allison hit a low where she questioned why this is happening and if God is listening. She told me she isn't sure how to pray because she is so sick. So, prayer warriors, your job is to inter-

cede for Allison because she is unable to pray
for herself.

Today we read Isaiah 43:2: "When you pass through
the waters, I will be with you; and when you pass
through the rivers, they will not sweep over you.
When you walk through the fire, you will not be
burned; the flames will not set you ablaze." Lord,
protect Allie.

02/21/2010 Email to Allie Speck's Prayer Warriors
Allison remains in the hospital. Blood counts are
improving slowly. She has a pain pump to help her
tolerate eating. The days are long.

Allison has begun to lose her hair. Even though
we were told to expect this, we did not expect it to
happen so soon. It is outward evidence of the battle
being waged in her body. She wants a short haircut
to make the journey to baldness less traumatic. Once
again, my heart is breaking.

Today we read Paul's words about how suffering
makes us stronger.

"...Therefore, in order to keep me from becoming con-
ceited, I was given a thorn in my flesh, a messenger
of Satan, to torment me. Three times I pleaded with
the Lord to take it away from me. But he said to me,
'My grace is sufficient for you, for my power is made
perfect in weakness.' Therefore, I will boast all the
more gladly about my weaknesses, so that Christ's
power may rest on me. That is why, for Christ's sake,
I delight in weaknesses, in insults, in hardships, in
persecutions, in difficulties. For when I am weak,
then I am strong" (2 Corinthians 12:7-10).

When we are weak, He is our strength.

02/23/2010 Email to Allie Speck's Prayer Warriors
Allison is home and got the short haircut she
wanted. She told us her hair physically hurts and

when she pulls it, it relieves the pain. Her hair
is coming out in handfuls. My beautiful daughter
will soon be bald.

I saw her smile today for the first time in awhile. She
has a beautiful smile, and I did not realize how much
I had missed it. I teased her about losing her hair,
eating soft foods and needing help to walk, telling
her she is my baby girl again. She laughed at this,
which is something else I have not heard recently.
We both smiled as we tried to make light of the current situation.

We are in the season of Lent when people give up
things as a sacrifice. Jokingly, Allison said she is giving up her hair for Lent.

MRI Results
We are disappointed. There is no change in the
tumors.

Last night, Allison pulled out the hair that remained
and slept with a hat on because her head feels cold. It
is a difficult thing to watch, but she seems okay with
it. I cannot believe how our lives have changed.

My heart is heavy tonight. Pray for peace for Allie.
She is having pain in her abdomen, and the last
thing we want is another weekend trip to an ER.
Our 19-year-old daughter deserves to have a normal weekend.

03/03/2010 Email to Allie Speck's Prayer Warriors
Allison has been doing more but tires easily. She has
peach fuzz for hair and originally said she did not
want a wig. However, when we went for dinner, she
wore a scarf and people openly stared at her. It broke
my heart. I wish I could protect her.

Today she went to the American Cancer Society and
got a free wig. It provides her with an option other
than scarves or hats. Tonight, she felt well enough

to go out with a friend and the wig is still on her dresser. I admire her strength.

03/07/2010 Email to Allie Speck's Prayer Warriors
Allison received chemo directly into the large tumor again. The doctor doing the procedure told us the tumor looked different. Allie asked, "Good different or bad different?" He says good different and told us not to be discouraged by no shrinkage after one treatment. We await the next scan.

Allison's Journal, March 8, 2010

I sit outside my house on a dining room chair I drug onto the porch. What a beautiful day I have found! A woodpecker pecks away in a tree. The wind blows gently, trying to turn my pages; bushes rustle; snow melts. A quote comes to my mind written by Anne Frank for when you feel misery or pain. She says, "My advice is 'Go outside to the fields, enjoy nature and the sunshine, go out and try to recapture happiness in yourself and in God. Think of all the beauty that is still left in and around you and be happy!'" I took her advice today and shuffled my scrawny bald body wrapped in pajamas, bathrobe and a winter hat outside. The sun hit me full on and warmed my body. All the familiar smells of home when I was healthy came rushing back. Somewhere someone is burning wood. I caught a hint of laundry on someone's line. I sense the end of winter and the rebirth of life in the world.

God speaks through His creation and today He has spoken peace into my soul. As the trees await summer, so do I, but I see the beauty in waiting. The quiet anticipation of the abundance of life that is to come. When I look at the beauty of nature I always think, "He didn't have to make it so beautiful, but HE DID!" The whole of creation, from the heights of the heavens to the depths of the sea— everything reflects God's majesty and so often we miss it. What wonderful advice to just sit and glorify God through nature. How healing to see the good He has made for us and to remember His promise to sustain us and hold onto us even through the longest winters.

"Do you not know? Have you not heard? The Lord is the everlasting God, the Creator of the ends of the earth. He will not grow tired or weary, and his understanding no one can fathom. He gives strength to the weary and increases the power of the weak....young men stumble and fall; but those who HOPE in the Lord will renew their strength. They will soar on wings like eagles; they will run and not grow weary, they will walk and not be faint"(Isaiah 40:28–31).

♥Allie

03/10/2010 Email to Allie Speck's Prayer Warriors
Allison's doctors delayed chemo so she could attend her high school's spring musical. Allie loves the stage and had the lead in her high school senior musical. God blessed Allie with an amazing voice, and she enjoyed being able to watch her friends perform. It was a nice distraction from the cancer journey. Allie also had visits from friends who are home on spring break. It was great to see her laughing and smiling even though we know she wants to be on spring break too.

We received an update on Allison's cancer treatment after a group of specialists reviewed her case. They feel Allie should receive the same chemo drugs given at a slower rate to decrease the risk of side effects. We are hesitant to get the same chemo, but we want whatever gives her the best possible outcome.

Allison's Journal, March 10, 2010

Cancer. It is such an ugly word. A scary word. Malicious. I would put that word in the same category. Cancer. It is still hard to wrap my head around. It seems so big. I feel like it is controlling my life. I fear that it could end my life. I think the reason I put off writing about my cancer was because I felt like it would be "the words I left behind." How can I make sense of this? It would seem like what I was writing would be my last legacy; my family would read through it and possibly use it at my funeral or cry over the words or try to get it published. All of those things are perfectly fine for them to do, but I felt if I wrote I would be fulfilling something. I would be making something God could use after I was gone...which meant He would not need me here. It is really twisted and hard to explain, but sometimes your mind thinks crazy things. I have to keep telling myself that what I have is treatable and that God still has plans for me. But, if His plan is that I would not be healed, if my death would further His Kingdom more than my life could, then I am at peace with that. My mom tells me not to think that way at all, but I feel like I need to sometimes. Of course, I am not always thinking about death and my cancer, but it does come to mind. Shouldn't I prepare my spirit for either outcome? Or does that mean I am not trusting God to heal me? In the end, I believe God has big plans for me. He is much bigger than cancer and He will lead me through whatever obstacles I face.

♥Allie

Allison's Journal, March 14, 2010

Well, I guess it is technically the 15th since it is almost 2:00 a.m. That means that today I go for my second round of chemo. I'm a lot less afraid this time. I guess because I know what I am getting into. I am just ready to go and get my yuckiness over with so I can get better and have some more good days. I think this time I will try to get out of the room and meet some of the kids on the floor.

Tonight my family and I watched *Joseph: King of Dreams*, an animated musical about the story of Joseph. I was reminded how God has plans for our lives even when we cannot see them being fulfilled. Joseph dreamed about his future years before they came true. He faced many trials that seemed like his plan from God would not be fulfilled. I feel a connection to Joseph's story. I KNOW God has a plan for my life, a plan much bigger than me, and I have faith He is already fulfilling that plan. You see, EVERYTHING that happened to Joseph was part of God's plan. It all worked together to fulfill a greater purpose. Thank You, Lord, for Joseph's story and for showing me You know better than I do about what is going on in my life.

Lyrics from *Joseph*: "You know better than I, you know the way, I've let go the need to know why. I'll take what answers you supply because you know better than I."

♥Allie

03/15/2010 Email to Allie Speck's Prayer Warriors
We arrived at the hospital for round two of chemo. Allie's brother, Andy, and her dad came along and stayed with us until Allie was admitted. It was nice to have them along, and it seemed to help Andy to see the process Allie goes through when she comes to the hospital.

Allie and I are reading *Hope Beyond Reason: Embraced by God's Presence in the Toughest of Times*, written by a pastor who successfully battled leukemia. He quotes the following scriptures in his book: "I will not die but live, and will proclaim what the Lord has done" (Psalm 118:17) and "For he will command his angels concerning you to guard you in all your ways; they will lift you up in their hands, so that you will not strike your foot against a stone" (Psalm 91:11–12). We are praying these scriptures over Allison tonight. Chemo has started.

03/16/2010 Email to Allie Speck's Prayer Warriors
Prayers have been answered! Allison had a good night. She feels "foggy" in her thoughts but no hallucinations. I believe the scriptures protected her.

God is with us in this valley, we know that. God is using Allison and this situation to touch thousands of people. Her mission has begun, and when she is well, she intends to share her story with every church that prayed for her.

Allison's plans after graduating college were to enter the mission field. We know that she is already on the mission field...and it is reaching far and wide. God has big plans for Allie, and, while they are not what we would have chosen, we are walking through this valley believing it is a miracle in the making.

03/17/2010 Email to Allie Speck's Prayer Warriors
Another good night for Allison, although today was
more challenging. We continue to ask God to protect
her from the side effects of chemo.

03/18/2010 Email to Allie Speck's Prayer Warriors
Another good night! I thanked God several times
that Allison has not had hallucinations. Two nights of
chemo remain. Nausea, however, has become an issue.

Pray for Tom as he travels to Baltimore to relieve
me so I can go to work. Allison became emotional
last night, and we read scriptures until she felt calm.
The nurses said they are glad to see Allie doing well.
They remember Allison's last chemo treatment for
all the wrong reasons.

03/20/2010 Email to Allie Speck's Prayer Warriors
Today is the first day of spring! We welcome new
beginnings! Allison completed her chemo and did
well. Several of Allie's nurses and doctors are now
wearing the "GOD IS BIGGER THAN CARL" bracelets
and praying for her. Allie's liver surgeon stopped to
visit. He commented on the cards he received prior
to Allie's surgery. He is amazed at the outpouring of
love. The surgeon's heart and mind will be in a different place the next time he operates on Allie.

This has been a rough week with nausea and fatigue.
No one should have to endure what Allison has experienced. Her spirit and determination amaze and
inspire everyone she meets.

Allison's Journal, March 22, 2010

Chemo is the devil! I received my second chemo Monday through Friday of last week. I came home Saturday.
I was vomiting nonstop; I would stand over the bucket,
and it would spew out. I could barely catch my breath.
On top of that I was so weak that I could not walk on
my own. After throwing up, I would feel so exhausted
that I thought I might die. One time I passed out from

exhaustion. And my throat is ulcerated and EVERYTHING hurts or is uncomfortable. Walking up the stairs wears me out so much that when I finally make it (with help from Mom, Dad or Andy), I lay at the top because I can barely breathe. One day at a time. This is seriously the hardest thing I have ever done. But I am going to make it! JEREMIAH 29:11!

♥Allie

CHAPTER SEVEN
PRAY, PRAY, PRAY

03/24/2010 Email to Allie Speck's Prayer Warriors
Allison is back in the hospital. She is barely able to walk one flight of steps. She woke up screaming with pain in her chest and cannot swallow her own saliva.

Please remember Allie's brother, Andy, as he tolerates sharing a parent while we take turns staying with Allie. I pray he feels our love and understands our desire to support Allie, who does not want to be left alone.

03/25/2010 Email to Allie Speck's Prayer Warriors
Allison remains in the hospital with a fever. I wanted to share a portion of my devotion today out of Dr. Jim Burns's HomeWord, written by Kelly McFadden. This scripture spoke to me about things happening in God's timing. John 11:43–44 says, "When he had said this, Jesus called in a loud voice, 'Lazarus, come out!' The dead man came out, his hands and feet wrapped with strips of linen, and a cloth around his face." If God can bring Lazarus back from the dead, then He can heal Allison completely of cancer. We want the blessing God has in store for Allison.

There are moments in life that only God can create, and they are called miracles. The story of Lazarus (which is one of Allie's favorites) shows that when

Jesus was told Lazarus was sick, He waited two days before going to see him. Why? Lazarus's sisters told Jesus when He arrived that if He had been there, Lazarus would not have died. Lazarus's sisters, Mary and Martha, saw Jesus perform miracles, so why would they doubt that Jesus could heal Lazarus? I think they are human, like us, and thought it was too late and so gave up hope. We often do the same thing. We want a miracle, but we don't always ask for it or expect it. Jesus wants us to hope in Him and trust Him in ALL things. Jesus is NEVER late.

03/27/2010 Email to Allie Speck's Prayer Warriors
Tonight, at Allie's high school, there is a fundraiser to help with her medical expenses. Allie wanted to attend but could not because she is in the hospital. She recorded a video to be shown during intermission to thank everyone for their support. We will be watching the event on Allie's computer.

As I sit here watching Allie sleep, I reflect on this journey that is scary, crazy, exhausting, rewarding, all-consuming and overwhelming...but through it all we know that God is with us. We have met many people we would not have met without this journey.

03/29/2010 Email to Allie Speck's Prayer Warriors
Allie was discharged today after six days! Her fever is gone, her pain is controlled and blood counts continue to rise. Pray for relief from her nausea and vomiting. We are exhausted, but we are home.

Allison was so sick after the second chemo treatment. While I was driving her to the ER, she looked at me with tears in her eyes and said, "Mom, I think I am dying." My heart dropped. I felt lost and had no words. I was scared. As a parent, you want to protect your child. I could think of no response other than to say, "Please don't give up. I love you!" And then I prayed because I did not know what else to do.

04/06/2010 Email to Allie Speck's Prayer Warriors
Happy Easter! Today we celebrate our hope of heaven. Allison felt well enough to attend church and dinner. We had a "Thanksgiving dinner" at Allison's request. It was an enjoyable evening.

Allison scheduled some professional pictures to document her cancer journey. The friend who took the pictures made Allie feel comfortable and beautiful, despite her scars and baldness. Life is good for the moment, and we are thankful.

Tomorrow, Allie has an MRI. We pray her tumors are shrinking. That would be encouraging as she faces the next round of chemo.

04/09/2010 Email to Allie Speck's Prayer Warriors
Woo hoo, prayer warriors!

Prayers are being answered! We give God all the glory for the call we received today. All of the tumors in Allie's liver are shrinking! We shed tears of joy. The chemo is working! What a wonderful feeling to get encouraging news! It is indescribable!

Earlier this week I heard the song "Praise You in the Storm" by Casting Crowns. The song spoke to me about Allison's situation. I found myself singing along and understanding that we should not only praise God in the times of peace and plenty, but we also need to praise Him in the storms.

Allie was interviewed by our local news. It is a great interview and shows Allie's strength, faith and determination.

04/17/2010 Email to Allie Speck's Prayer Warriors
Allison has had several good weeks. She is feeling decent and eating well. Andy started baseball, and life seems almost normal.

Last evening we received a call to schedule Allie's

third round of chemo. Allison has felt so good, she is anxious to see how great she feels with NO cancer in her body. She is encouraged by the news of the shrinking tumors, so she scheduled college classes for the fall semester. Our hope is that she will be done with treatment and have surgery in July so she can return to college cancer-free.

Allison's Journal, April 20, 2010

Am I too stubborn to take my own advice? I had just come to the realization that all of my worrying about the future is pointless. However, after being off chemo for four weeks and feeling so good, I began to forget what I learned. I started to slip back into my old habits of being stubborn and worrying. Today I was reminded of what I had learned. It may sound crazy, but getting treatments is actually enjoyable in one area: my family is much kinder. It is not that we are mean at all, but I think it makes us appreciate each other more. However, it is easy to cherish one another and live life with less abrasiveness when my suffering is constantly there as a reminder of just how short life can be. Cancer really puts things into perspective. But what about when I am better? I do not want to slip back into making life complicated. Maybe I need to be sick a little longer to really engrave this knowledge into my lifestyle.

   I am amazed at how God is using this to change me. I feel like a new person. I am much more confident and kinder. There are so many changes...even my way of thinking or seeing things. I cannot wait to see how changed I am by the end of all this. God is doing a great thing within me and with my life. For example, one friend says she is an atheist, but she has so many questions. She told me all the stuff that is going on with me has changed the way she thinks. She said reading my mom's emails and seeing my faith makes it hard not to believe. She said, "It is your faith that is getting you through this." I was blown away! I praise God for how He has used me to open her heart. I simply told her that with all I have seen and been through, in my mind, there is no way there could NOT be a God. I hope I am a good example for her. I am glad God put words in my mouth to respond because I had no idea what to say. I believe God made an impact on her through me.

♥Allie

04/21/2010 Email to Allie Speck's Prayer Warriors
Allie had the large tumor injected with chemo again today. She had a lot of discomfort during the procedure, but the doctor told us he is pleased with how things went. He said she looks better than during the last two treatments. This made her smile.

She ate with no nausea and is now asleep and looks comfortable. She has a pain pump, which must be working.

To close I want to share a quote from a book I am reading, entitled *Your Best Life Now*. It asks, "When God brings an opportunity across your path, do you step out boldly in faith, expecting the best? God's resources are unlimited. He is not limited by what you have or don't have. HE CAN DO ANYTHING, IF YOU BELIEVE!"

Allison's Journal, April 22, 2010

Did I forget to mention that on April 20th my brother, Andy, turned 14! He is growing up so fast, and I am so proud of him. He is such a Godly young man, and I hope he never changes. He has been so strong through everything that has been going on with me. He does not get jealous when I get more attention or when Mom and Dad have to be away with me. He does not complain or get angry. He hasn't talked much about how he feels, which makes me a little concerned that he is bottling a lot up. I know I used to be like that until I got sick. I did not talk about my feelings. I see a lot of myself in him even though we are very different. I pray that God guides him as He did me, and I pray Andy is a better listener.

♥Allie

04/25/2010 Email to Allie Speck's Prayer Warriors
It is a rainy, cold Sunday afternoon. Allison has been doing pretty well since returning home from her chemo injection. She has nausea with no vomiting. She is very weak and has not left the house since we got home.

Allie has a week off between treatments. We return to the hospital in three days for the third cycle of chemo. The tumor being smaller causes less pressure on her stomach; however, she is experiencing sharp pain in the area of the tumor, which we hope is an indication that the cancer cells are dying.

04/29/2010 Email to Allie Speck's Prayer Warriors
Allison has been admitted for her third round of chemo. She feels pretty good with less nausea.

We wanted to share that Allison's brother, Andy, who loves baseball, has an opportunity to throw out the first pitch at the Harrisburg Senators game. We cannot wait.

This amazing young man started a prayer table at school for his sister. During lunch, all the kids at the table join hands and pray for Allie. When Jesus said we should have faith like little children, I think this is what He meant. As parents, we could not be more proud of Andy as he realizes he can cast his cares on a God who loves him.

05/02/2010 Email to Allie Speck's Prayer Warriors
Allison has been amazingly tolerant of this chemo treatment. She repeatedly says she cannot believe how good she feels. We are so thankful and give God all the glory.

God tells us that "we have not, because we ask not" in James 4:2. We had an uneventful chemo experience because we prayed for it and believed it could happen. We can't just pray; we must also believe that God will answer. God is doing above and beyond what we have asked.

Hoping we will see some of you at the Senators game when Andy throws out the first pitch. He is so excited, and Allison hopes to feel well enough to attend.

05/04/2010 Email to Allie Speck's Prayer Warriors
We are home! Allison tolerated this chemo treatment the best so far. She is tired and weak, but home.

Allison is a shining example of how to travel through the valleys of life while maintaining a positive spirit.

05/06/2010 Email to Allie Speck's Prayer Warriors
We had an amazing evening at the Senators game! Allison is weak, but nothing would keep her from attending the event. The evening was perfect: our family together, beautiful weather, Andy throwing out the first pitch, and Allie well enough to attend. I shed a few tears as we celebrated a moment that we used to take for granted.

When you fix your eyes on Jesus, you will find He is the author and finisher of our faith, the beginning and the end, the Alpha and the Omega (Hebrews 12:2; Revelation 22:13). I love this quote from Corrie ten Boom: "If you look at the world, you will be depressed. If you look within, you will be distressed. But if you look at Christ, you will be at rest." Amen.

Allison's Journal, May 10, 2010

I want to take a few minutes to reflect on my journey. On November 3rd I wrote a note to God. I remember that night, as I was filled with the Holy Spirit and on fire to do something, anything, for the Lord. I remember writing, "Use me to Your glory." I thought I would go abroad soon for mission work. Little did I know my mission was right here. I closed my entry with, "Great I Am, my gift to You is my life. I lay it down willingly before You as an offering. Take it and use it." I was willing, and that is all God needed to hear.

My next entry was on November 4th (the next day), and I had gone to chapel at Messiah. The speaker talked about the importance of daily devotions to have a true relationship with God. She gave us a 21-day challenge to read a chapter of John every day, meditate, pray and keep a prayer journal. So, I did, and my spirit was strengthened and I was pulled closer to God. He showed me areas of my life that needed work and began molding me. Now, because I was sick in November, I did not finish in exactly 21 days. But the day I finished was December 10th, the same day I went to see the doctor about my "lump" and ended up having a CT scan to find this mass. Was that a coincidence? Nope.

♥Allie

05/11/2010 Email to Allie Speck's Prayer Warriors
Your prayers continue to be answered. Allison has been feeling well. She has not vomited once since the third round of chemo and the biggest answered prayer...no fever! This has been a wonderful post-chemo time that almost makes all the other times seem like an awful memory. Allie is scheduled for another MRI, and we are anticipating good results.

Allison's Journal, May 13, 2010

Tomorrow is my scan to see if the tumors are smaller. I hope they are! My mom talks all the time about thinking/believing things and they will happen. I think it might be true. If you dream about something long and hard enough, it can happen. I have never shared this before, but I used to daydream about what it would be like if I had cancer. I used to think of all the lives I could touch and how I could glorify God. (No lie, I am serious.) But I thought it would never happen, and guess what? Isn't it amazing how God prepares us? I think He may have put those daydreams in my head as preparation. I believe God speaks to me through my imagination. Lately as I fall asleep, I imagine how it will be when the doctors tell me I am healed. I must go to sleep soon because we have to be at Hopkins early tomorrow. I am praying for good news.

♥Allie

05/15/2010 Email to Allie Speck's Prayer Warriors
We have received encouraging news! The most
recent MRI shows shrinkage of the tumors. I have
attached a copy of the email sent by one of Allie's
doctors. Be sure to note #7 of the doctor's plan:

I have really exciting news. After everyone reviewed
Allie's scans, the verdict is in. We are going to do one
more round of chemo and then surgery. The surgeon
is pleased with our progress and thinks one more
cycle of chemo will put the finishing touches to make
the largest tumor more removable.

So, the plan will be:

1 – 6. Treatment details
7. Pray, pray, pray

Isn't it fantastic that the doctor included prayer in
the plan! Allison says if the surgeon goes in again, it
is for him to take ALL of Carl, not just a piece.

We serve an awesome God, and He will work for good
through this situation. In fact, He already has.

CHAPTER EIGHT

DANCE WITH THE DEVIL

Allison's Journal, May 18, 2010

Dear God,

A lot has happened since the last entry. Thank You for getting me through the past three chemo treatments. The surgeon looked at the last scan and thinks I will soon be ready for surgery. The finish line is in sight! It has been like a bike race. The first two chemo treatments were all uphill, and this last treatment was a nice downhill coast. As I look at the remaining treatments, I am praying I will be able to have surgery in July and return to college in August. After surgery, I plan to begin a "testimony tour" and speak at all of the churches that prayed for me.

I am reading Luke chapter 9 about when Jesus took two fish and five loaves and fed 5,000 people. It says that Jesus blessed and broke the fish and bread. In order to get the full potential, Jesus had to break them. As they were, they were what the disciples said, "just two fish and five loaves," but broken, they were literally more than what anyone thought possible. Broken, they became a miracle! Isn't it the same with me? I have been broken and now I can be a blessing to others.

"For the Son of Man did not come to destroy men's lives but to save them" (Luke 9:56 NKJV). No matter what, God does not harm us. This cancer is NOT to destroy my life, but to save it and to save others. Thank You, Jesus!

♥Allie

05/23/2010 Email to Allie Speck's Prayer Warriors
We were blessed this weekend. A softball tournament was held to benefit our family. Not only did it
raise funds to help with medical bills, but Allie also
was able to attend and participate. We formed a team
named the "CARL KILLERS." Allison said it was the
most fun she has had in a long time.

Thank you to everyone who came to support our
family. Each game had a volunteer umpire who
turned down paying games to support Allison. What
a boost to Allie's spirit! I cried as I listened to Allie's
beautiful voice as she and her friend sang "The
Star-Spangled Banner" to open the tournament.

I remember the day in February when the organizer
of this event called to tell us about his idea for the
fundraiser. I had to hang up during the call because
Allie began vomiting blood and passed out on our
kitchen floor. At that time, the organizer was hoping
Allie would be well enough to hand out trophies to
the winners. When I think where we were then and
where Allie is now, it is truly a miracle.

Watching Allie and Andy play softball was one of
my greatest joys during this time. When I think that
Allie could barely walk a flight of stairs a few months
before but was then able to swing a bat and hit a
softball, I was amazed and thankful. She did not run
the bases, but she was able to participate with her
brother and feel part of the event rather than just
be a spectator who is sick. I sat in my car and cried
tears of joy as I watched my children play softball
and enjoy life. For many people, moments like this
are taken for granted. But for our family, that day
was a precious gift.

05/26/2010 Email to Allie Speck's Prayer Warriors
We are home. Allison had chemo injected into her
large tumor today. The doctor "hit it hard" because
the surgeon wants the most tumor shrinkage possible
before surgery. As a result, Allison has a lot of pain.

The doctor who injected the tumor came to recovery and shared news with us that confirmed God's presence throughout this journey. He told us most patients referred to him with a tumor of Allison's size have no shrinkage of their tumor and usually cannot have surgery. The first time he injected Allie's tumor, he said it was like shining a tiny flashlight in a huge cavern. He did not believe his treatment would make a difference.

After saying that, he smiled and told us he heard about Allie's prayer warriors, and he believes the prayers are what made the difference! What a testimony! We know Allie's situation is no surprise to God. It was nice to see a smile on the face of a doctor who did not smile the first time he met Allie.

05/27/2010 Email to Allie Speck's Prayer Warriors
Allison is having A LOT of pain in her tumor and has spiked a fever of 102. She feels miserable and has not been able to get out of bed. She has moments of intense pain that cause her to cry out. It is one more difficult moment as a parent, knowing there is nothing we can do but pray.

05/29/2010 Email to Allie Speck's Prayer Warriors
We are preparing for a Memorial Day family gathering. Despite Allison's pain, the doctor feels it will be safe to travel a short distance. The doctors believe the pain is related to swelling of the tumor. Allie wants to make an overnight trip to be with family. Fresh mountain air, fellowship with family and a night under the stars may be the best medicine.

06/01/2010 Email to Allie Speck's Prayer Warriors
So much has happened in a few short days. We made the trip to the family gathering. It was one night away, but much needed and appreciated.

Sunday, we visited a church that has been praying for Allie. The road to the church was rough, causing Allie a lot of pain. She sat in the parking lot until the pain subsided enough for her to go into the church. She said she felt the devil was trying to keep her from attending the service. During the service, the leaders of the church prayed over Allie and anointed her with oil. This is the first step in what Allison hopes will be her mission field, to travel and share her testimony.

Today Allie was admitted for her fourth round of chemo. We received a call from the surgeon's office with a tentative surgery date of June 30th.

Our devotion today in *Grace for the Moment* was about Matthew 4:19, where Jesus said, "Come, follow me." God invited Mary to give birth to His Son, He invited the disciples to fish for men, He invited the adulterous woman to start over, and He invited Thomas to touch His wounds and believe. God prepares the palace, sets the table and invites His subjects to come. His favorite word is *come*. God says, "All who are thirsty, *come* and drink" (see John 7:37) and *"Come* to me, all of you who are tired and have heavy loads, and I will give you rest" (Matthew 11:28 NCV). He is a God who invites and a God who calls us to lay down our burdens.

We feel God is calling Allison to something bigger than we can understand. The two-story statue of Jesus Christ in the center of Johns Hopkins Hospital has His arms stretched wide and at the base of the statue is the same scripture from this devotion: "COME unto ME all ye that are weary and heavy laden and I will give you REST." We took a picture of Allie standing by the statue, touching the hem of Jesus's robe, giving Him her burdens.

Allison's Journal, June 1, 2010

Today I went for chemo. I walked out to the van and sat. I started to cry. I did not want to go, not again. I looked at my wrist and saw the familiar blue and red band that reads, "God is BIGGER than Carl." I choked out through the tears over and over, "You are bigger, You are bigger, You are bigger." For some reason, coming down this time was MUCH harder. I did not want to come. NOT AT ALL! But here I am, in a hospital bed, hooked up to an IV pump. No matter how much I don't want to come, I HAVE TO. Now that I am here, though, I want to get the chemo in and get Carl out of me! I AM DECLARING WAR! I really think this round of chemo is going to work. The surgeon is going to remove the big tumor after this round. I have a surgery date of June 30th. So soon!!

♥Allie

06/03/2010 Email to Allie Speck's Prayer Warriors
We are in the hospital. Allison is receiving her third night of chemo.

I am reading a book by Joyce Meyer about not being anxious. In summary, the book states our past experience does not determine our future. No matter what happens to us, God can take it and use it for good. It quotes another favorite scripture of Allie's, Romans 8:28(NKJV): "We know that ALL things work together for good to those who love God, to those who are the called according to His purpose."

The story of Joseph is another favorite of Allie's, and the book stated how Joseph's brothers meant evil toward him by selling him into slavery in Egypt. But God was with Joseph, and he became second-in-command to Pharaoh and was responsible for saving his own family and his brothers. Joseph kept his eyes on God and believed that God had a good purpose for his life.

Part of the passage states that sometimes we forget how big our God is. I thought about the bracelets we wear that remind us that "GOD IS BIGGER THAN CARL." God is bigger than any problem we have... including Carl.

06/07/2010 Email to Allie Speck's Prayer Warriors
We are home!!

Allison had no hallucinations. The doctors are amazed at the change in her response to the chemo. We KNOW it is God's hand moving in response to everyone's prayers.

One of the chemo drugs Allie receives is sometimes called "the red devil." This particular chemo turns her body fluids red and has been the cause of ulcers in her mouth, vomiting and severe pain due to its toxic effect. This chemo has been known to damage heart muscle and requires careful monitoring. We give thanks that Allison's tests have shown no indication of heart damage related to this drug.

I remember Allison's disappointment when she learned that the "red devil" would be included in her last chemo before surgery. She cried, knowing it would attack her cancer so aggressively that she may end up in the hospital. When I titled this chapter "Dance with the Devil," it was a reflection of the chemo attacking Allie's cancer. Looking back, I realize how ironic that the use of this "red devil" drug required close monitoring of Allie's heart. We were told it could damage her heart muscle and cause her problems later in life. Isn't that what the devil does? He attacks our heart, weakens our defenses and causes problems in our life. Through it all, Allie's heart remained strong, just like her faith.

Allison's Journal, June 7, 2010

I am home! How wonderful! I hate being cooped up in the hospital for five days. It is especially hard when it is so nice out and my friends are posting on Facebook how they are headed to the beach or out with friends or off to the pool. It makes me long so much for normalcy. What I would give to wake up and just feel good and normal and say, "Hey, I feel like going to the pool." And then I could hop in my car or on my bike and just go. I could eat and drink whatever I want and not worry about throwing up or taking a ton of pills. Being sick has definitely made me value "normal." I just cannot wait until this last round is out of my body and I can feel better again. Chemo makes it hard to connect to things. It makes me feel distant and changes all my senses. It is hard to explain, but the expression "chemo brain" is a real thing. Only those of us unfortunate enough to be given chemo understand the disconnect.

♥Allie

06/09/2010 Email to Allie Speck's Prayer Warriors
Every time Allie has gotten the "red devil" chemo, she ends up in the hospital. We went to the clinic today for follow-up lab work. Allie has been admitted due to pain, weakness and a very low blood count. We pray this is a short stay.

06/12/2010 Email to Allie Speck's Prayer Warriors
Allison is still in the hospital. The doctors are having a difficult time regulating her blood levels.

Allison has six IV pumps to receive all the medications and blood she requires. The chemo was extra toxic this time. Her mouth sores have worsened, and she has not had solid food for several days.

She was scheduled for an MRI that may need to be canceled. Surgery is set for June 30th. I will close with the saying Allie likes to repeat: "Don't tell God how big your mountain is; tell your mountain how big your God is!"

06/13/2010 Email to Allie Speck's Prayer Warriors
Allie's blood counts are slightly improved; however, she now has a fever and must remain in the hospital.

Pray for healing, successful surgery and Allie's return to college in the fall. We claim the scripture from Matthew 18:19 (NET) that says, "Again, I tell you the truth, if two or more of you on earth agree about whatever you ask, my Father in heaven will do it for you."

06/15/2010 Email to Allie Speck's Prayer Warriors
Allison remains in the hospital. This has been her longest stay. Her blood counts remain low, and the sores in her mouth and throat are worse. Her body cannot heal until her blood counts rise.

This setback has not stopped Allison from sharing her testimony. She was invited to be the guest speaker at Relay for Life, an American Cancer Society fundraiser being held at her high school. She spent this morning writing her speech. She told the doctors she needs to be discharged by Friday. She is determined to share her testimony.

She talked to me about what she should say, and God led us to this scripture in Mark 13:11 (AMPC): "Now when they take you [to court] and put you under arrest, do not be anxious beforehand about what you are to say nor [even] meditate about it; but say whatever is given you in that hour and at the moment, for it is not you who will be speaking but the Holy Spirit." Jesus said this to His disciples as He sent them out into the world to preach the gospel. We pray that Allison will continue to allow God to use her and speak through her.

Sadly, Allie's MRI has been canceled and will be rescheduled when Allie is discharged.

06/17/2010 Email to Allie Speck's Prayer Warriors
Allison remains in the hospital, day number eight. Her blood count remains low with no change. She has been stuck five times for IVs in the last three days. Everyone is discouraged.

As for the Relay for Life speech, Allison continues to write and has asked me to speak on her behalf.

06/19/2010 Email to Allie Speck's Prayer Warriors
Today is day ten in the hospital. Relay for Life is over. I shared Allie's words while her brother recorded the speech so Allie could watch it. She cried listen-

ing to her own words, so I know that my occasional
pauses during the speech to gather my composure
were justified.

Today our devotion in *Addicted to God* was from
1 Thessalonians 5:18: "Give thanks in all circumstances; for this is God's will for you in Christ Jesus.
"There is always a reason to be thankful. There is
a saying that goes, "I complained because I had no
shoes until I met a man who had no feet." No matter
what your circumstances, there is a reason to be
thankful *in* your circumstances. Your situation may
never change, but your attitude toward it can.

CHAPTER NINE

TRUSTING HIM

Allison's Relay for Life speech

Anyone who has ever been diagnosed with cancer, please raise your hand. Let's give them a round of applause.

Now, who has ever taken care of a cancer patient? Whether it be taking them to doctors' appointments, staying with them in the hospital, encouraging them, lifting them up when they are down, helping them emotionally or financially, if you have done any of these things, please raise your hand. I would like to give you a round of applause as well. Because we definitely need you. I don't think you know how important you are and how important it is that you come together at events like Relay for Life.

As I write this, I am in the hospital surrounded by numerous other kids whose lives have all been impacted by cancer. Some spend months at a time in the hospital away from home. They have numerous surgeries and procedures. They spend countless hours in MRIs, CTs and other scans. There are countless pokes, prods and medicines. Chemo and other treatments are administered, and days, sometimes weeks, of illness follow. Sometimes it can seem endless. Trust me, I know. And no matter how strong someone is, this isn't something a cancer patient can face alone. But the beautiful thing is, we don't have to face cancer alone.

I can remember after my first chemo treatment sitting on the edge of my bed crying and saying over and over to my mom, "I can't do it again." She held me and told me confidently, "Yes, you can. You have to. Just think, think of all the people who are praying for you, think of everyone who's supporting you." I did and still often do, knowing that they all believe in me and are trusting in God to heal me. The comfort and confidence I have just from knowing I'm not alone in my fight is what keeps me going. It amazes me how God never fails to show up when I need Him, and He usually does it through someone else. Through someone who stops by for a visit to encourage me when I'm feeling frustrated or helpless. Or through a card that says just the right thing or an event that meets a need. It's beautiful.

I see the same thing on the floor. There is so much hope and promise here. There are so many people coming and supporting the other kids. Families pulling together and cherishing each other. Simple things like balloons and cards decorating the rooms. Friends bringing encouragement and prayer. Foundations offering hope and support.

What I am saying is, a lot of times cancer patients are only as strong as their supporters. So, what you are doing is very important. I guess I just wanted to let you know what a difference you are making, and, most of all, I want to say thank you.

Even though I'm really disappointed that I can't be there, I think this really helps to show what Relay is about. Others pulling together to help when someone like me needs it. We're both fighting cancer tonight, just in different ways, and none of us are fighting alone. I know we are both headed for a victory. So, to those of you supporting cancer patients and those of you who have traveled or are still on the journey of cancer diagnosis, remember God is bigger than cancer.

06/20/2010 Email to Allie Speck's Prayer Warriors
Today is day 11 in the hospital. It has been a tough day for Allie. There were lots of tears and frustration. We are canceling the pre-op appointment with the surgeon. Allison is not mentally prepared for

surgery or to spend more time in the hospital. Please lift her up in prayer.

06/21/2010 Email to Allie Speck's Prayer Warriors
Today was so hard. Lots of tears and time spent reading devotions and healing scriptures. Allie has been in the hospital almost two weeks. She is angry and tired of being sick.

Tom and Andy were allowed to visit, and Allie's blood counts were high enough for her to go outside in a wheelchair. The weather was beautiful. My heart broke as Allie cried sitting outside in the sunshine in a wheelchair with her bald head and IV pump. She said they were tears of joy. She misses being outside, she misses her brother and she misses home. Family and home have become so precious.

We trust that tomorrow will be a better day with improved blood counts. Psalm 30:5b (NET) says, "One may experience sorrow during the night, but joy arrives in the morning."

I felt tired, sick and alone. I remember lying in the hospital bed. I had been hospitalized for two weeks. It was summer. All my friends were posting on Facebook about going to the pool, going to the beach, out with friends. Meanwhile, I was lying in a hospital bed, I couldn't eat, I couldn't sleep, no one could visit me because I was in quarantine, and I was throwing up. Chemo kills cancer, but it also kills the cells that fight infection and all the fast-growing cells in your body. My hair fell out, my fingernails fell off, the lining from my throat to my stomach dissolved, and I threw up chunks of my esophagus. It had been about two weeks since I had eaten. It had been months since I had seen my friends. I was basically vomiting all the time, and I had a bad infection in my stomach. I was tired, just tired. So very tired.

I remember throwing a fit and saying to my mom, "If God loves me so much, why doesn't He make it easier? I know He can come down and just heal me. I believe all of this could be over. But I am not even asking for that anymore. I just want Him to make it a little bit easier. But He won't." I felt alone, I felt abandoned. I was very close to giving up.

It was the next day that we were told by the nurse that my blood counts were high enough for me to leave my room for the first time in two weeks, which is a super big deal. This is like going to Disney World for a cancer patient. So, I could leave my room AND go outside. So, this would be like going to Disney World AND meeting the real Mickey Mouse. I should have been excited, but I was too upset, too angry, too fed up. Mom said, "No matter how you feel, we are going outside." At that point, I was too weak to walk, so she lifted me into the wheelchair, pushed me into the hallway, and went back to get her purse. She told me to wait there. Ha, where else am I going to go?

I was sitting in the hallway: miserable, feeling sorry for myself, having a pity party. Down the hall, I could hear screaming. Now, when I was diagnosed, I was 18, so I was put in the pediatric cancer unit where I will remain for the rest of my treatment. That means I am a 21-year-old sitting on a firetruck exam table. So, I am always in the pediatric unit and used to hearing kids cry, which is normal because obviously none of them want to be there. This was different. This child was screaming in pain. I thought, "What are they doing to that poor child?"

I looked down the hall and coming out of one of the patient rooms was a little girl, probably about six or seven years old, pushing a walker with Dora the Explorer stickers on it. She was bald with an IV pole, just like every other kid on the unit. Her leg was bandaged, and it appeared she had a tumor removed from her leg. I learned from one of the nurses that she was walking for the first time since her surgery. This was causing her a lot of pain. She did not want to be walking on it, and she made that clear to everyone on the unit. And she kept screaming, "It hurts, it hurts!"

And then I saw her dad walking just a little bit in front of her as she was coming along with her tiny walker. Her dad was walking ahead of her, saying, "Come on, you gotta keep coming. You can do it." And she is screaming at him, "Daddy, I hurt, hold me, I hurt!" He said, "I know, I know you hurt, but you have to keep walking." He had a big smile, but I could see the pain in that father's face.

My first thought was, "Oh my word, what that father must be feeling to see his daughter, someone he loves more than anything, someone he helped create, in that much pain. And he knows he can pick her up; he was strong enough. He can take her pain away, just like that. But the father knows that if he picks her up, she may never learn to walk. She could be crippled for the rest of her life."

I felt God speak to me in my spirit and say, "That is you and that is Me. I'm not ignoring your pain. I don't enjoy your pain. I feel your pain. I've experienced pain. I don't like it any more than you do. If you don't learn to walk in this, you could be spiritually crippled for the rest of your life." Knowing that did not make things easier. But what God spoke to me in that moment was, "It does not matter how you feel; I'm with you. I have you."

06/22/2010 Email to Allie Speck's Prayer Warriors
WE ARE HOME! Allison is finally home! She smiled

the whole way home. Tonight we spent time as a family and will enjoy sleeping in our beds. Thank you for your prayers. The scripture that promised joy in the morning was fulfilled.

Allison's Journal, June 24, 2010

Where to start? I got home Tuesday night from a two-week stay in the hospital. It took FOREVER for my blood counts to come up. Then I had a fever, so they gave me antibiotics, which killed my good bacteria, giving me C. diff, which is a nasty bowel infection with diarrhea. Oh, the things that chemo does to my body! It amazes me how complex our bodies are and how everything must be in balance.

My surgery was to be June 30th, but after the way this last treatment kicked my butt, I won't be healthy enough in time, so it is moved to July 7th. I also missed my MRI because I was too sick. I am ready for surgery but not excited. I remember how painful it was the first time.

I love being home! They cannot make me go back there for anything. They tried to make me stay today for a magnesium infusion. I said, "NO WAY!!! I will come back tomorrow." And I did.

To close, I want to share a scripture sent to me in a card.

"But now, this is what the Lord says—he who created you, Jacob, he who formed you, Israel: 'Do not fear, for I have redeemed you; I have summoned you by name; you are mine. When you pass through the waters, I will be with you; and when you pass through the rivers, they will not sweep over you. When you walk through the fire, you will not be burned; the flames will not set you ablaze. For I am the Lord you God, the Holy One of Israel, your Savior...'" (Isaiah 43:1–3).

❤Allie

06/25/2010 Email to Allie Speck's Prayer Warriors

Allie went to the clinic yesterday for blood work. Since it took so long to get the results, the doctor wanted to admit her overnight for an infusion. Allie politely said she had just spent two weeks in the hospital, and she was not staying overnight. She agreed to return the next day for the infusion, and the doctor agreed. I am so proud of her strength.

Allie's new surgery date is July 7th. This was a tough round of chemo. We are celebrating every second of being home. We have grown in our faith watching Allie walk this journey. Through her tears in the hospital, she told me, "I can do this, Mom. With God's help, I can do this."

06/29/2010 Email to Allie Speck's Prayer Warriors
As I read my devotion in *New Day, New You* this morning, I was thinking that Allison's surgery was to be tomorrow morning. I realized God was speaking to me again. The devotion was regarding God's perfect timing. It reminded me that God's timing is not our timing. We are often in a hurry, but He is not. He prepares a solid foundation to build our faith upon. We are under construction and God is the master builder. We might not understand what He is doing, but the Bible promises us that He has a good plan for each of us. God is never late, but He is not early either. He is right on time, so why don't we settle down and try to enjoy the journey?

As I flipped ahead in my devotional, I looked to the new date of Allie's surgery, July 7th. The title of that day's devotional was "God Meant It for Good"! Is that a coincidence? No way! This is a marathon, not a sprint.

MRI results
There is no significant change in the size of the tumor. My spirit was immediately dejected. Allison seemed calm. The surgeon made it clear that attempting to remove the biggest tumor puts Allison at high risk for bleeding and even death. It was a sobering conversation as we discussed the risks involved.

Allison's response to the surgeon was yet another inspirational statement. She said, "Now is the time for more faith than ever before!"

We left the surgeon's office and drove to Creation, a Christian festival that Allie loves. We stayed for the candle-lighting service. Seventy thousand people on a hillside holding candles and praising Jesus—WOW! Tonight, Allie celebrated life and Jesus. For a short time, I would like to believe she forgot about cancer.

07/06/2010 Email to Allie Speck's Prayer Warriors
Allison's surgery is set for tomorrow! God is in control, and we know what may be impossible for man is possible with God (Luke 18:27).

Allie is ready! She is ready to begin sharing her testimony of healing that could only come from God.

Allison's Journal, July 6, 2010

I had my MRI on Friday, and nothing shrunk.... However, the doctor did say the tumor appeared dead, and its consistency had changed. My surgeon is going to go ahead with the surgery. He stressed that this is a very high-risk and life-threatening surgery and will be just as difficult as the last time because the tumor did not shrink where it needed to. He will be taking the entire left lobe of my liver to get Carl and parts of the right lobe, depending on the smaller tumors.

So, the big question.... How do I feel about this? Well, I am not nervous. I am a little conscious of death. I have had daydreams about cancer taking my life. I have not told anyone that. It gives me a bit of an eerie feeling. There is so much more that I feel I can do for God on this earth. Well, I mean, there is more God can do through me. I have always felt called to something greater. To something beyond myself. Perhaps this was it, but I am so in love with the Lord that I feel there is more to come for me. Or maybe there is more to come after I am gone. I do not fear death; I fear not touching enough lives while I am here. If my death is what needs to happen to further the kingdom of God, then I will go to heaven rejoicing. I want more time here because I feel like I am not finished yet. I want to have more time to experience all the wonders God put on the earth for us. I feel like I have just begun to appreciate life and its beauty. I am blessed with so much to share with the world.

Initially I thought God would take away my tumor because that is what made sense to me. If He was a loving God, then that is what He would do. But as I face a second surgery, I have a whole different outlook. My thought is, "God, whatever You know is best for my life, that is what I want. Whatever happens, it will be the best thing."

Oh my gosh, I just looked at the scripture at the bottom of this journal page! "Daughter, your faith has healed you. Go in peace" (Luke 8:48). That IS the word of God. He has got this! We will do this! He will do this! I told God the other day, "I don't know the end of this, but I know that what You have planned for my life will be beautiful." God has more for me. I am ready!

♥Allie

CHAPTER TEN
CARL IS GONE!

07/07/2010 Email to Allie Speck's Prayer Warriors
We give all glory to our Lord Jesus Christ as Allison is cancer-free. Allison is in ICU and doing well. All of the tumors have been removed. Thank you for your prayers. GOD IS WITH US! He will never leave us or forsake us (Hebrews 13:5). Thanks for keeping the faith with us.

07/08/2010 Email to Allie Speck's Prayer Warriors
We continue to celebrate the victory of complete and total removal of all cancer from Allison's liver. Here are the joyous details....

When Allison went to the OR, we sat in the waiting room receiving periodic updates through phone calls. Five hours later, we were called into the same consultation room as before to meet with the surgeon.

This time, however, the surgeon walked in with a huge smile on his face, holding his "GOD IS BIGGER THAN CARL" bracelet. He announced that Carl had been completely removed and the surgery went well. He shared that Allison prayed with the entire team before her surgery. Everyone involved in Allie's surgery witnessed her faith at work!

After surgery, Allie was transferred to the ICU. She received ten units of blood during the surgery. The surgeon did say Allie was at risk for complications after surgery, especially bleeding.

An hour later we were allowed to see Allie. She looked like she had been in a battle. Her entire body was swollen with fluid, and the breathing tube had created a huge fluid-filled blister on her bottom lip. She could barely open her eyes due to swelling. Her first question was, "Did he really get it?" When we confirmed that the surgery was a complete success, she began to cry and repeated over and over, "Thank You, Jesus!" We celebrated with her. God was and is and always will be BIGGER than Carl.

Despite the joy of the miracle, the night in the ICU was rough. Allie had an incredible amount of pain. She was transferred to a regular room today by wheelchair. She has amazing strength! The surgeon visited today and said her remaining liver is functioning normally even though 60 percent of her liver was removed to get all the cancer.

Allison had a special visit from one of her oncology doctors who is a strong prayer warrior. She arrived wearing her "GOD IS BIGGER THAN CARL" bracelet. We joined hands, and she led us in a beautiful prayer, thanking God for Allison's healing and blessing her testimony to be shared all over the world.

Faith and prayer bring miracles from God the Almighty, the Great Physician, the Maker of heaven and earth.

I remember sitting at Allie's bedside in ICU, praying for pain relief and thanking God for the joy of Allison's healing. I cried many tears of joy and hope as I held her hand and reassured her that the surgery was successful and that her pain would subside. It was a very long night, and I felt exhausted. But that part of the battle had been won. I tried not to let Satan overwhelm me by thinking too far into the future and watching Allie battle the pain of recovery. God had delivered our daughter. There was hope for tomorrow.

07/10/2010 Email to Allie Speck's Prayer Warriors
The surgeon is pleased with Allie's progress. Allie's liver will grow to normal size in about two months! God created our bodies in such an amazing way!

Allie may be discharged in two days. She is nervous about the long ride home. Two more cycles of chemo have been recommended to ensure destruction of any cancer cells that may be left in her body. We are hopeful these treatments will be completed in time for Allie to resume college in September.

Allison is still celebrating the victory and occasionally looks at us with a big smile, saying, "Guess what? He got it all!" She appreciates your support and prayers. We serve an awesome God! This journey has an end in sight, and for that we are thankful.

I want to share an inspiration from the book I am reading, *Be Healed in Jesus' Name*. It says that the name of Jesus is above every other name and contains more power than anything in existence. We are told that one day, every knee will bow and submit to His authority in heaven, on earth and under the earth (Philippians 2:10). There is more power in the name of Jesus than there is power in the name of cancer or any other disease. John 14:14 (NKJV) tells us that Jesus says, "If you ask anything in My name, I will do it." HE DID IT!

07/12/2010 Email to Allie Speck's Prayer Warriors
Allison is leaving the hospital today! Five days after having 60 percent of her liver removed, she is walking, eating and ready to go home. The large incision is painful, but we are thankful for medication and the healing properties of our body created by God.

Home never looked so good; Allie is cancer-free and the mountaintop is in view. We could not have endured this journey without the support of our prayer warriors and the grace of our Lord Jesus Christ.

07/14/2010 Email to Allie Speck's Prayer Warriors
Allison rode to the hospital exit in a wheelchair and walked two blocks to the townhouse where we were staying. AMAZING! She rested while we packed for home.

Arriving at home, we were greeted by a huge banner in the front yard declaring, "CARL DOESN'T LIVE HERE ANYMORE!" Allison laughed out loud.

The surgeon called to tell us the tumors had clean edges, meaning no cancer cells were left behind! Miraculous!

God has provided timely scriptures and songs throughout this journey, and today was no exception. The devotion in *New Day, New You* addressed the question, why does God wait so long? The scripture was Matthew 19:26 (AMPC): "All things are possible with God." The devotional was about Abraham and Sarah waiting for their promised child. They waited 20 years from the time God promised Abraham he would have a child. God gave Abraham and Sarah a baby when Abraham was 100 years old and Sarah was considered barren.

Sometimes when you ask God for something, He lets you wait so long that the only thing that can possibly produce what you asked for is a miracle. God is an awesome God. Nothing is too hard for Him. We waited, and God delivered our miracle.

07/16/2010 Email to Allie Speck's Prayer Warriors
Allison's last two days have been tough. She is vomiting and has a bowel infection. Her blood work shows dehydration and anemia. Please pray she does not need to go to the hospital.

07/19/2010 Email to Allie Speck's Prayer Warriors
We went to church on Sunday, even though Allie
was exhausted. She continues to vomit, and her
weight is down to 116 pounds. It is sad that she cannot enjoy this time of celebration. She will be starting home IV therapy.

My devotional *New Day, New You* spoke to me by
stating that all things work for good (Romans 8:28).
That scripture did not say that all things ARE good,
but it does say that all things work together for good.
In Romans 12:16 the apostle Paul tells us to adjust
ourselves to people and things. We must learn to be
the kind of person who plans but doesn't fall apart
if the plan doesn't work out the way we want. A
positive person can decide to enjoy the situation no
matter what happens.

That is exactly what Allison is doing: she is trying
to enjoy herself even though things are not going as
planned. This journey is certainly not over, but we
declare that the battle has been won!

Allison's Journal, July 20, 2010

I AM CANCER-FREE! There is so much to say, but I am
pretty tired. The main thing you should know is God
created a miracle. The surgery was a complete success.
Not only did the surgeon remove Carl, my big tumor,
but he also removed all the smaller tumors too! They
tested the tumors, and they were all the same type of
cancer, so I don't have to worry about other kinds of
cancer. I recovered so well. My incision was made right
along my old incision, although it needed to be a little
bigger to get the tumors out.

I am going to be okay. More than okay. These are
some of, or maybe THE, hardest things I have ever
had to go through, but it is through testing that we
get a testimony. Good is going to come out of this.
God has granted me such peace about it. NO, it
is not easy, and yes, I still struggle and want to see
Him and talk to Him, but I need to understand that

I have given this to God. I need to stop trying to fix things myself.

I listened to Joyce Meyer, a Christian speaker, the other day; the sermon was entitled, "What to do when it seems like God isn't doing anything." It was exactly what I needed to hear. It talked of suffering and waiting for answers. It spoke of Jairus and his dying daughter and Lazarus who died waiting for Jesus to come. Sometimes we don't need a healing; we need a resurrection. Lazarus was dead two days before Jesus went to him. Jesus was dead three days before His resurrection. There is some "waiting in the grave," but a resurrection day does come! I realized there was a Saturday between Good Friday and Resurrection Sunday. My Saturday of waiting with my cancer seemed endless, but my resurrection day DID come, and the same is true for all of our struggles. So, I will not be worried or afraid, because God has got it!

♥Allie

07/27/2010 Email to Allie Speck's Prayer Warriors
Thank God Allison is feeling better. The home IV therapy has given her energy, and tomorrow will be three weeks since her surgery. If she remains stable, chemo may begin next week. Pray for her spirit to be refreshed. She is strong but carries a heavy load as she anticipates more chemo.

My devotion in *New Day, New You* today was regarding Ephesians 3:20 that says God is able to do exceedingly above and beyond all that we could dare to hope, ask or think, according to His great power that is at work in us.

God works through us, so we have to cooperate. We need to be daring in our faith and in our prayers. Some of us are not believing for enough. We need to stretch our faith.

07/31/2010 Email to Allie Speck's Prayer Warriors
Allison's follow-up with the surgeon is complete. She returns to the oncology team to finish chemo, which

is scheduled for 8/5. Allie cried when they discussed the chemo plan. I cannot imagine how she feels.

As Allie faces more chemo and was feeling down, she was thrilled to be invited by friends to the beach. She loves the beach and left this morning. I was nervous about the trip, but God gave me peace. Allie needs to get away before chemo.

08/04/2010 Email to Allie Speck's Prayer Warriors
While at the beach, Allison took the opportunity to do something she has always wanted to do. She went parasailing! She never stops seeking adventure. She went 500 feet in the air in a harness four weeks after liver surgery! The trip to the beach was just what she needed. She is tan, refreshed and excited to show us that her eyebrows and eyelashes are growing back.

Last week Allie was invited to speak at Impact, a Christian gathering for youth. Many young people come to know Jesus through the testimonies that are shared. It was a two-hour drive, but Allison was thrilled to have the opportunity to share her testimony.

08/07/2010 Email to Allie Speck's Prayer Warriors
Two days ago, we arrived at Hopkins for Allie's admission for chemo. Because there was no bed available, we sat in the clinic most of the day. God used that time to allow us to meet a young teenager with a recurring brain tumor. She was an athlete and is now in a wheelchair. She has been treated at Hopkins for over four years! Her appointment was to set up hospice services, as her mom told me she was given six months to live. My heart broke. I cried with this mom as I asked God to provide them with strength for the days ahead. After hearing her story, waiting to be admitted for chemo took on a new perspective.

Chemo has gone as well as chemo can go. Allie has felt well enough to visit other children on the unit and give them friendship bracelets that she made. She is always thinking of others.

08/09/2010 Email to Allie Speck's Prayer Warriors
Allison is having mild side effects and will receive her final dose of chemo tonight. We should go home tomorrow.

During our devotions, we reflected on the families who are here. Each one has a different journey and outlook. Some see a trial that becomes a blessing while others see a disaster that cannot get worse. The devotion was about how your attitude makes a difference.

The following story is about two men in the same hospital room. Mr. Wilson was in a bed by the window. He was allowed to sit up in bed for one hour a day. His roommate, Mr. Thompson, had to lie flat on his back. Remaining still was part of their healing. This meant no TV and no radio. So, they talked a lot about their lives. Every afternoon Mr. Wilson, the man by the window, was able to see outside for an hour and he would describe everything he could see in detail. Mr. Thompson, who could not see outside, lived for this hour. Mr. Wilson talked about the park with a lake where ducks and swans swam and children sailed boats. He described the flowers and trees, the look of the city skyline. He mentioned the people: young lovers, older couples, families and their activities. One day there was a parade, and Mr. Thompson became jealous that he could not see it. He was ashamed of his thoughts, but he became unhappy and felt that he should be by the window. One night Mr. Wilson, the man by the window, became sick and started to cough. He was unable to call for the nurse, and Mr. Thompson did nothing to help him. In the morning, Mr. Wilson was dead. As soon as Mr. Thompson thought it was decent to ask, he asked to be moved to the window. They moved him the next morning. The minute the nurse left the room, Mr. Thompson painfully propped himself up on one elbow and strained to look out the window. To his surprise, it faced a blank wall.

Attitude makes all the difference. Jesus is our hope. In Him, we know that despite difficulties we are assured victory over death. Praying for all families facing difficult days.

08/11/2010 Email to Allie Speck's Prayer Warriors
We are home, and tonight Allison felt well enough for us to have dinner with a friend. Her prayer before the meal brought tears to our eyes as she thanked God for her blessings.

College classes start August 31st, and Allie has a dorm room where she will stay as soon as chemo is complete.

08/15/2010 Email to Allie Speck's Prayer Warriors
Allie's surgeon called to say how honored he was to be part of her care team. He was glad to hear she was doing well. Per Allie's request, he told her he would be sending her pictures of the liver tumors. She prayed with him at the end of the call.

Each day is a blessing. Allie and I attended a wedding on Saturday, and we attended church as a family on Sunday. Andy had the opportunity to go to the beach with a friend. We are blessed! We are looking forward to a concert being held at our church on Saturday to help our family with medical expenses. Allison will be sharing her testimony. We are excited to see her missionary role begin.

08/16/2010 Email to Allie Speck's Prayer Warriors
We had a setback today. Allison woke up with a sore throat and fever and stayed in bed, which is unusual. By afternoon, her temperature was 102, and she was delusional. She was admitted to the local hospital tonight and will be transferred to Hopkins when she is stable. She is very sick with a blood infection. Everything happened very fast, and we are concerned. Please pray for a quick recovery.

08/17/2010 Email to Allie Speck's Prayer Warriors
Allison became stable enough to be transported by ambulance to Hopkins. She has been admitted and

seems to be slightly improved. We pray that God will allow Allie to be home and strong enough to share her testimony.

08/18/2010 Email to Allie Speck's Prayer Warriors
During Allison's journey, there have been moments when Allie was very sick or we were given discouraging news. It was during those times that we got on our knees and cried out to God for mercy. This admission was one of those times. When moments like this come and everything is stripped away, God is our only hope.

Allie's blood counts have improved, and her fever is down. We are waiting for the order, and then she can go HOME! We know that answered prayers are the reason for her prompt response to treatment. Allie is asking for prayers that her voice will be strong enough to sing the song she wrote for her testimony. Thank you.

08/22/2010 Email to Allie Speck's Prayer Warriors
It is Sunday and we are blessed! Allison was discharged Thursday night from Baltimore. At 10:00 p.m., a home health nurse arrived at our house to give her first IV antibiotic and trained us in how to give it every eight hours.

Friday morning Allie felt well enough to go to the Joyce Meyer Conference. She attended both the morning and evening sessions.

Saturday, our entire family attended the concert where Allie shared her testimony. God's Spirit was felt as about 120 people attended. Allie was able to end the evening singing the song she wrote. I had tears in my eyes most of the night as I considered how God had orchestrated the entire event.

Allison's victory is a direct result of your prayers and God's grace. My devotion yesterday in *New Day, New You* was from 1 Peter 5:8-9 (AMPC): "Be well balanced...be vigilant and cautious at all times; for that enemy of yours, the devil, roams around like a lion roaring...seeking someone to seize upon and devour. Withstand him; be firm in faith...knowing that the same (identical) sufferings are appointed to your brotherhood...throughout the world."

We are told to defeat the devil by being rooted and grounded in Christ. When problems arise, we are not to assume that the Lord will intervene without an invitation. We are to pray and ask God to change our circumstances. Then we must remain faithful and constant, allowing God to intervene. Satan will try to overcome us through deception and intimidation. But how can the devil threaten someone who does not fear?

Allison stated in her testimony that she was afraid of chemo until God told her not to fear but to pray and trust Him. God bless each one of you, and thank you for praying for Allison and believing in her healing. We are blessed beyond what we deserve.

Allison's Journal, August 25, 2010

There is something absolutely beautiful about the silence of my bedroom in the summer. Night noises drift through my open window. I lie there and listen to the soft singing of crickets, and a piece of me mourns that I could never write anything as breathtaking as this, for God says in silence what I could never begin to express with words.

There is something friendly about silence, as if it says to you, "Oh yes, I remember you. You were the little six-year-old who filled me with your laughter." Silence has always been there to envelop you in soft, open arms as it did in the womb. Silence is my oldest friend.

♥Allie

08/27/2010 Allie's email to one of her nurses at Hopkins

I don't know if you know, but after my last chemo, I did end up back at Hopkins with an infection. I am on IV antibiotics until Monday, and I start college

on Wednesday. Other than that, I am doing REAL-
LY well. I actually rode my bike two miles today! Of
course, it was pretty much all flat, and when I got
home, I just dropped down in the driveway until
I could finally breathe again. HA HA. And then I
spent the rest of the evening relaxing. I was thinking, as I lay in my driveway (with my neighbors
watching and probably thinking I was dead), that
this time last year I could ride my bike eight miles
with hills and then run two miles without thinking
about it. Now two miles feels like a marathon. But
it's a process, and I guess I have to be patient. I'm
just a really "get up and go" person, and it's hard to
do that when you have no "get up and go." LOL. I am
really excited to see how college goes. :) I'm ready
to feel semi-normal again. Hope you are doing well
and that you enjoy the parasailing pictures I am
including, just for fun.

♥Allie

08/27/2010 Email to Allie Speck's Prayer Warriors
Allie had an appointment at Hopkins, and things
are looking good. Praise the Lord! Her antibiotics
were reduced to every 12 hours, and her weight is
up to 125 pounds. I cannot tell you how emotional
it felt to sit in the same office where we were told
in January that she had cancer and to see her
smiling and cancer-free in August. God has truly
been with us through this storm. At the end of the
visit, Allie's doctor held our hands and offered a
beautiful prayer of thanks and blessing for our
entire family. This mother's heart almost exploded
with joy.

Allie returns to college on Wednesday. The staff have
been so helpful, and we know Allie was drawn to
Messiah for a reason. We thank God that all of her
classes are in the same building this semester. We
are all one phone call away from tragedy. I pray, if
you are required to carry a burden like Allie's, that
you could look to Jesus for comfort and guidance. He
is the only way to peace.

09/01/2010 Email to Allie Speck's Prayer Warriors
Allie is back at college and loving every second.
She will never take ANYTHING for granted again...
driving, classes, eating and especially feeling
healthy. She is ready for the word *cancer* to disappear from her life.

CHAPTER ELEVEN
SECOND CHANCES

Allison's Journal, September 4, 2010

I have not felt this human in a long time. I know this is most likely a distraction: a beautiful unknown road that veers left. A road I may stare down for a while, and then I'll pedal on wondering for a while, every time my lefthand aches to turn, who that road may belong to. I don't know, but I do know the road ahead is mine.

WOW! Our God is amazing, and I need to remind myself that He is number one in my life. Not school, not friends and not boys...HAHA, though they have come back into the picture. I AM BACK AT COLLEGE! I have classes Monday, Wednesday and Friday. I have a dorm room with two roommates, but I cannot live there until chemo is done. I have one more treatment left. I should be done by now, but I got a blood infection. I was delirious and don't remember most of the details, but I got treatment during another hospital stay. I am good as new! I am hanging out with friends and playing board games. Tomorrow I am going kayaking with the Outdoors Club. I want to dive into everything that life has to offer. Cancer has wasted enough of my time already.

I am working hard to focus on God and live this wonderful life that He has blessed me with and given me a second chance at. I am enjoying my theology class and learning more about what I believe and why I believe it.

♥Allie

09/06/2010 Email to Allie Speck's Prayer Warriors
Happy Labor Day! What a beautiful day! Allison is at college while Andy has friends over, enjoying a slip-and-slide party. As I listen to the chatter of teenagers and their innocent laughter, I thank God for the joy I am feeling! We are blessed with a home, health, friends and family.

Allison is doing more than she should before her last chemo treatment. I consider the risks of her getting sick, but I realize she has already missed out on enough of life. She attended Outdoors Club and signed up to go kayaking. Yesterday she was floating on the Susquehanna River and had a blast. Nothing is going to hold this girl back! She is living life to the fullest and thanking God for every opportunity. This morning as I kissed Allie good-bye on her way to classes, I paused to realize how blessed we are!

09/10/2010 Email to Allie Speck's Prayer Warriors
Allison is doing well at college and is preparing for her last round of chemo. The email below is from Allie's oncology doctor and prayer warrior:

Dear Allison,
The reason for doing these two cycles of chemo is really more than preventative. At this point, we know the surgeon removed all the tumors. What we don't know is if there are individual tumor cells hiding somewhere. Your type of cancer is known to leave residual tumor cells sitting around. It only takes one tumor cell to divide and grow into a tumor. So, the purpose of these cycles is to destroy any trace of tumor cells. I want you to return to college and have a normal life. But when I think about a normal life, I am thinking beyond college and onto a lifetime of dreams fulfilled: your calling to ministry, international relief work, children, grandchildren, a legacy. I don't want recurrence of this tumor to interfere with whatever God has planned for you.

After reading this email, we know exactly why God led us to Johns Hopkins. Not only is Allison's oncology doctor a skilled physician with a compassionate heart, she also is a Christian who believes in God's plan for Allie's life.

09/17/2010 Email to Allie Speck's Prayer Warriors
Today we drove to Hopkins for another chemo admission. Allie and I both felt apprehensive about this admission, and when we walked on the unit, Allie wrinkled her nose and said, "It smells like chemo." We are here until Tuesday. Pray for treatment to be uneventful and to kill any remaining cells. This chemo treatment requires Allie to use the bathroom every two hours to protect her kidneys. Five days of this rigorous schedule results in total exhaustion. We will not miss this.

09/19/2010 Email to Allie Speck's Prayer Warriors
Allison is tolerating her chemo well and is working on college assignments. Her Bible verse for today was 2 Timothy 1:7 (NKJV), which we claim: "For God has not given us a spirit of fear, but of power and of love and of a sound mind." One nurse mentioned how cancer survivors live in fear from one scan to the next. We will not live in fear. God will be our strength.

09/21/2010 Email to Allie Speck's Prayer Warriors
We are leaving Hopkins today, and Allie has had a few prayer concerns she would like to share. Her tongue is swollen, which is often a chemo side effect that causes severe pain and an inability to eat. The other concern is low blood levels. Pray for her body to remain strong with no side effects.

One doctor this morning told us to go home and pack a "hospital bag" just in case we need to return. We will prepare for the worst and pray for the best. God is in control, and we have faith that He will protect Allie. We claim Hebrews 11:1 (NET): "Now faith is being sure of what we hope for, being convinced of what we do not see."

Allison's Journal, September 22, 2010

I AM DONE WITH CHEMO! I had my last infusion Monday night. This is so amazing! All that is ahead of me now is a life with no chemo and no cancer! That is an amazing feeling, the best feeling in the world! I AM DONE! It is part of my past. It is over! No more needle sticks, shots, sleeping in hospitals, getting sick, missing out, being in pain. IT IS OVER! I can grow hair! I can make plans! I can live at college! I can do ANYTHING! How great is the Father's love for us! My journey with cancer is over, but my real journey is just beginning!

♥Allie

09/23/2010 Email to Allie Speck's Prayer Warriors
We got home from Hopkins in time to watch Andy play soccer. Tom drove Allison to school on Wednesday because she was too weak. Her sore throat and swollen tongue have not worsened, and her blood work remains stable! Allie went to church this evening with friends and quite honestly, her social calendar has no time for a hospital admission. She has been contacted by several churches to share her testimony. She is excited to spread God's Word.

09/30/2010 Email to Allie Speck's Prayer Warriors
Allie had a follow-up appointment today where she got two units of blood and a flu shot. She hates the needles but will endure them to stay out of the hospital. This is the first follow-up appointment that Allie was not in the hospital and able to attend. Thank You, Jesus!

Allison's Journal, October 4, 2010

Life after cancer seems so overwhelming, or maybe underwhelming. I have had a hard time adjusting. I don't know how to switch back to normal. I was just in the battle of my life, and now I am supposed to be normal? I realize it is impossible for you to understand if you have never battled cancer. I told my doctor that I should not be depressed after beating cancer. My doctor says this is a common thing for cancer patients to experience. She also said most patients don't jump right back into life with both feet in the deep end like I did, either. LOL. But she knows that is the kind of person I am. She told me it is common for strong women like me to expect too much of ourselves and become over- whelmed and disappointed.

I feel the need to reconnect with God. I was so close in my suffering, and I feel distant now. I almost miss the days where all I could do was rely on God to get me through. I have learned a lot about myself. I am looking forward to a camping trip this coming weekend.

♥Allie

10/11/2010 Email to Allie Speck's Prayer Warriors
Allison is commuting to college and hopes to be back on campus soon. Her recent blood work was great! Pray for her MRI results on 10/19. We are ready for life to return to our "new normal." Family time is sweeter and small blessings more noticeable.

It is amazing how many times Satan will set a trap for us, meaning it to harm or destroy us. But when God gets involved, He takes what Satan meant to destroy us and turns it for good. Our mess becomes our message. Our misery becomes our ministry. God can use our experiences with pain to help others who are hurting. God is using Allison's situation to reach so many people. We are proud of her faith.

Allison's letter to another young woman battling cancer, October 2010

I know what it is like to be terrified and to face your mortality at such a young age. I know what it is like to be frustrated and so tired that you just want it all to stop. I know what it's like to feel like people don't understand or to feel all the eyes in the room staring at your bald head. But because I know all of those things, I now have a perspective that I NEVER would have had otherwise. I feel it is a blessing to be able to view the world with a cancer patient's perspective. We will see the world and the trials in it a lot differently than others. It's like Mary

Tyler Moore said, "You can't be brave if you've only had wonderful things happen to you." Even the Bible says to delight in our sufferings because they develop perseverance. Now, I'm not going to write to you and tell you to "see cancer as a blessing" because I know what it is like to have people say that to you when you are in the sweat and grime of fighting cancer and you just feel like telling them, "Oh yeah? You get down here and try it and YOU tell ME how much of a blessing it is!"

I am just trying to say this: Don't get so bogged down in your trials that you lose sight of the end goal. Just because test results may come back bad or you feel sick, don't forget that God has a plan. The one verse I held onto was Jeremiah 29:11: "'For I know the plans I have for you,' declares the Lord, 'plans to prosper you and not to harm you, plans to give you hope and a future.'" So, try to keep a positive attitude. That helps a lot, and it doesn't mean you never complain and are always happy. It means get angry, complain, vent, be sad...be whatever you feel, BUT THEN, let it go and remind yourself: He knows the plans He has for YOU, and they are much greater than cancer. Cancer cannot stop God's plan. Period. Just don't let cancer stop you from living life. Know your limits, but try to keep some normalcy. Go shopping, go to church and plan a trip when you are feeling well. I am here if you want to talk.

Second Corinthians 4:16–17 says, "Therefore we do not lose heart. Though outwardly we are wasting away, yet inwardly we are being renewed day by day. For our light and momentary troubles are achieving for us an eternal glory that far outweighs them all." I am praying for you, and I KNOW, just like 2 Corinthians says, the glory that comes after this will be SO much greater than the pain we have suffered.

Love and prayers,
Allie

Allie's testimony, October 17, 2010

Good morning. Wow! That song was awesome! Romans 8:28 has been one of my strength verses through everything, and when I opened the bulletin and saw that was the song right before I came up, I said, "Thank You, Jesus!" It was the word of encouragement that I needed today.

Can we bow our heads in prayer, please? Lord God, I thank You for the testimony that You have blessed my life with and that I have the honor to share it in this church today. Thank You for how You have blessed me and my family. I give You praise, Lord, that I am healthy and able to be here to share what You have done in my life. I ask that all of the glory goes to You, Lord. Speak through me and do not let me become prideful of my experiences, but let me honor You. In Jesus's name we pray. Amen.

I believe some of you have received some emails about me, but most of you don't know me. I am going to share with you one of the most wonderful, but also most horrible, thing that has ever happened to me. I became sick during my senior year of high school, but no one could find anything wrong. So, I went to college with a plan that God was going to use me to do something involving missions. I kept praying to God and asking Him to show me how He wanted to use me. I just felt like I wasn't getting any answers. I was like, "Please just tell me; I am listening. All You have to do is tell me, and I will go." I kept saying, "Use me, I want You to use me."

During finals week of my freshman year, I noticed a lump in my abdomen. I saw my doctor, who sent me directly for a CT scan that evening. There was a football-sized tumor on my liver. The doctors were pretty sure it was cancer and gave me six months to a year to live.

We found a surgeon at Hopkins who was willing to attempt surgery. I went into surgery believing that God had an amazing plan for my life. My mom had started an email chain to keep close friends updated so they could pray for me. That email chain has grown to over 200 people, who send to over 200 people, and they send to over 200 people. As a result, I have people all over the world who have heard my story and are praying for me.

So, I went to surgery, and, when I woke up, my mom was there and told me not only did he not get the tumor, but it also was cancer. I started to scream, cry *and throw a fit. I just didn't even know what to think. Not once did the thought of cancer enter my mind.*

My diagnosis wasn't very good, but we had faith. But at that moment in that hospital room, I felt lost and abandoned. I said, "God, I thought You were going to use me to do something, but You're too late. The tumor is too big. It is too complicated." Each day I get a Bible verse that comes via text to my phone. My pastor was visiting and had just prayed, "Lord, please show Allie that You are here and help us understand." My phone dinged with the verse for the day, and it was Proverbs 3:5: "Trust in the Lord with all your heart and lean not on your own understanding." I thought, "I don't understand, but God does, and He has a plan."

Then came chemo. I was more scared of chemo than I was of cancer. I had a very bad reaction to the first chemo. It caused me to hallucinate. I had horrible dreams where voices told me repeatedly, "Chemo is prolonging your death." I woke up the next day terrified, and I prayed, saying, "Lord, I cannot spend this journey living in fear." The one thing I have learned is that we have nothing to fear but fear itself. I know that sounds cliché, but if I had just put my trust in the Lord and not been fearful, I believe chemo would have been easier for me.

Then, I developed physical side effects. I could not eat for about two weeks. It was very painful. I ended up in the hospital, and my hair fell out after one treatment. It was so much harder than I thought it would be. But God revealed Himself to me in those times, and I held onto His promise that He had a plan for me. Even when the scans were bad and the doctors gave me little hope, I knew I was going to be healed.

As treatment continued, things didn't get any better. I would pass out from weakness. My parents had to lift me into bed and the tub. I got so frustrated with God during that time and told Him I did not understand. It was then that God appeared through a little girl with cancer struggling to walk as she begged her father to carry her. I knew how she felt. I wanted God to take me out of my situation, but God said, "You need to walk through this WITH Me."

On July 7th, I went for the second liver surgery. I was told it was life-threatening and the surgeon may need to take 60 percent of my liver. But God gave me peace, and I woke up feeling different. My mom confirmed that the surgeon had removed all the cancer. I had no cancer in my body. I would doze off and every time I woke up, I would say to whoever was in the room, "Hey, guess what? They got it!" I was overjoyed.

Even though the journey is long and really hard, God has a purpose for you. All we have to do is trust God with our lives and believe that He knows what He is doing even when we think He doesn't. It's like Jairus in the Bible who tells Jesus that his daughter is sick, yet Jesus takes the time to stop and heal a lady who had been sick for 12 years. I bet Jairus was like, "This lady has been waiting for 12 years; she can wait another 24 hours. My daughter is dying! Come heal her." But Jesus stopped, and Jairus was told that his daughter had died. Jesus said to Jairus, "All that is necessary is that you believe." Jairus believed Jesus could heal his daughter, and she was healed.

One thing I want you to take away from my journey is that you do not need to fear anything and that you can trust God with everything. Just like the band sang in their opening song, God causes ALL things to work together for good for "those who love him, who have been called according to his purpose."

I want to close by saying thank you for praying for me. I want to thank God for all the people He has placed in my life and that I was able to come and share my testimony with you. God bless you.

10/20/2010 Email to Allie Speck's Prayer Warriors
I write with a mixture of emotions. We were told there are areas on the MRI that "lit up" in Allie's liver and lungs. These areas could be due to inflammation or movement, but it was a lot to process. Allison demonstrated her typical stoic behavior, stating she will not entertain thoughts of cancer unless there is a confirmed finding. Her faith and trust amaze me.

A CT scan has been scheduled for tomorrow. Please pray that these areas are not cancer. She shared her testimony this past Sunday to over 300 people at a church in Lebanon. We are hoping for the best but know that God will equip us for the path ahead, whatever it holds.

As I sat to write this email, I found an email from the mother of the girl we met at Hopkins who was arranging hospice care due to her inoperable brain tumor. The update simply gave her daughter's name, her date of birth and her date and time of death.

I cried as I read it. Humbled at how full life is for Allison and what a blessing she is to us and the world. We must make the best of every day. Please pray for peace for this child's family. They walked a path most of you will never experience. I cannot imagine how her mother feels. My heart is broken.

10/21/2010 GLORIOUS CT SCAN RESULTS!
We give God glory and thanks! Allison's doctor gave us two thumbs up in the waiting room after seeing Allie's scan results. There is no sign of tumor growth. Allison will have another MRI in two months. Allie's "End of Chemo" party is scheduled for November 18th.

Satan throws roadblocks at us and challenges our faith daily. We must keep our eyes on Jesus! Allie's faith never wavered. We know there is a roller-coaster ride ahead, but we have wonderful company.

Allison's Journal, October 27, 2010

Guess where I am writing to you from? MY DORM ROOM!! I am officially living on the college campus again. I also found out that I have been accepted into a biology class that will be studying the ecosystem of Florida in January. I will be camping and studying biology for three weeks in Florida. How exciting!

♥Allie

I remember thinking what a difference a year can make! A year ago, we were taking Allie from doctor to doctor, trying to find out why she was not feeling well and was losing weight. We had no idea what lay ahead of us, and perhaps it is good that we did not know. We learned the true meaning of faith and trust.

11/19/2010 Email to Allie Speck's Prayer Warriors
This update comes with tears of joy and thanksgiving! We attended Allie's "End of Chemo" celebration yesterday. I remember asking when Allie started chemo if they would sing to a 19-year-old. The answer is YES! My morning devotion from *New Day, New You* was regarding Matthew 9:28b: "He asked them, 'Do you believe that I am able to do this?'"

There have been many times in life when I have been discouraged and not known what to do. Whatever the situation, I have often asked God, "What do You want me to do?" The answer is, "Only believe." Hebrews 4:3 tells us that believing brings us into the rest of God. Once we enter that rest, it is wonderful, for although we may still have a problem, we are not frustrated by it because we believe God will deliver us.

Allison's oncology doctor made a speech at Allie's "End of Chemo" party, saying, "I feel lucky to have been your doctor. I am blessed to have had you in my life. I am more open to believing and trusting, and I learned so much from you. I am inspired by you, every day. You are going to do great things."

The nurse who gave Allie her first and last chemo treatments presented Allie with a "Purple Heart" bead, the final bead to complete her "Beads of Courage" strand. There was not a dry eye in the room. Then, Allie's liver surgeon arrived, surprising everyone. We had Allie's favorite chocolate cake with peanut butter icing and captured the moment with a group picture of Allie's caregivers.

When I look back on how things followed God's plan, I am amazed. Allie's liver surgeon said, "You have no idea what an inspiration you have been to me and my staff!" He said how disappointed he was that the January surgery was unsuccessful. But we realized that if the surgery had been successful, we would not have met the oncology team who were all part of God's plan. Plus, Allison's successful surgery was July 7th, 7/7. The number seven in the Bible signifies perfection and completeness. Although Allie would have chosen not to experience chemo and all the suffering it involved, that experience put her where she is today and exposed her to people she would not have met otherwise. As Ralph Abernathy said, we may not know what the future holds, but we know who holds the future.

12/17/2010 Email to Allie Speck's Prayer Warriors
Great news! Allison's MRI shows no signs of cancer in her liver! We give God ALL the glory and give Him our thanks.

Allie will be taking a college biology class in January that involves traveling to Florida. She is excited to be sleeping in a tent in the Everglades for three weeks. Allie sees adventure; I see alligators. However, anything less would not be an Allie adventure. This young woman has traveled all over the world by herself, including Australia and Europe. God will protect her.

My thoughts during this time return to a year ago when we knew there was a mass on Allie's liver but had no thought that it was cancer. We had no idea where this journey would take us. A phone call on Christmas Eve from a friend led us to Hopkins, and the rest is history! This past year has been extremely difficult but a blessing overall. My morning devotional in *New Day, New You* declared that God's way is best! We know this firsthand. If you are saying, "Why, God?" or "When, God?" remember that God wants our trust, not our questions. Trust requires unanswered questions. When faced with a difficult and unclear situation, we need to say, "Lord, this does not make sense to me, but I trust You."

Allison's Journal, January 5, 2011

I am in Florida! We got up at 4:30 a.m. to swim with manatees. Once I was in the water with them, it was one of the most amazing experiences of my life. They are huge wild animals in their natural habitat. I was afraid at first, but then they swam up to us. They are such gentle and trusting creatures. As we patted them, they rolled over so we could rub their stomachs. Truly miraculous!

After our day swimming with the manatees, we took an evening walk on a long boardwalk that went out into the marsh. It was very dark, so we could see the stars beautifully. I was trying to walk and look at the stars at the same time, but it was not safe, and there were people in front of and behind me, which made walking complicated. So, we all stopped walking and just looked up. It was so much easier to enjoy the heavens. It was at this point that I thought, "This is like life." Often, I long to look, to think upon and aspire to heavenly things, but I get so distracted by the things around me that I keep looking down and fumbling in the dark. All the while, what I long to do is to gaze upon the heavens and bask in God's presence. When we are able to stop the earthly distractions and take time to be still, look to the heavens and seek to dwell with God, we are at peace. That is what this trip is for me, and I am so very thankful.

♥Allie

On January 13th, while Allie was in Florida, she remembered my birthday and called me. She reminded me that a year ago today we were told she had cancer. Allie's life is a testimony of what faith can do.

Allison's Journal, January 13, 2011

One year ago today, I was lying in the ICU, experiencing some of the worst pain I have ever felt (physically and emotionally) with a cancerous tumor inside me the size of a football. Now, here I am only ONE YEAR later, hiking through the Everglades, wading through marshes, sleeping in tents and just LIVING (biologically and vibrantly). I am overwhelmed by God's goodness and healing power. I was brought to tears this evening just thinking about it. The tears, however, weren't just joyful; there were some sad ones, just thinking of the kids on the floor at the hospital still going through that hell. They are on my heart every day and especially today. I need to visit the floor again soon.

♥Allie

01/26/2011 Email to Allie Speck's Prayer Warriors
Allison is safely back at college. They left the Florida Keys and drove 24 hours in a 15-passenger van to get home. She looks amazing! Tan, happy and healthy with a new growth of hair. What an amazing experience!

Allison will be taking five classes for the spring semester. Her next MRI is in March. She is moving forward at a very fast pace, but we know that God keeps up with her. Here is to a New Year with new adventures!

02/03/2011 Email to Allie Speck's Prayer Warriors
Life is so normal I need to pinch myself to make sure it is real. Last night Allie attended a three-hour lecture and then took a two-hour swing dance class! Her enthusiasm and adventurous spirit make me smile.

02/12/2011 Email to Allie Speck's Prayer Warriors
Allie's visit to Hopkins was great. We had a wonderful visit with her doctor, who wanted to hear all about Allie's trip to Florida. It was wonderful to sit and watch a tan, healthy Allie tell of her adventures and stories. At the end of that discussion, Allie asked about going to Kenya in May. She was told it is possible as long as her scans are clear and her port is removed before leaving the country. Allie is excited.

CHAPTER TWELVE
LIFE INTERRUPTED

Allison's podcast interview at Messiah College (now Messiah University), February 2011

Question: When did this all begin? When did you have feelings that something was wrong?
Allie: It all started the middle to end of my senior year of high school. I was sick all the time. I had a fever every day. I was tired. I kept telling my mom that I did not have any energy and just did not feel well. She took me to the doctor multiple times, but they could never find anything. Blood tests, checkups—everything came back normal. So, I graduated high school and started college in the fall. I found a lump in my abdomen. My mom made me a doctor's appointment, and I was sent for a CT scan that same day. That evening we got a call saying they had found a large mass on my liver, and I would need more tests. Everyone asked me how I reacted. I was actually kind of glad they had found something because I was sick all the time and knew something was wrong. I thought, "They found what was wrong, and now they can fix it." I never thought it was cancer. That thought never crossed my mind. I figured it was a lump and could be removed. I found out it was cancer in January, after they tried to remove it but couldn't. I woke up from anesthesia, and my mom told me they did not remove the tumor and that it was cancer.

Question: When you first heard the word *cancer*, how did that make you feel?

Allie: When I first found out, I was scared. Cancer is a pretty scary word, no matter what context you hear it in, whether it is you or someone you care about. But I knew that God had a plan for me through everything, and I just put my trust in Him, knowing He would lead me through whatever He brought me to. It was scary, but I had confidence that I would be okay.

Question: Were you ever afraid of dying?

Allie: I was, in the very beginning. It was a scary time. Some doctors told me I had six months to a year to live. The diagnosis was grim. They painted a dismal picture. So, I thought about death, but I knew I would go to a better place if I died. It did make me sad to think of leaving my family if that would happen.

Question: Can you talk about the treatment you received?

Allie: I went to a local hospital, and they told me my cancer was too complicated and there was nothing they could do for me. So, my mom took me to Johns Hopkins for a second opinion. That is where I had my first surgery, which was unsuccessful. So, I went to the pediatric oncology unit, where I received six rounds of chemotherapy. They gave me two very strong chemotherapy drugs. It was a really long, hard road. Probably one of the hardest things I have ever done in my life.

Question: With chemotherapy, you lost your hair. Was that difficult for you to experience?

Allie: I was never really upset about losing my hair. I knew it was part of the process. I think I was surprised that it happened so fast. I got my first treatment, and within a week I had no hair. My mom loves my bald head. She loves to rub it. HAHA! Everyone tells me I have a beautiful bald head. It has never really bothered me too much.

Question: Your treatment required you to spend a lot of time in the hospital. Tell me what that was like.

Allie: That was especially hard, since most of my treatment was over the summer, and all of my friends were
on vacation, swimming in pools. I wasn't allowed to swim
in pools, and I wasn't allowed in the sun, because the
chemo made my skin sensitive. It was boring and frustrating at the same time. The one benefit was meeting lots of
people in the hospital. The kids are amazing! You will never
meet anyone like the kids in a pediatric oncology unit.
They are mature beyond their years. Amazing little people!
The parents are strong, and the nurses are committed to
providing quality care. I would not want to do it again, but
I am thankful for the people I met along the way.

Question: What kept you grounded and strong through
all of this?
Allie: Definitely my faith. I clung to God and went to Him
with everything. My family, especially my mom, took
care of me all the time. I don't know what I would have
done without my mom. My friends were supportive too.
They sold T-shirts and held fundraisers. The community
rallied around and helped us financially. Friends provided support to my little brother if he needed a place to
stay while my parents were with me. The support was
incredible! It is hard to express how much that support
meant to me and my family.

Question: Do you view your life differently now than
before you were diagnosed with cancer?
Allie: I do. I have said that cancer was one of the worst,
but also one of the best, things that has happened to
me. It gave me a new perspective on life that I would
not have had without cancer. Once you face death
and realize how short life can be, you realize how much
you want to enjoy the time you have. There were days
in the hospital when I hadn't eaten for weeks, vomiting,
tired, sick and frustrated, and I would think how I would
love to wake up, feel normal and just eat. I wouldn't
even care what the food was, just to enjoy a simple meal
without pain or sickness. So, every morning that I wake
up and feel normal, it is a great day! Every time I sit down
to eat, I am thankful to not throw up or feel sick. Every
night that I sleep in my own bed and not a hospital bed

has made me thankful for all God has blessed me with. I believe I took those things for granted before cancer.

Question: What have you learned about yourself through this experience?
Allie: I learned that I am stronger than I thought I was. If you would have asked me a few years ago how I would handle a cancer diagnosis, I probably would have answered, "Not very good." I mean, it is a hard situation to imagine. But I have realized the importance of my family and friends, of keeping them close and letting them know how much they are appreciated.

Question: You are now cancer-free! Can you tell me about getting the news that you no longer had cancer?
Allie: I got the news after my second liver surgery in July. I woke up from surgery and of course the first thing I said was, "Did they get it?" My oncology doctor was there and said, "Yes, they got it all!" It was one of the happiest moments of my life. The nurses were cheering. I remember my family and my mom coming in. Of course, I was still groggy from anesthesia, and I kept asking each person over and over. But it was the greatest feeling in the world! I no longer had to carry that fear anymore. It was gone.

Question: Now that cancer is gone, how hard has it been to adjust to your normal life?
Allie: It has been pretty difficult getting back to the norm because your body is worn down from the fight. You have to take some time and build yourself back up. My cancer doctor thinks I do things too fast. She says, "Normally cancer patients start at the shallow end and wade back into life, but you, Allie, you just jump in the deep end with both feet." HAHA! I feel like I want to get back into life and experience it fully, right now, as much as I can. Cancer took away a large chunk of my life, and I don't want to waste any more time. I am ready to get back to college, be with my friends and family, and enjoy the life that God has blessed me with.

Question: Would you say this experience has had an impact on your spiritual life?

Allie: Absolutely! It strengthened my relationship with the Lord. I realized that I can go to Him with everything and trust Him completely. The main scripture I held onto through this journey was Jeremiah 29:11. It kept coming up over and over. I held onto that because I believe God has great plans for me and He knows what they are. God is much bigger than cancer. I believe this journey showed me that God does use all things for good. He does want what is best for us and will give us what is best for us if we trust Him.

Question: You refer to this experience as a journey. Tell me about that.
Allie: This journey was a necessity in my life. It was something that I needed to go through to make me stronger and to give me this perspective that I never would have had otherwise. It was absolutely the hardest thing I have ever done physically, emotionally and spiritually. But I am a stronger person because of it. I believe my story can touch others. I want to share my journey and show others what God can do if you put your trust in Him and give Him the glory through your life.

A letter from one of Allie's college roommates, February 10, 2011

Hello, Allie.
It seems like forever since I have seen you. I cannot wait until you are back on campus, living a "normal" life. But here's the thing: your life isn't "normal" and you haven't lived it normally, and that's what is so cool about your situation. Through it all, you and your family haven't lost faith. You have persevered, and that is not something you see every day. In fact, I would call that rather extraordinary—nothing "normal" about it. I pray that you continue to heal and continue to shine your light like we are called to do in Matthew chapter 5. You are amazing! Keep strong!

Allie's response to questions from a reporter about her cancer, March 2, 2011

I think it is important that people know that cancer isn't a death sentence; it is simply a calling to live with more vivacity. I do not want to waste a minute simply living a ho-hum life. I was not going to let cancer stop me from chasing down the dreams and plans God has set in place for me. If anything, cancer has allowed me to run with more confidence. I am not as afraid of failure or death or pain because I have faced the worst of those things and discovered I can make it through them. I have also learned that God is not going to take me home until He is finished with me on earth. By bringing me through cancer, He has shown me that He is not finished working through me, and that has given me confidence. I am not afraid of dying because I know He will protect me until it is my time, and, if I die, I am not very concerned because that meant it was my time and then I get to go be with Jesus. I think I have lost or perhaps forgotten what things were so scary about death in the first place. Don't think I am some irrational daredevil who tempts and teases death. I am simply saying that that fear of stepping out in faith is gone. Cancer pushed me out headfirst into faith, and God caught me; so now stepping out is much less intimidating. I just love sharing what God has done for me and what my friends and family have done for me. It is such a beautiful thing to me that I want others to really understand it. And do not in any way make me out to be an extraordinary or outstanding person! I still doubt, I still fear, I questioned and I was frustrated. I am very much human and still very stubborn. I just have gained more confidence to work through those things and realize I will be okay.

Allison's Journal, March 2, 2011

So, I have been super busy! I have been traveling to different churches and sharing my journey. So far, I have been well received. Everyone has been very encouraging, and several thanked me, saying they were touched by my testimony.

I AM GOING TO KENYA IN MAY! SO EXCITED! This is my dream trip! I have always wanted to do mission work in Africa, and now I am finally going. I am thinking about all that I need to do before the trip...I need to find a job, apply for a scholarship for the trip, get my laptop computer checked, find my extra battery and buy extra SD cards for my camera. Yikes!

I have been healthy and working on getting back in shape. I weigh 150 pounds! I am getting stronger, and I am making time with God a priority in my life. This is the happiest I have been in quite some time. Anyway, I need some sleep, something I am a stranger to lately. HAHA!

P.S. I am going to start writing a book about my journey.

♥Allie

Allie's testimony, March 2011

Good morning. Thank you for praying for me. I am here to share my testimony. I have believed for a long time that God would use my life in a big way to glorify Him, and I thought that meant being a missionary and going overseas, which is still one of my goals. When I was in elementary school and they asked us what we wanted to be when we grew up, my answer was a missionary. I have always wanted to do something great for God.

After I graduated high school, I wanted to go to a Christian college. I was accepted at Messiah and jumped right into mission work. I went to inner-city Harrisburg to hand out food to the homeless, and I was organizing a trip to Nicaragua. I was enjoying getting involved and connected, but I didn't feel well. I had lots of tests, but they all came back negative. No one could find anything wrong.

At the end of November, I noticed a swelling in my stomach that I showed to my mom. She was very concerned and scheduled a doctor's appointment.

More testing found a large mass and two smaller tumors in my liver. I was referred to a local hospital where the doctor said he was not sure anything could be done, and he thought it was cancer. My mom decided we would get a second opinion.

Through an amazing series of events that was nothing short of a miracle, my mom spoke with a doctor at Johns Hopkins on Christmas Eve. I was seen by the liver surgeon the day after my 19th birthday and was scheduled for surgery on January 13th. I believed that he would remove the tumor. I was confident. I had faith. I prayed. People told me God was going to work a miracle in my life. I was going to be healed. I was not worried at all.

The morning of the surgery, my friend texted and reminded me that I always wanted to be a missionary. She said, "Look at this as your mission. So many people are watching and praying for you. God will be glorified through your healing." I thought, "Exactly! God will heal me, and I can go back to school and pick up MY plan where I left off." So, I went into surgery believing that I would be healed, but God had a different plan. Those are words I have come to understand: BUT GOD. I had a plan, BUT GOD had a better plan. I thought it was time to be healed, BUT GOD was not done working in my life.

I woke up from surgery, and my mom was there to tell me that the surgeon could not get the tumor and that it was cancer. I started to cry, scream and basically throw a fit. To me that meant I had months to live. Mom explained that they could treat the cancer with chemo. I trusted God and struggled with understanding why He had not healed me and why I had cancer. I wasn't angry; I just did not understand. I took the opportunity to use this trial to be drawn closer to Him and learn to trust in His grace; that was sufficient for me.

I met with the oncology doctors, who made me believe my cancer could be treated. We came up with a plan. The next step was chemo. I did not want to do chemo. I had seen chemo in movies and other people who went through it. People asked me if I was scared, and I said no. I wasn't lying. I wasn't scared; I was terrified! So, I started chemo, which caused hallucinations. My mom said I was thrashing in bed, screaming, and there was a roomful of nurses trying to keep me safe. I felt like what I was seeing and hearing were my fears manifesting through my dreams and visions. I gave all my fears to God. I said, "I don't understand and I am afraid, but I trust You with whatever You are doing with my life."

Along with the mental side effects, there came physical side effects, which were no walk in the park. I lost my hair, and I developed ulcers in my throat and stomach. I could not eat. I was so weak that I would lie in bed for days. It was miserable. During one of my longest admissions, I was stuck in my room and was so sick. At the end of week two, I said to my mom, "God could make this so much easier. Why can't I just feel normal? Why doesn't He?"

It was a few days later that God led me to the story of Lazarus in John chapter 11. "Now a man named Lazarus was sick." He was the brother of Mary and Martha. "So the sisters sent word to Jesus, 'Lord, the one you love is sick.' When he heard this, Jesus said, 'This sickness will not end in death. No, it is for God's glory so that God's Son may be glorified through it.' Now Jesus loved Martha and her sister and Lazarus." Because He loved them, "when he heard that Lazarus was sick, he stayed where he was two more days." When I first read this, I did not understand it. BECAUSE HE LOVED Lazarus, He waited two more days. WHY? Why wouldn't He go immediately and heal him? Then after two days, Jesus said to the disciples, "Let's go to Lazarus." The chapter continues, "'Our friend Lazarus has fallen asleep; but I am going there to wake him up.' His disciples replied, 'Lord, if he sleeps, he will get better.' Jesus had been speaking of his death, but his disciples thought he meant natural sleep. So then he told them plainly, 'Lazarus is dead, and for your sake I am glad I was not there, so that you may believe. But let us go to him.'" So, Martha meets Jesus on the road. "'Lord,' Martha said to Jesus, 'if you had been here, my brother would not have died. But I know that even now God will give you whatever you ask.'" Later, when Jesus saw Mary and the Jews weeping, "he was deeply moved in spirit and troubled. 'Where have you laid him?' he asked. 'Come and see, Lord,' they replied. Jesus wept. Then the Jews said, 'See how he loved him!' But some of them said, 'Could not he who opened the eyes of the blind have kept this man from dying?'" Jesus went to the tomb and asked them to remove the stone. "'But, Lord,' Martha said, 'by this time there is a bad odor, for he has been there for four days.' Then Jesus said, 'Did I not tell you that if you believe, you will see the glory of God?'"

When I read this story, I understood why Jesus waited. Jesus was not late. He was not surprised by Lazarus's death. It was not an accident. Jesus waited because He loved them and wanted them to see the true glory of God. What I realized is, sometimes you don't need just a healing; you need a complete resurrection. You need to get to the point where you are in the deepest, darkest place because it is in that dark place that you will see God's light. God spoke to me through this passage, and I realized that God was working through everything that happened to me. God knew exactly what I needed. One of the verses I repeated to myself was Jeremiah 29:11. The other verse I held onto was Romans 8:28. In that scripture it doesn't say that God works through good things; it says He works through ALL things for good. Even things we see as not good.

During my two-week stay in the hospital, I wrote lyrics to a song that God put on my heart. I shared them with my friend, and she wrote the music. I am going to share that song with you now:

Lyrics:
When trials seem to get the best of me,
Jesus says, "Come and rest in Me."
Even when things don't go as planned,
God is faithful, I'm still in His hands.
Lord, Your ways are higher than my ways;
All of creation shows me this.
Star breather who created the nights and days,
Who am I to question, who am I to doubt who You are?

You're God the Almighty, You fashioned each cell
that is in me.
You spoke the world into being, every mountain,
every seedling.
You crafted our race; Your hands smoothed the clay,
That sculpted the ones I lift to You,
Then descended to save this people of dust.
Lord, who am I not to trust in You.

When sorrows like sea billows roll,
I know You are in control.

Though I don't understand, and I can't comprehend
all of the things that You do,
I've learned not to lean on my own understanding.
Instead, Lord, I lean on You.

You're God the Almighty; You fashioned each cell
that is in me.
You spoke the world into being, every mountain,
every seedling,
You crafted our race; Your hands smoothed the clay,
That sculpted the ones I lift to You,
Then descended to save this people of dust.
Lord, who am I not to trust in You.

Thank you to everyone who prayed for me. As you know, I am now cancer-free. I am grateful for your support and encouragement.

To hear Allie's song, "The Journey," and see the video she created, please go to this YouTube link: https://www.youtube.com/watch?v=KqP6ZnCUfwY.

It was early March when Allison called me and said she was having pain in her abdomen and dizzy spells. She wanted me to ask if her scans could be ordered sooner. I was immediately consumed with fear. I sent an email to Allie's oncology doctor detailing the symptoms and asking for earlier scans. The doctor encouraged us to keep the next appointment and not worry. I prayed and asked God to give Allie peace and strength as she awaited testing. I had an ominous feeling. I remember crying as I typed the email to Allie's doctor and being thankful that Allie was not there to see my emotions.

03/18/2011 Email to Allie Speck's Prayer Warriors
This is a difficult email to write. Allison had an MRI and CT scan yesterday. It has been six months since her last chemo and eight months since her surgery. The doctor took us into a room, closed the door and said, "I have bad news." The MRI shows a mass in the liver and two in her lung. Allie's first words were, "God brought me through this before and He will bring me through again." The doctor has recommended different chemo and possibly radiation.

> Life was returning to normal, and this feels like a
> sucker punch to the gut. However, we still claim
> Jeremiah 29:11. We have witnessed part of God's
> plan, as Allie has been sharing her testimony. She
> is scheduled to speak locally this Sunday, and she
> was asked if she would still speak after hearing that
> her cancer had returned. Allie's response: "Why
> wouldn't I? God is still in this."

I remember waiting for the usual thumbs-up signal from Allie's doctor after reviewing the scans to let us know that everything was good while we waited for an exam room. The thumbs-up signal never came. Instead, we were taken to a room, and Allie's doctor entered quietly, looking down and saying words I will never forget: "I have bad news." My eyes immediately filled with tears that I tried to hold back as I watched Allie's reaction. It was devastating! She was on the brink of a normal life, and we were being thrown back into the cancer world again. WHY? What purpose could this possibly serve? My first thought, after watching Allie handle the news as stoically as she always has, was to activate the prayer chain and get people praying. We needed support. We needed prayers. We needed God.

> **03/23/2011 Email to Allie Speck's Prayer Warriors**
> Thank you for all the support we have received. Allie
> gave a beautiful testimony at a local church on Sun-
> day. While driving to the church, Allison felt God had
> a message for her. Suddenly a bald eagle swooped
> across the road in front of her, carrying an animal in
> its claws. She slammed on the brakes and watched
> the bird soar. She said the scripture Matthew 6:25-
> 27 immediately came to mind: "Therefore I tell you,
> do not worry about your life, what you will eat or
> drink; or about your body, what you will wear. Is not
> life more than food, and the body more than clothes?
> Look at the birds of the air; they do not sow or reap
> or store away in barns, and yet your heavenly Father
> feeds them. Are you not much more valuable than
> they? Can any one of you by worrying add a single
> hour to your life?" How perfect!

> That same evening, I attended Bible study, and we
> read Psalm 103:1-5. "Praise the Lord, my soul; all
> my inmost being, praise his holy name. Praise the

Lord, my soul, and forget not all his benefits—who forgives all your sins and heals all your diseases, who redeems your life from the pit and crowns you with love and compassion, who satisfies your desires with good things so that your youth is renewed like the eagles." I saw this as God's confirmation that He is with us. The eagle was a symbol to Allie and to me to encourage our faith and to remind us that we serve a God who is able.

Allie shared that the return of cancer should not diminish the glory of her first healing because that was a miracle. Her faith is amazing! Rather than become angry, we have watched Allison and Andy trust the Lord's plan for the future.

Allie's surgeon wants to operate next week to remove the liver lesion. There is much to absorb, as we were also told further review of the CT scan showed nine to ten "spots" in her lungs that are new. We are reactivating this prayer chain, where we can lay our burdens down. Our motto is "God is able!"

03/27/2011 Email to Allie Speck's Prayer Warriors
We are trying to keep up with all that is happening. Allison is scheduled for liver surgery on Tuesday. Once she has healed, chemo will start around April 21st.

The book I am reading, *You Were Born for This*, discusses how Jesus's disciples asked why they couldn't perform specific miracles and were told they were limited by their unbelief. Jesus said, "If you have faith the size of a mustard seed, you will say to this mountain, 'Move from here to there,' and it will move; nothing will be impossible for you" (Matthew 17:20 NET). Jesus did not say with faith in God, you CAN say to a mountain, "Move." He said if you have faith, you WILL say to the mountain, "Move."

The difference between belief and unbelief is demonstrated in Matthew 14 (NKJV) in the story of Peter, who stepped from a solid boat onto the water. It was a stormy night as the disciples sailed across the Sea of Galilee. Suddenly a figure appeared, walking on the waves. They thought it was a ghost. But Jesus called out, "It is I; do not be afraid." Then Peter said, "Lord, if it is You, command me to come to You on the water." So, Jesus said, "Come." And when Peter stepped out of the boat, he walked on the water. Can you imagine what that first step felt like? All of the other disciples stayed in the boat. Only Peter took a step of faith and only Peter experienced a miracle.

Even though Peter was brave at first, he became fearful, took his eyes off Jesus, and began to sink! Peter cried, "Lord, save me!" And *immediately* Jesus stretched out His hand and caught him, and said to him, "O you of little faith, why did you doubt?" (Matthew 14:31 NKJV).

So, no matter how we feel, if we don't take the first risky step, we will never experience the miracle.

Allie wrote a Lenten devotional for our church. At the end of it she wrote, "If you are going to walk on water, you have to get out of the boat!" She wrote that in February. This story was God confirming our need to step out in faith.

03/29/2011 Email to Allie Speck's Prayer Warriors
Allison had surgery, and everything went well. She went to surgery about 9:30 a.m., and about 12:45 p.m. we met with the surgeon. He was smiling! My heart leaped with joy. He said, "Mission accomplished!" He removed the lesion seen on the MRI and two small spots deep within the liver. He saw nothing else. Thank God!

We waited two hours to see Allie. Despite her pain, she pointed to the sky, gave a thumbs-up and whispered, "God is good!" I love her continued faith. She always looks so young in that hospital bed. The mother in me just wants to take away all the hurt.

03/31/2011 Email to Allie Speck's Prayer Warriors
While Allie was in surgery, we learned that a girl she
graduated with died in an accident. This hit hard
for Allie and her friends. Allie spoke with friends by
phone, crying and sharing with each other. During
our prayer time, we asked the Holy Spirit, our great
Comforter, to provide peace that passes understanding for the family. Allie hopes to be home to attend
her friend's service.

Allie is recovering well despite some pain and a
fever. She did get a private room and a wonderful
nurse whom we knew. We know God prepared the
way. I was able to sleep by her bed.

Yesterday Allie asked if she would have visitors while
at Hopkins. I told her it was unlikely, since we are an
hour and half from home. God had other plans, as she
received a visit from our pastor and one of her favorite nurses. God knew just what Allie needed.

A poem written by Allison entitled "What Is Love?"

Love is when your hair falls out
and you become skin and bones
and your social skills are shot
and you can't even stand on your own
and the one you thought you loved leaves you
and you are alone.

Here is love.
Look at it,
that sobbing mass of bones
there in the quiet darkness
with a pillow soaked in tears.

Can you see?
If you can't, then maybe you don't know what love is.
So let me tell you.

Love is what took those bones and broke them.
Love is what took that life and wrung it almost dry.

Love is what led that mess of sin into the darkness,
and then love is what takes its hand and walks it to
the window.
Love is what pulls back the curtain
and lets in the light.

Love is what whispers,
"There is still beauty in the world."
Love is what reveals darkness
in its rawest form
and then painfully wrenches it from the one it belongs
to.
Like falling into a cactus patch,
painfully, thorn by thorn,
love pulls out what was never meant to belong,
sometimes taking bits of flesh with it.

And then in the end,
when you are left alone and broken,
Love is what slowly reforms,
reconstructs
and reveals
that you are stronger than you know
and you were meant for more than this.

And because that love is so great,
it shows you this.
True love is nothing like you had expected,
but more than you could have ever dreamed.

Allison's Journal, April 10, 2011

So, I have cancer again. I found out in March. It is in my
liver and my lungs. I had surgery on March 29th, and the
surgeon removed all the cancer from my liver. I started
chemo this past Thursday, and it is not supposed to be as
rough as my previous chemo. So, how do I feel? Originally
I was okay with it. I just wanted to get things moving and
start fighting. I was optimistic. But as time has gone on, I
am not sure how I feel. No one else seems to be optimistic.
How do I feel about cancer? I don't know. How do I
feel about life? Overwhelmed. My family is quiet, and I

have not heard much from my college friends. No one wants to date a girl with cancer. Not to mention that I have cancer again. If you can answer how I feel, then you know better than I do myself. I think I am going to go with the emotion of anger. Lots of it, in different categories. Defiant anger, frustrated anger, desperate anger, confused anger. Sometimes I feel numb, mostly because I don't know how to feel at the moment. Right now, I feel tired. Good night.

♥Allie

CHAPTER THIRTEEN
GOD WITH US

Allison's Journal, April 2011

This is my desperate prayer from the shower.
It is not You that I don't believe in; it's me.
I am not strong enough to bear what You have
given me.
I am not whole enough to keep You in me.
I am cracked and broken, and You leak out and I
lose You.
God says, "Then let Me fix you."
But I don't know how.
I don't know how.

♥Allie

04/02/2011 Email to Allie Speck's Prayer Warriors
The day after Allie got home from her liver surgery,
she invited friends to create a scrapbook for the family of her friend who passed away. It was bittersweet
watching them share stories and memories of a life
taken much too soon.

Today was Allie's friend's funeral. It was a long and
exhausting day. We went early so Allie could give
condolences to the family and find a seat. She sat for
five hours while guests paid their respects. She has
a slight fever and pain, but she persevered to hon-
or her friend and support the family. No one could

believe that she had liver surgery three days ago.
She slept three hours on the ride home.

The theme of the funeral was, "What Choice Will Your
Heart Make?" When we face trials in life, we have
a choice how we handle tragedy. We sang "Blessed
Be Your Name," which reminded us to praise God
through blessings and trials. So, in times of trial, what
will your heart choose to say? Do we praise God only
when the sun is shining and the world is right, or do
we praise Him in the darkness too?

Pray for Allie as she anticipates chemo, schedules
classes and cancels her trip to Kenya, which is a
huge disappointment. Missionary work in Africa
was her dream of a lifetime, but we believe she will
achieve that dream eventually.

I remember taking Allison to the funeral and watching her push through
the pain and the fatigue to make sure the family knew how much her friend
meant to her. Allie was always giving to others, even when she was in need
of support herself. Her act of inviting friends to our home to create a beautiful memory scrapbook for the family and attending the funeral were selfless
acts of love and respect. She was 20 years old, but she demonstrated faith
and wisdom beyond her years. Those attending witnessed a strong young
lady who put friendship and family before personal pain and suffering.

04/06/2011 Email to Allie Speck's Prayer Warriors
Allie has her first chemo treatment tomorrow. We
took her to college on Tuesday and Wednesday to
attend class. Taking her to the campus helped to
ease some of the stress related to everything she
needs to accomplish before the end of the semester.
She is working hard on several term papers.

04/08/2011 Email to Allie Speck's Prayer Warriors
Allie had a CT scan that required her to drink two
bottles of contrast. After the first bottle, she told the
technician she felt sick and asked if the scan could
be done soon in case she vomited. The technician
said she needed to finish both bottles. Not long after
asking, Allison threw up and, despite the nausea,

grabbed the second bottle, started drinking and said, "Let's do this." They were able to complete the scan after she finished the second bottle. Her strength amazes me!

The preliminary results show the pelvis and liver to be clear. The lung shows no new lesions, but the current lesions are slightly larger. The doctor says it is good that Allie started chemo.

04/16/2011 Email to Allie Speck's Prayer Warriors
Allison received her second dose of chemo. The doctor was amazed how well her liver incision had healed from two weeks ago. She felt well enough to work on a college paper. Allie is tired and short of breath but has no nausea or vomiting. We pray she remains stable until her next chemo treatment.

Allie attended a Spring Fling dance at Messiah last night. She has returned to campus until she has to come home for chemo. She is trying to live a normal life and finish this semester. Her professors have been supportive, and we know exactly why God placed her at Messiah.

This scripture spoke to me today. First Thessalonians 5:16–18 says, "Rejoice ALWAYS, pray continually, give thanks in ALL circumstances, for this is God's will for you in Christ Jesus."

04/21/2011 Email to Allie Speck's Prayer Warriors
Andy turned 15 yesterday! We celebrated his birthday by watching old home movies. It was fun to look back on carefree days and laugh at the memories. It was a wonderful evening celebrating Andy and the joy he brings to our family. We also attended Maundy Thursday services at church. Allie and Andy colored Easter eggs after church. I guess you are never too old to color eggs.

04/27/2011 Email to Allie Speck's Prayer Warriors
Tomorrow Allison will receive another round of

chemo if her blood counts are good. Allie did fairly
well after the first chemo. She had rough days, but
they resolved. She was able to attend class at Messiah, and she started a job in a clothing store. It is the
perfect job where she can combine her love of people
with her sense of fashion. We are happy for her.

As Allie endures new chemo, we begin a time of
waiting. We know that God can heal Allie, but we
don't know the timing of His plan. When we are faced
with a delayed answer from God, what do our actions
say about our belief in God while we are waiting?
We pray that our faith shows trust that God knows
exactly what He is doing.

05/02/2011 Email to Allie Speck's Prayer Warriors
Allie received her chemo and is tired and queasy but
stable. The biggest effect was losing her hair again.
She left for college with hair and came home bald.
She said her hair hurt so she started pulling, and it
came out in clumps. Her biggest concern was cover-
ing her head for work. Today she wore a hat to work
but felt confident enough to remove it and worked all
day without it.

She finishes final exams this week and is looking forward to working and enjoying her summer vacation.
Andy is working on a 1962 truck he bought with his
dad. Allison enjoys helping them with the project
when she feels well. We are anxious for some summer family time together.

05/08/2011 Email to Allie Speck's Prayer Warriors
Happy Mother's Day! Allie was able to sing in church
today, despite being slightly short of breath. Her
beautiful voice is a gift from God. I love watching her
sing as much as I love watching Andy play baseball.
My children bring me great joy. I am blessed.

Allie sang the Chris Tomlin song "Faithful." The lyrics were perfect: "Faithful, forever You are faithful.
Shelter for the fragile soul. You lift us up, You hold

us all together. You are faithful, God." The words brought tears to my eyes. I was reminded that God is forever faithful and a shelter for Allie's fragile soul.

05/09/2011 Email to Allie Speck's Prayer Warriors
Last night Allie complained of lightheadedness and shortness of breath and had a fever, so I called the doctor. We were sent to the local ER. When I told Allie we needed to go to the Emergency Room, she said, "I don't want to go to the hospital. Besides, it's Mother's Day and you don't want to go to the hospital either." I said it was after midnight, so it was technically no longer Mother's Day. Begrudgingly she left for the hospital.

The first nurse recognized Allie and said they had a call from Hopkins to expect her. Within an hour, she was in a room with an IV and got an antibiotic. Her counts were good enough that she was discharged home at 3:30 a.m. God's hand was upon her.

05/19/2011 Email to Allie Speck's Prayer Warriors
Allie went to Hopkins today for chemo. Her platelet count needed to be 50,000 to get chemo, and her last check was 23,000. Today her platelets were 216,000! Allie's doctor said that each of Allie's 200 prayer warriors must have asked for a 1,000-point increase in her platelets. We were blessed to be home in time for a family dinner.

The remainder of Allie's treatment will be determined by her scan results. We pray the scans show improvement. God wants us to come to Him with our requests and then BELIEVE that He can do all we ask and more. We believe Allie can be cancer-free...again!

Mark 11:22-23 says, "'Have faith in God,' Jesus answered. 'Truly I tell you, if anyone says to this mountain, "Go, throw yourself into the sea," and does not doubt in their heart but believes that what they say will happen, it will be done for them.'"

06/01/2011 Email to Allie Speck's Prayer Warriors
Last Thursday Allie received chemo and completed
her last final exam. Her semester is officially complete! Praise the Lord! Driving home from Hopkins
we heard tornado warnings on the radio. The winds
rocked the car while rain and hail smacked the wind-
shield. We drove cautiously, encountering several
downed trees and power lines. Tom and Andy were
on a baseball field during the storm, but we found
them safe at home. We have had no electricity for
several days, but thank God no one was hurt.

Allie developed a fever and ended up in the Emergency Room on Memorial Day. She was given an antibiotic and sent home. Today she woke up with severe
abdominal pain that resulted in a trip to Hopkins'
Emergency Room. We arrived around 7:30 p.m. Allison was admitted for a bowel infection and given two
units of blood. They plan to do her scans here once
her pain is controlled.

06/02/2011 Email to Allie Speck's Prayer Warriors
God has heard your prayers. Allison may be discharged home today. The MRI of the liver shows no
tumors, and the best news is that her CT of the lungs
shows shrinkage of the lesions in her lungs! Since
the lung lesions are responding to chemo, she will
continue to receive the same chemo.

When Allie had her MRI last night and was out of the
room, I had a serious talk with God. I spoke from the
depths of my heart, asking Him to heal my daughter
completely and allow her to serve Him. After praying, I opened the book I was reading, *Right People,
Right Place, Right Plan,* to a chapter titled "RIGHT
PLAN." Each chapter opens with a scripture, and
the scripture for this chapter was Allie's: Jeremiah
29:11. I felt God responding to my prayer for Allie.
He has the right plan.

The book said that God's plan often comes through
unexpected events that force you in a direction you

never would have gone. This journey is definitely not a direction we would have chosen. It also said that we get busy grabbing at ordinary things while God is planning extraordinary things for us. It referenced another of Allie's favorite scriptures: Romans 8:28.

When Allie came back from the MRI, she said it was the most peaceful MRI she has ever had. She said that she knew everything was going to be all right. I am so thankful for scripture and for a God who listened to this mother's heart.

06/09/2011 Email to Allie Speck's Prayer Warriors
Allison had an appointment at Hopkins today and has been cleared for a week's vacation in Florida. We are so excited; we leave tomorrow! We had Disney tickets in 2010 but had to cancel our trip when Allie was diagnosed. Allison loves Disney, and we booked a special breakfast with Cinderella. She might be the only bald 20-year-old dining with Cinderella, but we believe you are never too old to enjoy some Disney magic! The whole family is looking forward to getting away.

There is a Children's Hospital in Florida that is familiar with the Johns Hopkins doctors, since lots of kids with cancer choose Disney as their Make-A-Wish destination. It is a bittersweet situation, but we have their contact information in case Allison needs medical attention during our vacation. We pray she does not.

Allie will resume chemo on June 23rd with two more rounds and then scans in July. Decisions will be made after the scans. Life is a never-ending series of events, with one event dependent on the next. We pray that God will bless us with an uneventful vacation and that we will return with a refreshed attitude.

A story written by Allison entitled "Let It Wash Away"
   "Ew...what is that thing?"
   He was referring to me.
   "What is wrong with you?"

He was asking me.

"That is so rude! What is your problem?"

That was my mom.

For the first time, I thought I might cry over my baldness.

I usually don't mind it. I didn't even cry the first morning I woke up to a pillow that was hairier than my uncle's back. I didn't choke up the night I picked the majority of my hair from the shower drain or the evening that I threw the last of it into the garbage. I honestly don't remember being the least bit upset. I could tolerate the staring and the bold questions, the occasional rude remarks and looks of pity. Of course, I didn't think I could escape them on vacation, but in a place as big and magical as Disney World, I figured there were bigger spectacles than a bald 20-year-old girl. Apparently, I was mistaken. In fact, most of this trip I felt like I was one of the main attractions. Heads swiveled everywhere I went. It was as if people's noses were made of metal and my bald head radiated a magnetic force that overpowered any social graces that someone may possess. It was understandable. I admit to letting my eyes linger on others that, like me, don't quite blend into the crowd.

I am so used to people staring at me that I have placed them into categories:

Avoiders: These are the ones who stare at me until I look in their direction, at which point they avert their eyes quickly and try to pretend as if they were not staring.

Pity Smilers: People in this category will stare until I look at them and then give me the pity smile. You know, the one where they slightly raise their eyebrows, smile without showing any teeth, and succeed in making me feel like I am on a slow march toward death.

Talkers: These usually result in either a very cathartic or very awkward experience. These are people who are brave enough to talk to me. When I catch them looking at me, they usually feel compelled to tell me something or ask me about my "condition." Sometimes this just results in a story about how their aunt's friend's sister died of cancer, but sometimes I actually get to make a nice connection with new people.

The Unashamed: These are my favorite because they will continue to stare like I am some type of animal in a zoo. Even if I look directly at them, they won't react. They just keep on staring with their mouths open. I enjoy this because I love to stare directly back into their eyes and see how long it takes them to feel uncomfortable.

In the time it took me to create this list, I became accustomed to people acting differently around me. So, I expected things like this to happen. In fact, I usually enjoy answering questions and sharing stories, but this comment was different. It cut deeper than any I had heard so far. Maybe it was because I was already in a bikini and not feeling overly confident. (Believe it or not, I have normal insecurities beyond my baldness.) Or maybe his comments hurt more because the lazy river we were in was freezing, and my body's sensations were heightened to feel every needle prick of icy water, so this sudden stab hurt more than usual.

For the first time since I attended a local fair, and the clown in the carnival dunk tank made fun of my bandana, I wished I had hair. For the first time since I was told I had relapsed, I felt worried that it would be like this forever. For the hundredth time that day, a part of me wished I didn't have cancer, and for what seemed like the millionth time in my life, I fought against the urge to let this make me bitter.

I told myself the same things I had told myself many times before. Some people just don't understand, and if you don't help them, they never will. All of this was helping me grow, as long as I would let it.

So, I planted my feet on the bottom of the lazy river and slowed my inner tube, causing the kid to float past me and on down the river to his grandma, who was shaking her finger at his remark. My mom began to yell after him until I cut in.

"It's okay, Mom. Just let it go." And I did.

06/20/2011 Email to Allie Speck's Prayer Warriors
It was a bittersweet return to Pennsylvania yesterday. We had a magical time at Disney and hated to leave. The weather was hot with temps in the 100s.

We had a beautiful villa and rented a scooter for Allie to limit her fatigue while enjoying the parks. Lots of sunscreen kept Allie's head from getting sunburned.

What a nice break from work, chemo and hospital visits. We met some wonderful people in Florida: some while waiting for rides, some in the parking lot, and some at a restaurant. One of the waiters adored Allie and has joined the email list. It is amazing how God puts people in our path who listen to Allie's inspiring story and are moved to become a faithful prayer warrior. We are refreshed and ready to fight.

06/26/2011 Email to Allie Speck's Prayer Warriors
Allie was too sick to work but did go to Hopkins on Thursday to receive chemo. She did well, and we were able to attend a Phillies game, courtesy of a gentleman who sent us four tickets to a home game. The seats were amazing, the weather was beautiful and the Phillies won! It was a memorable event we will cherish. What a blessing!

On Saturday Allison asked if she could drive to Ocean City, Maryland, to stay with some girlfriends who went to the beach. Our initial response was no. We were concerned about her driving by herself, but she persisted, so we prayed and ended up saying yes. We cannot live in fear. She arrived safely in Ocean City and spent the day on the beach. They visited the wild horses at Assateague Island and walked the boardwalk. She was thrilled! There are times when you must let go and trust God. This was one of them. She came home today exhausted but with a smile that made it all worthwhile.

Tom and Andy left today for a weeklong mission trip in York, Pennsylvania. They will be working in the community, showing God's love. I am so thankful that Tom and Andy can share this opportunity together. Please pray that they will experience God and see His hand at work.

Allison has been busy sharing her message of hope. This world is full of hurting people with a hole in their spirit that only God can fill.

07/07/2011 Email to Allie Speck's Prayer Warriors
Allison reminded us that one year ago today she was declared cancer-free! Today we celebrate that miracle and hold fast to the hope that God will perform another miracle. We serve a powerful God who can do far more than we can ask or imagine.

Allie received chemo and did not end up in the ER with a fever. She does have nausea, fatigue and a sore throat, which does not allow her to work. She spends most of her days on the couch. We had a small Fourth of July picnic. She was frustrated that she had to leave the picnic several times due to illness. However, we are thankful that she was able to enjoy fireworks and some board games. It was nice to welcome friends into our home.

I am reading Joyce Meyer's book *Never Give Up!*, which talks about people who did not give up. Henry Ford went broke five times before he succeeded in the automobile business. Walt Disney was fired from a newspaper job for a lack of ideas. Abraham Lincoln lost several elections before becoming the president of the United States. God created each of us with a purpose. People who are called to greatness meet great challenges. God never promised us life would be easy. In fact, His Word guarantees we will face adversity (John 16:33). But He promises to be with us.

07/18/2011 Email to Allie Speck's Prayer Warriors
Last weekend we went camping with people from our church. We ate together, played together and on Sunday worshiped together. It was wonderful! Best of all, Allie felt well enough to participate. Last year Allison made the trip but was getting IV antibiotics for a blood infection and, because of the needle in her port, could not get in the pool and was so weak she fainted. This year we celebrated her being able to get

in the pool and join the group for campfires, mountain pies, s'mores and board games. It was a wonderful time of fellowship with beautiful weather. God definitely provided.

Allison received chemo last Wednesday. While she was getting chemo, Tom took Andy to have his wisdom teeth pulled, and he did well. He even spoke in church yesterday, sharing his testimony from the "Week of Hope" in York. We are so proud of him.

Exciting news: Allie found a car! She is the proud owner of a monthly car payment! Welcome to adulting. God's hand has shown our family favor, and we are thankful. Allie loves when she feels well enough to drive, and now she has her own car to enjoy.

On Wednesday Allie goes for chemo, and the following Wednesday she will have an MRI and CT scan. We are expecting good results. I am reading a book by Jentezen Franklin about prevailing prayer, which is having the tenacity to hold on until something happens. The book says one of people's greatest weaknesses is a lack of commitment for the long term. The cheetah can run 70 miles per hour; however, it has one problem: it has a small heart and tires quickly. If it doesn't catch its prey quickly, it won't survive. Some of us have a cheetah approach to prayer. We lack the determination to sustain our effort for the long haul. We burst out in prayer, but it does not last. We need an eagle's heart. Isaiah 40:31 (NKJV) says, "Those who wait on the Lord shall renew their strength; they shall mount up with wings like eagles, they shall run and not be weary."

Many of you have been praying prevailing prayers for Allie and our family from the beginning of this journey that started a year and a half ago. The eagle that flew in front of Allie's car on her way to share her testimony was a sign to her that God hears our prayers and will sustain us. We are thankful for our amazing prayer warriors.

07/26/2011 Email to Allie Speck's Prayer Warriors
Things have been crazy. Allie had a horrible headache
Sunday morning and said she felt like her head might
explode. We took her to the Emergency Room and a CT
scan showed no reason for the pain. She was admitted
and given some blood to see if the headache improved,
which it did. She was discharged Monday morning.

Monday evening, while I was at soccer practice with
Andy, Tom called, saying Allie's legs and abdomen
were very swollen, and he thought she might need to
go back to the hospital; however, the doctors started
a water pill that seems to be helping.

Tomorrow we head to Hopkins for a CT scan and
MRI. We are expecting good results.

07/30/2011 Email to Allie Speck's Prayer Warriors
We got the MRI results of the liver yesterday afternoon. It shows no signs of disease! The CT of the
lungs shows lesions in both lungs, but they are
smaller, meaning they are responding to chemo.
Allie will need to continue chemo, two weeks on and
one week off, until there is no more disease. This will
inhibit her involvement on campus, but she wants to
do whatever gives her the best outcome. Her doctor
agreed to a two-week reprieve from chemo so Allie
can go to the beach. She was so happy!

We were disappointed that the lung lesions remain,
but this scripture spoke to me: "Being confident of
this very thing, that He who has begun a good work
in you will complete it until the day of Jesus Christ"
(Philippians 1:6 NKJV). God has started a work in
Allie, and He will use it to His glory.

08/21/2011 Email to Allie Speck's Prayer Warriors
A lot has been happening, and most of it is good.
Allison and Andy were invited by different families
to go to the beach. Andy went to Ocean City, Maryland, and Allie went to Myrtle Beach. They both had
a wonderful time. While they were away, Tom and I

went to Gettysburg and Fallingwater on day trips.
We all feel refreshed. We used to take these moments
for granted, but not anymore.

On August 17th we took Allie to Hopkins for a CT scan
and chemo. The scan was to ensure that the two-
week break from chemo did not result in growth of
her lung lesions. We are happy to report there were
no changes. Allie began her sixth round of chemo. We
will return to Hopkins next Wednesday for the second
part of her chemo, then she has a week off. This cycle
of chemo for two weeks on and one week off will continue until the doctors decide to scan again. During
Allie's week off, she will begin classes at Messiah. We
moved a few things into her apartment, and she is
excited to get back to school. Pray that side effects
will be minimal and that she will not require hospitalization. She hopes to arrange virtual classes so she
doesn't miss class due to chemo.

I want to share a portion of Pastor Parker's sermon
from last Sunday that spoke to my mother's heart.
It was based on Matthew 15:21-28: "Leaving that
place, Jesus withdrew to the region of Tyre and
Sidon. A Canaanite woman from that vicinity came
to him, crying out, 'Lord, Son of David, have mercy
on me! My daughter is demon-possessed and suffering terribly.' Jesus did not answer a word. So his disciples came to him and urged him, 'Send her away,
for she keeps crying out after us.' He answered, 'I
was sent only to the lost sheep of Israel.' The woman
came and knelt before him. 'Lord, help me!' she said.
He replied, 'It is not right to take the children's bread
and toss it to the dogs.' 'Yes it is, Lord,' she said.
'Even the dogs eat the crumbs that fall from their
master's table.' Then Jesus said to her, 'Woman, you
have great faith! Your request is granted.' And her
daughter was healed at that moment."

What I heard was a mother who never gave up. She
was persistent in her request to the point of annoy-
ing the disciples.

Pastor Parker pointed out that in verse 23, it says that Jesus did not say a word to the woman. We all know that there are times when we are praying, and it seems that God is silent. The question posed to us was, when we don't hear from God, do we stop praying or asking, or do we continue to petition God with our request, knowing that an answer is coming in His timing and not ours?

I will never stop asking and petitioning God for Allie's healing.

Allison's Journal, August 24, 2011

I had scans last Wednesday. All my tumors were the same size, which is good. There was no growth during my time off chemo. Today while getting my chemo, the group Maroon 5 visited the pediatric oncology floor! I had my picture taken with Adam Levine! It was so cool! Adam told me he liked my glasses. I told him he should see how good they look when I have hair. He caught my humor and actually laughed. I only wish I did not have to have cancer to meet Adam Levine, but I guess I will just consider it a perk, since there aren't too many perks when you are a young person with cancer.

♥Allie

09/08/2011 Email to Allie Speck's Prayer Warriors
Allie is asleep at home. She received chemo yesterday at Hopkins and will return next Wednesday for more chemo. She tolerated the treatment well, but we got home late, so she decided to stay home and return to college this morning. She is in an apartment with four girls and loves it. They have their own kitchen where she can prepare meals and their own bathroom. It is an ideal situation!

Allie is scheduled for an MRI and CT scan on September 22nd. The results will determine our next step. Allison is ready to be done with chemo and enjoy college. Every scan has shown a decrease in the lung lesions and nothing in the liver. We continue to trust God.

Pray for Allie to endure this battle, for it is a battle, and we intend for her to win. Some days the trips to Hopkins and the hospital, the sickness associated with chemo, the financial struggles and the disruption of life become overwhelming. Those are the times we must give our struggles to God and allow Him to fight for us.

A story written by Allison entitled "Normal"

I pushed the heavy doors that opened into a world of sterile, shiny metal; white tile floors; and rubber gloves—all lit by fluorescent lights. It smelled like hand sanitizer. I stopped in the vital sign room and waited for the nurse to finish with the patient before me. A little bald girl about two years old sat in her mother's lap while the nurse wrapped the tiny blood pressure cuff around her arm.

"We are going to give your arm a little hug, okay?" the nurse said as she pushed the start button.

The little girl really didn't need an explanation. She sat, unfazed, because she knew the drill as the nurse took her temperature, blood pressure and heart rate and wrote down all the numbers. To this little girl, this was normal. For a moment, I let my mind wrap around the fact that to this two-year-old girl, this was normal. This was her life. Vital signs, pills, needles, chemo, IV poles and nurses—all of it was simply day-to-day, ho-hum normal. She looked up at me, and I smiled at her and waved. She raised a chubby hand and opened and closed her fingers. My heart brightened at her response.

I stepped to the side to let a boy get past me with his IV pole. He looked to be between 11 and 14 years old, an age that was difficult to determine by looking. He was pale and appeared very tired as he shuffled down the hall to the teen room. I could see by the fluids hanging from his pole that he was getting blood today. This meant by the time he left he would be a completely different kid. It blows my mind how something as simple as a unit of blood can make such a change in someone. He came in looking like a wet dishrag and would leave revived and animated. I had seen it happen a million times and had experienced it myself more times than I can count. I did not doubt that this boy already knew how much better the blood would make him feel. After all, this was his normal.

The nurse was ready for me, and I sat in the chair. Height, weight, temperature, blood pressure and heart rate were recorded. Then I headed back to see my nurse, Pam. She got out the needles and tubes and accessed my port. It is insane the things they put you through to make you better. I thought about this as she pushed an inch-long needle into the port in my chest, just beneath my collarbone. I remember a time when the port seemed foreign to me, like a piece of alien hardware stuck in my body. Now it was normal.

Pam flushed my port, and I tasted the familiar salty flavor of the saline as it rushed from my port into my bloodstream. She drew back, and the clear liquid in the tube turned red. "Yes, great blood return!" Pam said with a smile.

She talked to me about her trip to see Andre Agassi be inducted into the tennis Hall of Fame as she drew multiple tubes of blood for testing. When she finished, I headed down the hall through another set of doors into the clinic where the exam rooms and chemo rooms are located. I picked my favorite room, with the view of the city of Baltimore, and Pam hooked up the first chemo drug of the day. I followed the chemo's path as it wound its way from the bag into my body. It looped its way like a roller coaster through what seemed like miles of tubing, disappearing under the gauze dressing on my chest where it flowed through my port and into my bloodstream.

I pulled out my book and began to read as my mom did the same. This was all just a normal Wednesday for me. This is where I was the Wednesday before and where I would be for many Wednesdays to come. To me, this is normal. It is hard to remember a time when my life wasn't dictated by scans, medicine and doctor's appointments, even though that was only a year and a half ago. I can barely remember the "normal" that existed before this one. But I guess that's how it is with normal. When it changes, you are bewildered at

first, but then it all becomes routine, and it is easy to
think that it always has been that way. But the wonderful thing is, it won't always be that way! Someday,
hopefully soon, my normal will change, and this routine
will be something I look back on and gape at the fact
that this was once my "normal."

Allison's Journal, September 21, 2011

So much has happened this past year and a half, and
you are full to the brim with ups and downs and back
and forths and changes and constants. It has been
such a time of growth for me; I am a very different person since the day I opened this new journal and started
writing. I have needed you! In the end, I have learned
that God is with me and what is meant to be will be...
when the time is right. I am so thankful for all that I have.
We will chat in my next journal.

♥Allie

CHAPTER FOURTEEN

WE NEED YOU, GOD

Allison's Journal, September 23, 2011

I had scans today, and everything looks the same. My lung tumors are small but still there. I am scheduled for two more rounds of chemo and another scan. I feel down after this scan. What is taking God so long? Why must I keep going through this? What is the point? I am sick of this. The more I think about it, the angrier I feel. I have been in a weird mood this evening. I could not motivate myself to do any of the reading I need to do, and I have a quiz tomorrow. Perfect! Can't God even grant me a little motivation? I don't mean to sound selfish, but I have been VERY patient. I have avoided being angry, but why? WHAT DO I NEED TO DO? What will make God take this cancer from me? Six more weeks of chemo and then scans that will probably look the same. Why?

Yeah, that's fine. NOT. I am not okay with wasting my prime years fighting cancer. I have done my best to praise God through my circumstances and sometimes I feel like I have been hit by a two-by-four. What is happening? I wasn't angry until I started writing, but I am sick of sitting back and accepting it. I am angry. I need to just go to bed.

You probably think I am a horrible and ungrateful person, but I never complain. Even my roommates just said to me, "I have never heard you complain one time." I don't get angry. I give God glory and I look for reasons to be thankful, but today I am sick of this. I am done. I am going to bed hoping that tomorrow brings a new attitude.

♥Allie

Allison's Journal, September 24, 2011

Okay, I am better today. I think I slept off my anger. HAHA! It actually was a terrible night's sleep. The last two nights I have had trouble sleeping. I was so uncomfortable and restless that I got up at 3:45 a.m. and took a shower and a pain pill and then was finally able to sleep.

I have hit the reset button. I want to express how much I appreciate my family: Mom, Dad and Andy. They have been through so much with me. They have lived my cancer nightmare too, and they have never complained (at least not in front of me). I am so thankful for their love and support. Today is a new day! Let's do this!

♥Allie

09/25/2011 Email to Allie Speck's Prayer Warriors
Allison went to Hopkins for an MRI and CT scan. She is tired and has a lot of ankle swelling. She was given blood, which gave her some energy. She is busy with classes and works four-hour shifts at the clothing store as well as three days a week at Messiah making phone calls to ask for donations. I never dreamed our girl would get paid to talk on the phone. What a great job for her!

The MRI results were good. Allie's liver remains free of tumors. The CT of the lungs continues to show lesions that are mostly unchanged. The doctors feel the chemo is keeping Allie's cancer "stable." Personally, we were disappointed to hear "stable disease." We want a miracle. Watching Allie juggle chemo and college has been hard. She misses three classes to go for chemo. One of those is a once-a-week lab that she makes up at 6:00 p.m. when we get home from Hopkins. Since she needed blood, we left Baltimore at 5:30 p.m. and she missed the lab. It is frustrating to watch Allie struggle to get to class when there are students skipping class for no reason. She works so hard to maintain what many students take for granted.

I was feeling discouraged that Allie needed more chemo, so I asked God for some encouragement. It will be two years in December that Allie has been undergoing treatment for cancer. Some days it feels much longer. I was tearful driving to work when I heard a song on the radio called "Strong Enough" by Matthew West. I believe it was God's answer to my request for encouragement. The lyrics reminded me that when I don't feel strong enough, God will be "strong enough for the both of us." When we hit rock bottom and feel broken, we still have a God who is strong when we are weak.

The song ends with Philippians 4:13 (NKJV): "I can do all things through Christ who strengthens me." Allie presses on. I am the one who needed reassurance that God was still with us. My human side needed encouragement. I must keep trusting and not be discouraged. Thursday begins round number eight of chemo.

10/07/2011 Email to Allie Speck's Prayer Warriors
Yesterday Allie went to Hopkins for chemo. She is tired, with swelling in her legs and feeling some nausea, but she has been able to live in her apartment at Messiah and attend classes. She continues to work three days a week at college and a few hours on weekends at the clothing store. She is amazing!

So, we have a new plan. Allie's doctors feel she has seen the maximum effect of the chemo, so they scheduled her to meet with a lung surgeon on 11/04. She has a tentative surgery date of 11/08. The plan is to operate on one lung, allow recovery time, and then operate on the other lung. Our prayer is that all lesions can be removed.

While waiting with Allie, I read about God's promises. I was reminded that He has promised to take care of us and that His plan will ultimately result in good. I have learned that God does not always share what He is going to do and that is how we learn to trust Him. Our unanswered questions have led us to trust God. And we certainly have our share of unanswered questions!

Pray for the surgeon and the staff who will be part of Allie's new care team. Allie plans to stay in class as much as possible and finish this semester. Allie will be victorious against cancer again!

Allison's Journal, October 8, 2011

There is turmoil within our family, and everyone seems to have problems that my mom has to deal with. I wish I could be more helpful to her and take some of the burden off her shoulders. But with college, work and chemo, I am doing my best to keep my life together. Life is messy, frustrating and upsetting, and I wish I could fix it.

♥Allie

10/23/2011 Email to Allie Speck's Prayer Warriors
Last Sunday Allie started having diarrhea. We thought it might be the same bowel infection she had before. She called from college, saying she felt terrible. The doctor at Hopkins said to head to the Emergency Room. Her magnesium and potassium levels were very low. After receiving several boluses of electrolytes and pain medication, she felt better. Allie stayed overnight, and I stayed with her. Allie was discharged home the next day and felt well enough to attend Andy's last soccer game. His team won. It was a great ending to a difficult season. Andy was glad Allie could be there to celebrate with him.

Fall semester started on Thursday, and Allie was frustrated that she was in the hospital. I pray for the day she will be a normal college student. Her legs are swollen, causing her a lot of discomfort. It breaks my heart. On a happier note, she was home this weekend and got to see Andy attend his high school homecoming dance. Allie was a proud big sister and took lots of pictures. Andy looked handsome!

Today Allie shared her testimony at another local church, even though her legs were painfully swollen. She was even able to sing the song she wrote about her journey. The church members anointed Allie with oil and prayed for healing. It was a good day, even though I know Allie was uncomfortable.

As I dropped Allie off at college tonight, I sat in the car and cried. I wish I could take her disease. There are few things harder than watching your child suffer. A good friend sent me encouragement from her devotional by Sarah Young. It said to be prepared to suffer. All suffering has meaning in God's kingdom. Pain and problems are opportunities to demonstrate our trust in Jesus. Bearing your circumstances bravely is one of the highest forms of praise. When suffering strikes, remember that Jesus can bring good out of everything. Your suffering gains meaning and draws you closer to Jesus. Joy will emerge from the ashes.

Today during Allie's testimony, she shared a profound thought that summed up that devotion. She said, "Suffer well, for others are watching." Such wisdom beyond her years.

Allison's Journal, October 24, 2011

I have so much pain in my stomach, plus diarrhea. This has been going on for almost two weeks. I don't understand it. The doctor thinks my bowel is swollen from the chemo. I hope this swelling resolves soon. My ankles look like they belong to an elephant. I have gained ten pounds of fluid. I am ready to feel normal again.

♥Allie

10/29/2011 Email to Allie Speck's Prayer Warriors
Allie's leg swelling remains an issue, but that has not stopped her from attending class and working.

She wears compression socks and has been living in
sweatpants and slip-on shoes. We are thankful that
the pain has decreased.

Allie is preparing for surgery and was granted an
exception to schedule her spring classes early, since
class schedules open the day of her surgery. Allie
could not be in school were it not for the gracious-
ness of the staff at Messiah.

Allie and I met a young lady who is battling cancer.
My feelings are very hard to put into words. My
heart breaks for the suffering this young woman has
endured. Her mom and I discussed how difficult it
is to watch our daughters experience the evilness
of cancer and know what it has taken from them.
We pray there will be a day when cancer no longer
dictates the lives of children and young adults. As
moms we prayed together for peace that passes
understanding as our families face the unknown cancer journey together.

Allison's Journal, October 29, 2011

My heart is broken. My mom and I met a young lady
who is battling cancer and her mother. We met at
the mall just to talk. She is dying, and her wish is to live
long enough to see her sister's baby be born. We have
communicated through letters and email, but this was
our first meeting. She is beautiful, but so sick. She was
so thin; her thighs are as big as my arms. She told me
she has not eaten solid food since February. She is fed
through a tube in her stomach. But when I looked into
her eyes, I saw the most beautiful spirit and so much
strength. She is engaged but knows she will not live
long enough to be married. Her mother says she never
complains. I cannot wrap my head around the horror
she has been through.

    As I talked with her, I told her that I hope to start an
organization for newly diagnosed cancer patients to
help them locate doctors and services. She said, "If
there is anything I can do to help, please let me know."

My heart broke. I cried the whole way back to college.
I pray she will live to see her sister's baby be born. God
be with her.

♥Allie

11/05/2011 Email to Allie Speck's Prayer Warriors
We left Hopkins yesterday discouraged. After waiting an hour and 45 minutes to see the surgeon, he
told us Allie's surgery date is November 22. Allie
rearranged her schedule to accommodate surgery
on the 8th. She was upset, as this schedule change
will create more stress for her. She had moved
home from college, notified her jobs and professors,
and I had scheduled off work. This throws a wrench
into all those plans. It was an emotional letdown for
everyone. The surgeon also told Allie this surgery is
painful, but he will do his best to alleviate her pain.
It appears Allie will be spending Thanksgiving in
the hospital.

The other disturbing fact presented was that the
CT scan may not show all the lesions. If he finds
30 or more lesions in the lung, he will not proceed with surgery and will deem Allie's cancer
advanced. He told us this happens in 20 percent of
patients. As a mom, this information hit hard and
made me fearful.

I sent Allie's oncology doctor an email saying, "Our
meeting with the surgeon was a reality check as well
as confirmation that we need to trust God because
this is out of our control. I am going to take a walk
and have another talk with God."

11/20/2011 Email to Allie Speck's Prayer Warriors
Allie's surgery is at Hopkins on the 22nd at 7:30
a.m., which means we will leave our house about
3:30 a.m. Andy will be home alone, so pray that he
gets the bus on time and can focus on school. The
surgery should take between three to five hours.
After the surgery, I will stay with Allie, and Tom
will come home to be with Andy. Since Allie will be

in over Thanksgiving, Tom and Andy plan to visit if Allie feels well enough.

Allie had an appointment with the oncology clinic on Thursday, and overall things looked good. Her swelling is intermittent and depends on her activities. Allie told the doctor she is physically and mentally ready for surgery. The doctor prayed with Allie at the end of her visit. It was a beautiful, heartfelt prayer and the best medicine she could have provided.

My devotion, *Jesus Calling*, spoke to me about Allie's surgery and life in general. It basically said to leave the outcomes up to God and to follow where He leads without worrying about how it will turn out. Think of life as an adventure with God as your guide and companion. Live in the present. When the path leads to a cliff, be willing to climb with God's help. When the path comes to a resting place, take time to be refreshed. Our ultimate destination is heaven, so focus on the path just before you and leave the outcomes to God.

Allison's letter to the young woman with cancer, November 2011

Hello.

I wasn't sure what type of bracelet you had, but I chose a bead that will fit any bracelet. I hope you like it! I wanted to get you one that sparkled because when we met in person, I could see God's light shining so brightly in you. People used to say similar things to me, and I would think, "Well, I am not doing anything special, and I don't feel God's light shining through me." But after meeting you, I now understand what they were saying because when I looked at you, I saw God's love and light and I knew that He had His hand on you, and He still does.

I liked the way the blue bead faded to clear, which made me think of the Bible verses of 2 Corinthians 4:16–17: "Therefore we do not lose heart. Though outwardly we are wasting away, yet inwardly we are being renewed day by day. For our light and momentary troubles are achieving for us an eternal glory that far outweighs them all."

I am praying for you, and I KNOW, just as these Bible verses say, the glory that comes after this will be so much greater than the pain we have felt.

Love and prayers,
Allie

I remember receiving an email from the young lady's mom thanking Allie for her letter and gift. The young woman's obituary indicated that she had died on November 23, 2011, at the age of 25, surrounded by her family. It was a moment to pause and consider the gift of time and how alive Allie was despite her ongoing journey. Meeting that young lady and her mother changed my life. Her life made a difference. We can all hope that our lives would do the same if we were faced with the same suffering. May she rest in peace knowing she fulfilled her purpose.

11/24/2011 Email to Allie Speck's Prayer Warriors
Surgery is complete. The surgeon removed 21 lesions from Allie's left lung. Allie spent a long night in the ICU and was moved to a regular room last night. Allie woke up asking if the doctor got all of the lesions. She smiled hearing that he did, but there is concern that there were more lesions than what the CT showed. The doctors agree that Allie should move forward with surgery on her other lung in four to six weeks, depending upon her recovery.

The chest tube is a source of much discomfort. Allison was moved to a regular room and sobbed until the pain from the move could be brought under control. It breaks my heart knowing there is nothing I can do but pray.

Tom and Andy are celebrating Thanksgiving with family. We look forward to seeing them. When Allie's chest X-ray shows an inflated lung, the tube can be removed, and we can go home. Have a blessed Thanksgiving!

11/27/2011 Email to Allie Speck's Prayer Warriors
We are still at Hopkins, and Allie is having a lot of pain from the chest tube. Every time she coughs,

moves or hiccups, the pain is severe. Yesterday her
X-ray showed air in the chest where it should not be.
Pray for this to resolve so we can go home. Tuesday
will be a week, and Allie is ready to get home and
finish her semester.

Tom and Andy visited with a delicious plate of
Thanksgiving food. On Thanksgiving Day in the hospital, our family made turkeys using colored construction paper. This was Allie's idea when she found
out there were 25 patients on the floor for Thanksgiving. It was great family time! We made a turkey
for each patient. Allie put her name and room number on the back with a Thanksgiving greeting. She
had the nurse distribute one to each patient. Several
patients stopped by Allie's room to thank her for her
thoughtfulness. We are grateful that Allie continues
to think about others even when she is suffering.

11/28/2011 Email to Allie Speck's Prayer Warriors
Last night was a rough night. Allie spiked a fever
and, as the evening progressed, became delirious
and had a lot of pain. She was hallucinating and
talking to people who were not there. While getting
up to go to the bathroom, Allie's chest tube became
disconnected, causing severe pain. It took several
hours before Allie was comfortable and able to rest.

Her chest X-ray still shows an air leak. Please pray
for Allie to endure this trial and be discharged soon.

11/29/2011 Email to Allie Speck's Prayer Warriors
Allie remains at Hopkins. Tom relieved me so I
could come home to work. I felt guilty going home
without her. The air leak remains, and Allie has
developed chronic hiccups that are quite painful.
Despite the pain and the frustration of the long
admission, Allie is in decent spirits. She has overcome so much in 20 years.

12/01/2011 Email to Allie Speck's Prayer Warriors
Praise the Lord, we are home! Allie's chest tube was

pulled this morning. It was confirmed today that the 21 lesions removed from Allie's lung are the same cancer that was on her liver. She will proceed with the second lung surgery on December 20th. Allison's 21st birthday is December 28th, and she plans to celebrate at home with family.

Sometimes we focus on a problem rather than on Jesus, who is the solution to our problems. In the story of Martha and Mary, Martha is busy preparing for company, cooking and cleaning while Mary sits at Jesus's feet and listens to Him. The scripture in Luke 10:41–42 reads, "'Martha, Martha,' the Lord answered, 'you are worried and upset about many things, but few things are needed—or indeed only one. Mary has chosen what is better, and it will not be taken away from her.'" Jesus told Martha not to be "worried and upset" about the many things of the world. Instead, "only one" thing is needed.

That one thing is having a personal relationship with Jesus. Absolutely nothing else is as important, and I thank God that Allison has that relationship.

12/06/2011 Email to Allie Speck's Prayer Warriors
Allie needs prayer. She was just taken into emergency surgery at Hopkins due to complications with her lung. We do not know where this path is leading, and it is scary. We were told that Allie joined hands with the surgical team and prayed with them before they put her to sleep. Her faith is incredible. I am so proud to be her mom.

12/07/2011 Email to Allie Speck's Prayer Warriors
About 9:30 p.m., the surgeon came out and told us that Allie did well. She developed an infection at the chest tube site that spread into her lung. The lung was scraped clean of infection, and she has two new chest tubes. She is in ICU but got out of bed today. She feels better since the infection was removed from her lung but is disappointed to have two chest tubes.

Allie told us about praying with the surgery team prior to surgery and said she saw a tear in the surgeon's eye. She said she prayed for peace and comfort for herself as well. Today one of the aides on the floor stuck his head in Allie's room and said, "I want to encourage you today. You are to receive the peace from God that passes all understanding." Allie shouted with joy, "That is exactly what I prayed for last night!" and the aide replied, "God sent me to provide you with confirmation that He is with you." How beautiful and amazing our God is!

12/09/2011 Email to Allie Speck's Prayer Warriors
Allie has pain, and we have had very little sleep. The smaller chest tube was removed, and she was moved out of ICU with the larger chest tube. The bad news is that during the transfer, Allie developed an air leak. We pray it resolves quickly.

12/11/2011 Email to Allie Speck's Prayer Warriors
"Therefore we are always confident and know that as long as we are at home in the body we are away from the Lord. For we live by faith, not by sight. We are confident, I say, and would prefer to be away from the body and at home with the Lord. So we make it our goal to please him, whether we are at home in the body or away from it"(2 Corinthians 5:6-9).

We claim this scripture because Allison's body is an earthly body that continues to heal. So, whether we are at Hopkins, home or work, we will continue to try to do things that please God. The small chest tube site has an open area that gets packed twice a day, which is a painful procedure for Allie. Her lung deflated when the chest tube was clamped, meaning the tube stays in another day. We are disappointed but pray we are home for Christmas. Tom and Andy completed our annual search for the perfect Christmas tree, and it is at home waiting for decorations.

12/12/2011 Email to Allie Speck's Prayer Warriors
Allison's air leak remains. The surgeon decided to

move her next surgery to January; however, Allison had registered for a January class, so she will need to cancel it. Once the tube comes out, Allie can go home. She is excited at the thought of being home for Christmas! However, this afternoon Allie was placed in isolation due to a bowel infection. Sometimes our requests seem never-ending. We are not alone.

Allison's Journal, December 15, 2011

I had surgery on my left lung on 11/22. I had a lot of pain and felt bad. I made it home after about a week because of an air leak. I had a fever in the hospital, but it went down. But when they pulled my chest tube to send me home, it smelled bad and there was pus at the opening. I questioned the doctor, who said it was normal and put a dressing over it and sent me home. At home I developed another fever and ended up in the Emergency Room. An X-ray showed I had pneumonia, a partially collapsed lung and pus around my lung. I was taken to Hopkins by my mom, but I don't really remember much of the trip. They took me into emergency surgery, and I remember being very scared and praying with the surgical team. One of the nurses held my hand as I went to sleep.

So here I am. The pneumonia is clearing, and my lung reinflated, but I have a new chest tube with another air leak. I am finally going home tomorrow WITH THE AIR LEAK. They put a valve on the tube, at my request, and I am going home, home, home in the morning. I cannot take another day here. I keep breaking down and crying. My dad is here with me, and he held me, asking me what was wrong. I told him the truth. I am tired of being sick. I just get so tired sometimes. My dad said, "We do too." He said Mom was exhausted when he came to relieve her, and he was angry with God, but this is the time we need to pull together and be stronger. It pains me to think of the sadness and stress I have brought on my family with this cancer. I hate to be a burden. It kills me. I know they don't see me as a burden, but the truth is I cause them pain, even if it is not purposefully. Where will we find rest? Sometimes it seems there is no rest in sight. We get breaks from it for a time, but it always comes again, and we are weary. I am afraid, so afraid, that I will have cancer my whole life. Spending the rest of my life in and out of illness. Dragging my family, my future husband and possibly children in and out of hospitals. I pray with my whole heart that this is not my future.

　Why can't life be simple like it is for other people? People whose biggest worry is school or work or relationships. But even as I write this, I feel bad for it. I AM blessed. My situation could be so much worse. My despair lasts only for a short time. Tomorrow I will be home. I am SO happy. I know I will cry. I miss Mom, Dad, Andy and HOME! I miss being with my family. I just talked with my dad about how blessed we are and how we often forget. He agreed, and the sorrow seems to have lifted for now. I am sleepy. Good night and I look forward to being in my own bed the next time I write.

♥Allie

12/16/2011 Email to Allie Speck's Prayer Warriors
ALLIE IS HOME! She told the doctors on Friday that she was going home with or without the tube. She came home with the chest tube. Pray for the air leak to resolve so the tube comes out before Christmas. She is also receiving IV antibiotics every four hours around the clock. BUT SHE IS HOME!

What an emotional day! When I came home from work, Allie hugged me, crying, and said, "I am so glad to be home. I missed you!" My heart was over-whelmed. We enjoyed the evening as a family. She is weak but spent the evening opening mail she received while in the hospital, and then we had a family dinner together. Tonight, she sleeps in her own bed. For all these things, we are thankful.

12/21/11 Email to Allie Speck's Prayer Warriors
THE CHEST TUBE IS OUT!!
We are thankful for your prayers that were heard and

answered. Today Allie had a chest X-ray. When she saw the surgeon, he smiled and said, "Let's pull that tube out for Christmas!" He told Allie to expect a fair amount of discomfort when he pulled the tube because it had been in so long. However, one quick pull and Allie said it was minimal discomfort. After another chest X-ray, the surgeon said, "What are you still doing here? Get out of here and have a Merry Christmas!" It is the best news we have had in quite some time. We will celebrate Christmas at home and return to Hopkins in January for the right-lung surgery.

My devotion was perfect for today. It is based on the scripture from John 11:40 (NKJV): "Jesus said to her, 'Did I not say to you that if you would believe you would see the glory of God?'" This is from the story of Lazarus, a Bible story that is often part of Allie's testimony. Lazarus was restored from death to life. Allison is also trusting the Great Physician.

12/30/2011 Email to Allie Speck's Prayer Warriors
"For to us a child is born, to us a son is given, and the government will be on his shoulders. And he will be called Wonderful Counselor, Mighty God, Everlasting Father, Prince of Peace" (Isaiah 9:6). This scripture summarizes Christmas for us. As we celebrated Christmas in our home, we were thankful, but Allie is having anxiety related to her upcoming surgery. Emotionally, it was a difficult time. She has been through so much, and Satan attacked her thoughts with doubt and fear. We prayed against it, and she immediately felt relief. Please pray for peace as she faces surgery on January 5th.

In response to the anxiety and fear Allie experienced, I found the following scripture in 1 Peter 4:12, 16: "Dear friends, do not be surprised at the fiery ordeal that has come on you to test you, as though something strange were happening to you....If you suffer as a Christian, do not be ashamed, but praise God that you bear that name."

A great joy was being able to celebrate Allie's 21st birthday on December 28th. We painted pottery at Color Me Mine with family and friends, and, for a few hours, thoughts of hospitals, cancer and surgery were replaced with joy, laughter and celebration. Happy 21st, Allie! We love you! The world is a better place because you were born.

CHAPTER FIFTEEN
LIFE AMID TRIALS

A poem written by Allison entitled "Expiration Date"

I feel a slight empathy for
that pack of cheese in the refrigerator door.

"How old is this?" my brother yells.
I shudder because I know how they'll tell.

"Just check the expiration date!"
And out it goes, if it's a week too late.

Six months to a year is what they stamped on me,
an expiration date they could guarantee.

I run my hands over the naked skin
that replaces where my hair had been.

I shake my head and smile; what did they know?
They stamped that on two years ago.

And thankfully no one has checked to see
if the expiration is out on me.

01/05/2012 Email to Allie Speck's Prayer Warriors
Today's surgery almost didn't happen due to Allie
having diarrhea and the surgeon thinking her bowel
infection had returned. The surgeon actually canceled

the surgery. We were devastated. Allie explained that she felt better and begged to be put back on the schedule. Within ten minutes, the surgeon called to say surgery was on. What a roller coaster!

Allie is in surgery now, and we pray God is cradling her in His arms. My scripture for today was 2 Corinthians 5:7: "For we live by faith, not by sight."

We had to leave Andy at home to get ready for school despite having a double ear infection and a reaction to an antibiotic, causing a rash. My heart is split in two today, half with Allie in Baltimore and the other half at home with Andy.

Allison's surgery lasted four hours. The surgeon removed nine tumors from the top lobe of her lung and two from the middle lobe. He attempted to remove a large tumor from the bottom lobe, but he found 14 more "spots." So he decided to remove the entire lobe completely. He said the lung reinflated nicely, and she has been transferred to ICU. We are disappointed that the scans are not showing all of the lesions that were found by the surgeon, but we continue to trust that God knows the details.

01/07/2012 Email to Allie Speck's Prayer Warriors
Allie is struggling with a lot of pain and difficulty breathing related to the recent lung surgery. When she gets enough pain medication to make her comfortable, her breathing becomes shallow. Then they take the medication away and make her take deep breaths, which is very painful. It is a horrible situation and so difficult to watch her struggle when they deny her pain medication. The night in ICU was tortuous.

Tonight she was transferred to a regular room and had a wonderful visit with Andy and one of his friends. We took them to see the statue of Jesus Christ in the center of the building. As we paused at the feet of Jesus, I felt true peace for the first time in a while. I left that statue with a better attitude and a renewed appreciation for God's grace.

My devotion from yesterday in *Jesus Calling* reminded me that Jesus can do far beyond all that we can ask or imagine (Ephesians 3:20). He wants us to come with positive expectations, knowing that there is no limit to what He can accomplish. We should not be discouraged when prayers are unanswered. Time is a trainer, teaching us to wait upon Jesus.

01/08/2012 Email to Allie Speck's Prayer Warriors
Allie is still battling for good pain control, plus her tube has a big air leak that needs to resolve. The final concern is that the amount of fluid draining from the tube is excessive and may be infected. It seems like Allie experiences the difficulties and never the easier path.

Her walking has been limited, and she still requires oxygen. Pray that God will correct these things so Allie can get home and back to college. There is power in prayer, especially where two or more are gathered. So far, her spirit is good, and we will continue to focus on the positive outcomes.

01/09/2012 Email to Allie Speck's Prayer Warriors
Two things today confirmed that God is hearing your prayers. My devotion in *Jesus Calling* was about Jesus being for us. It reminded me that, with God's help, we can overcome any obstacle and that we were not promised an easy path in life. In fact, the Bible guarantees we will have trials and tribulations. We are to look to God for help during those times. The second confirmation was an email I received from a prayer warrior who has learned so much from Allison's journey. She spoke of Allie's wisdom and depth of character that could only come from suffering.

When Allie stated that she would not stop sharing her testimony when her cancer returned, this prayer warrior was reminded of the miracles in her own life that helped her to see how God was sustaining her. This email allowed us to know the impact Allie's testimony is making. God has such a BIG plan for Allie, and this is just the beginning of her journey. There are people all over the world being changed by Allie's faith and testimony.

01/11/2012 Email to Allie Speck's Prayer Warriors
Allie remains at Hopkins. Tom drove down so I can work tomorrow. The air leak is slightly smaller but still too significant to remove the tube. The tests performed on the chest-tube fluid showed no infection. Thank God!

Allie prayed before I left for home, thanking God for a kingdom that is unshakeable. That reminded me of Psalm 55:22 (NKJV): "Cast your burden on the Lord, and He shall sustain you; He shall never permit the righteous to be moved."

01/15/2012 Email to Allie Speck's Prayer Warriors
Allie remains in Hopkins. I am with her until Tuesday and then must return home to work. My prayer is that God will allow Allie to come home with me. We are expecting good things to happen.

01/18/2012 Email to Allie Speck's Prayer Warriors
I am home, but Allie remains at Hopkins. She is in good spirits, despite the fact that her air leak remains. Please, please pray that God allows Allie's body to heal itself. She told me yesterday that God has given her a peace and contentment about being in the hospital. She is working diligently to finish the overdue work required to complete the fall semester. She has two finals to take and two papers to write. Pray for clarity of thought as she completes these assignments while on pain medication.

01/21/2012 Email to Allie Speck's Prayer Warriors
Allie is still at Hopkins. Her lung surgeon is planning a procedure to reduce the air leak. If this procedure does not work, Allie will need to go back

to surgery. This has been a long process. Today Allie will be here 16 days.

Last night, I relieved Tom and upon arriving home he found about three inches of water in our finished basement due to a hole in our hot water heater. What a mess! I am thankful that I am married to a patient husband who does not get upset when things like this happen.

01/23/2012 Email to Allie Speck's Prayer Warriors – safe email to open
Please be aware that my Hotmail account was hacked and emails were sent asking for money. I apologize for any inconvenience this may have caused you. My account is safe now; you do not need to be concerned about opening my "Allison Updates." I truly believe that Satan is afraid of this email chain and the power of all of the prayer warriors, so he attempted to shut it down.

01/25/2012 Email to Allie Speck's Prayer Warriors
Allie tolerated the procedure on her lungs. The surgeon says he might be willing to send Allie home with a partially collapsed lung if she does not require oxygen. However, this means she will come home with the chest tube. It is not what we wanted, but at least she would be home.

01/26/2012 Email to Allie Speck's Prayer Warriors – Allie is coming home! ! !
Allison's chest tube is connected to an external valve. She is on her way home right now! We are overjoyed.

Allie starts the spring semester at Messiah on Monday. Pray for her to be able to attend classes with the chest tube. Thank you so much for praying Allie home. She also had an MRI while at Hopkins to check her liver. We are awaiting results.

02/03/2012 Email to Allie Speck's Prayer Warriors
Allie went to class at Messiah, but she said that her

chest hurt more than usual. As the day progressed, her pain increased. At 2:00 a.m. she woke up in pain and was unable to take a deep breath. We headed to the local ER.

Her chest X-ray showed a partial collapse of her right lung. They tried using her chest tube to rein-flate the lung, but it was clogged. Allie was admitted to get her pain under control. It was recommended that the surgeon who inserted the chest tube be involved, so Allie was transferred to Hopkins by ambulance this morning.

The surgical team at Hopkins attempted to clear the clogged tube, and the procedure seems to have worked. She is awaiting a chest X-ray to confirm that the lung has reinflated.

My devotion *Jesus Calling* reminded me that Jesus tells us He is with us and for us. We face nothing alone! When we feel anxious, it is because we are focusing on the visible world. Instead, we must fix our eyes not on what is seen, but on what is unseen.

The last day and a half we have experienced despair, frustration, anger and fear. We continue to keep the faith and trust that God is with us.

02/06/2012 Email to Allie Speck's Prayer Warriors
Allie was discharged from Hopkins late on Saturday afternoon, and the chest tube appeared to be work-ing. Sunday morning Allie stayed home from church, but she developed chest pain in the afternoon. It appeared the tube was blocked again. Because Allie was stable, we drove to the Hopkins' Emergency Room, where her surgical team was waiting.

An X-ray confirmed that her lung had collapsed again. They attempted to clear the tube, but it was unsuccessful. They decided to insert a new tube, which resulted in immediate lung expansion. Howev-er, the pain that Allie endured during the procedure was excruciating. She was very angry with the residents who performed the procedure and told them she was not given enough pain medication.

I am thankful that God's mercies are new every morning. Allie is resting despite spasms of pain from the new tube. We are hoping to be discharged tomorrow. Today the surgeon pulled the old chest tube that had been in for over a month and put a valve on the new tube. The chest X-ray shows an inflated lung and no sign of an air leak.

Please pray for no more setbacks to Allie's recovery. We do not understand this journey at all, and the suffering seems unbearable. We try daily not to lean on our own understanding, but to trust God.

I remember them taking Allie to a procedure room in the Emergency Room for placement of the new chest tube. We were both scared, and I prayed with her before she left. When they brought her back, her face was swollen and blotchy from crying. She sobbed in my arms, telling me that she felt everything they had done, including punching a new hole in her chest. She told me she begged the doctors for more sedation. My heart broke in two as I sobbed with her and apologized for their lack of concern. I was angry and frustrated and felt that I had failed to be her advocate. Yelling at the doctors would not change the pain she had suffered, but I did tell them how their lack of compassion was a disappointment to me. I wanted to make them hurt the way they hurt Allie. That moment when she was returned to me, sobbing and in pain, still haunts me to this day.

But I remember the next day those same doctors entered Allie's room to observe while the surgeon examined Allie. As they prepared to leave, Allie said she wanted to say something to all of them. She very calmly stated that what they did to her in the Emergency Room should never happen to anyone. The pain she felt was horrible. They need to learn to listen to their patients and respond with compassion. She reminded them that she was not a procedure, but a person who suffered due to their lack of concern. She told the surgeon that none of them would perform any procedures on her ever again. I was so proud of her, as I knew that her calm demeanor and well thought-out words had more impact on those doctors than any angry outburst ever would. I prayed that would be the last time Allie would suffer such agony, especially at the hands of those who were supposed to help.

02/08/2012 Email to Allie Speck's Prayer Warriors
"No one will be able to stand against you all the days
of your life. As I was with Moses, so I will be with you;
I will never leave you nor forsake you" (Joshua 1:5).

I opened my email this morning to find this scripture. We are reminded that God is with us, even
through the difficult days.

Allie was discharged yesterday with the new chest
tube. We got home about 5:30 p.m. She is having A
LOT of pain due to the new tube; it is a tender area
and the trauma of the insertion created sore muscles
and ribs. Pray for pain relief. We will travel to Hopkins on Friday for a chest X-ray.

While the tube is in, Allie will not be attending classes. Pray that she does not get too far behind with her
studies. She is doing all she can to keep up with her
required work. She got her grades for the fall semester, and they were all A's! She is an amazing example
of what you can do despite your circumstances.

Andy made honor roll despite our upside-down
house and also won third place in the science fair. We
are so proud of him. He has been a big help at home
and texts his sister regularly. Say a special prayer
for him as he is suffering through this journey too.
Days are tough, but he never complains.

02/10/2012 Email to Allie Speck's Prayer Warriors
THE CHEST TUBE IS OUT! Thank God! We had a joyous evening spent around the dinner table, laughing,
praying, sharing and rejoicing. Today was a mountaintop experience. Allie will catch up with school,
and life will return to our "new normal." Never
underestimate the power of prayer or the strength of
your family. God is always worthy to be praised.

02/25/2012 Email to Allie Speck's Prayer Warriors
Allie's journey since the chest tube removal has
been a bit of a roller-coaster ride. The first hurdle

was weaning her off the narcotics used to keep
her pain under control. Last weekend she got a GI
bug that caused vomiting for two days. She was in
misery and actually asked to be taken to the hospital. I took her to the local ER for IV fluid with
nausea medicine, which helped. She came home
that same evening.

We celebrated when she drove herself to college for
the first time since November! Driving is something
we take for granted, but to Allie it was a celebration
of freedom and a step on the road to recovery.

On Thursday Allie saw her oncologist at Hopkins.
It was an emotional visit. She listened while Allie
shared her concerns. The outcome of the visit is that
Allie has decided not to start chemo at this time. Her
liver appears clear, and her lungs have too much
scar tissue to allow accurate scans. The next scans
are scheduled for March.

During the visit the doctor told Allie more than once
that she is wonderfully and fearfully made. The next
morning, my daily scripture was Psalm 139:14: "I
praise you because I am fearfully and wonderfully
made." I see this as God's confirmation that He created Allie and He knows the plan. We pray the plan is
a life free from cancer that celebrates the faith and
trust developed during this trial.

Allie is taking five classes at Messiah. We believe that
she "can do all things through Christ who strengthens" her (Philippians 4:13 NKJV).

03/01/2012 Email to Allie's oncologist
Allie left her afternoon class early due to pain
in her back. She is on her way home. The pain is
bad, and she is anxious. I cried on my way home
because I don't know what to do for her. I really do
not want to take her to the ER. I will let you know
if this episode does not subside with pain medication. The pain seems more frequent, and I hate

that it has disrupted the small bit of normalcy she was experiencing.

I don't mean to be abrupt, but I am mad. I want God to deliver her to health, and it isn't happening. Thanks for listening.

03/01/2012 Second email to the oncologist later that day
Allie came home and felt better without pain medication. She used a heating pad, ate some dinner and plans to attend Powerhouse at college tonight, which is a music worship service. I should be relieved that she is trying to lead a normal life. It just feels like we spent the past four months in a hospital or Emergency Room, and I am so very tired of it all. Forgive me for the first email I sent without evaluating Allie. She looked better than what I expected when she got home.

Thanks for letting me express my concerns. Our family needs a vacation on a deserted island as far from hospitals as possible and some health and wellness infused into our home.

03/06/2012 Email to Allie Speck's Prayer Warriors
Between Allison and Tom, we have been in the Emergency Room four times in the last three weeks! Two visits for each of them to receive IV fluid and nausea medicine to combat a GI bug. Andy was sick for about 24 hours. Thankfully I was spared, for God knew if I got sick, our entire household would collapse!

Tom, Andy and I leave for North Carolina tomorrow with Andy's high school baseball team for spring training. Allison is staying home to attend classes. Please pray that everyone remains healthy. Allie's goal is to be back in her apartment at college after spring break.

Allie will spend her spring break seeing the lung surgeon to have an outpatient procedure at Hopkins to remove the valves that were inserted to correct her air leak. We pray there will be no complications.

03/19/2012 Email to Allie Speck's Prayer Warriors
"Dwell in Me, and I will dwell in you....Just as no branch can bear fruit of itself without abiding in... the vine, neither can you bear fruit unless you abide in Me. I am the Vine; you are the branches. Whoever lives in Me and I in him bears much (abundant) fruit. However, apart from Me...you can do nothing" (John 15:4-5 AMPC).

Apart from Christ we can do nothing! But in Christ... ALL things are possible! Even through our darkest times, God was abiding in us. But it is also our job to abide in Him, even when we don't feel like it and life seems overwhelming. This is not easy to do. We had many days we wanted to give up. But we didn't, and here we are on the other side of the valley, looking back at a journey we hope to never take again.

It is with great joy that I tell you Allison has moved back into her apartment at college. She looked so content to be back where she belongs. We pray she can finish the semester there. Last Friday we traveled to Hopkins for Allie to have three valves removed from her lung that were used to seal her air leak. Everything went smoothly, and Allie woke up saying, "I cannot believe how much easier I can breathe!" We were thankful for a simple procedure with no complications. The lung surgeon told Allie she looked great, gave her a hug and wished her well.

On March 22nd Allie will return to Hopkins for a CT of her lungs and an MRI of her liver. We are praying for a day filled with good news. We are ready to move forward. Allie is stronger than anybody we know, and she draws her strength from God. She abides in Him, and He in her.

To God be the glory! We extend our appreciation to each of you for your prayers, support and faith.

03/23/2012 Email to Allie Speck's Prayer Warriors
Allison had the CT scan and MRI on Thursday, and
the results were not what we had hoped. Please read
the update below written by Allie.

I have struggled over how and when to tell everyone the results of my scans. Today I read a devotion
about the carnality of our flesh and the war that is
waged within ourselves. The flesh longs to explain
away what it does not understand, to hide the unde-
sirable parts of itself. But those who walk in the spirit stand bare before the Lord and wholly trust. Easier
said than done, right? Well, allow me to stand bare.

The doctors determined that I have new lesions in
both of my lungs. Surgery is no longer an effective
option. There is a new chemo drug they are offering
that is a pill I would take every day. Its side effects
are mild, and I will not lose my hair or become vio-
lently ill. Right now, in the eyes of many specialists,
it looks as if I will be battling this cancer for a long
time, possibly my entire life. That is their opinion. I
choose God's truth over that opinion. Yes, God has
gifted doctors to aid in our healing, and He does
work through them, but I feel in my spirit that, in
this instance, I need to wait on the Lord.

What does this mean? It means that I will not be
starting the chemo they recommend right now. I
have decided to wait three weeks and get another
scan. In that time, I will receive no treatment or can-
cer-related medication. I trust wholly in the Lord's
goodness and grace. He is greater than any medicine, any doctor and any surgery. He can see what
we cannot find, heal what we cannot fix, redeem
what we see as unredeemable. I don't claim any
special understanding or revelation. I simply claim
God's love. I believe in my depths that He can heal
me. I believe without a doubt that in three weeks my
scans can be clear. That is not through any special
faith or work of my own. It is by the mercy and healing of God. I have not given Him complete control

over this. I did not feel, up until now, that I should not act upon the doctor's opinions. However, there is a knowing in my spirit that tells me it is time to wait on the Lord. He is not done here.

I would ask that you believe with me. Thank God for what He has already done. Praise Him for the clear scans I will receive. Do not become angry because you do not understand. Let your spirit rest in the assurance that God has nothing but good things planned for us. Do not pity me. I am healed. Do not treat me as if I am sick. I am healed. Do not act as if God has stopped working. He has not and will not.

This is not me giving up. This is me surrendering all to Christ in the only way I know how. When I handed the reins to God alone, my mind was flooded with assurance from His Word in Romans 4:18: "Against all hope, Abraham in hope believed," and John 20:29b: "Blessed are those who have not seen and yet have believed." The woman who had a bleeding disorder for 12 years sought help from various doctors. She then turned to Jesus, believing that if she touched His robe, she would be healed. When she did, she was SUDDENLY made whole. Jesus said, "Take heart, daughter...your faith has healed you" (Matthew 9:22). I heard these words in that moment when I made my decision. As I said before, I don't claim any great faith that brings this about. I simply know God's love.

At Powerhouse last night (Powerhouse is a student-led praise and worship service at Messiah), God's Spirit was moving in an amazing way. We sang "Your Great Name," a song by Natalie Grant, which assured me that this is what I need to be doing. I know God will heal me.

Father God, I thank You for Your sustaining grace. I thank You for the prayer warriors, the men and women of courage whom You have raised up through this battle with cancer. I praise You for Your goodness and amazing love. I thank You for the healing I have received from You. Continue to make my body whole. Continue to pour out Your grace. In the Psalms You say that You will give us the desires of our hearts. You say in the Gospels that if we only ask, we will receive. You know the desires of my heart. I ask, in Jesus's name, that in three weeks my scans will be clear and that all cancer will be completely gone from my body forever. Thank You, thank You, thank You for healing me. I ask this humbly and wholly. Amen.

"O precious is the flow
that makes me white as snow;
no other fount I know;
nothing but the blood of Jesus."

"The Lord's love never ends; his mercies never stop. They are new every morning; Lord, your loyalty is great. I say to myself, 'The Lord is mine, so I hope in him.' The Lord is good to those who hope in him, to those who seek him" (Lamentations 3:21–25 NCV).

Blessings,
Allie

03/29/2012 Email to Allie Speck's Prayer Warriors
When Allie received the news that her cancer was back, she asked you to thank God for what He had done and thank Him for the healing He would provide. The focus of her message was thankfulness and praise. *Jesus Calling* from that day encouraged us to have grateful, trusting hearts. Practicing trust and expressing gratitude allows us to experience peace despite our circumstances. This describes Allie's attitude.

Thank you! We are overwhelmed by the support of our community and prayer warriors. Allison is doing well at college and is back to work at both jobs. Cancer should have a hard time keeping up with this girl and her schedule. We share her desire to be healed and feel a peace regarding her decision to wait on God. The day after the disappointing visit to Hopkins,

Allie received an exciting email. She was accepted
for a summer internship with HOPE International,
a mission organization in Lancaster, Pennsylvania.
Her writing sample was so good that they promoted
her to the position of executive writing assistant to
the president. She is excited by this opportunity. She
will be provided with housing in Lancaster, Monday
through Thursday, and can come home on weekends.
We pray for an amazing experience and thank God
not only for what He has done in her life, but also for
what we are expecting Him to do.

Please pray for Andy, who suffered an elbow injury
at baseball practice. Even though Andy cannot play,
he attends every practice and game and encourages
his team from the bench. His coach texted him to say
how much he appreciates Andy's positive attitude.
We are so proud of him!

04/15/2012 An update from Allie
I want to thank God that He blessed me with so many
caring and dedicated prayer warriors! Every time I
stop to think about it, I praise God. It is an amazing
gift to have so many lifting me before the Lord daily.
Few are given such a blessing.

I had my scans on Thursday. I have trusted and kept
my eyes on God these past three weeks and prayed
my socks off. I meditated on God more in these past
three weeks than I ever have and was blessed with a
peace I have never had. As I sat on the exam table, I
was not afraid or anxious like I expected I would be.
When my doctor came around the corner, I knew in
my spirit before she spoke that my scans were not
clear. She informed us that all of the tumors were still
there and that they were pretty much the same size. I
didn't think anything right away except for "Okay. So,
what is the next step?" I didn't cry or get angry. I was
not devastated; disappointed, of course, but okay.

Tears came to my eyes initially, but they were tears
of peace, if that is even possible to imagine. You see,

two weeks earlier I had had a dream in which my oncologist came in and told me this exact news. It was God's gracious way of preparing my spirit, I believe. Of course, after the dream I still believed in a healing, but I've realized that the peace God has given me may not mean I will be immediately taken out of my circumstances. It may mean that I would be given wings to fly above them.

I discussed with my mom and the oncology doctor what I should do next. We discussed the option of a new chemo drug that specifically targets my type of cancer cells. I wrestled with the fact that I want to continue to trust God completely, but at the same time this chemo drug looks promising—and God heals through medicine as well as miracles. My mom put the situation into words in a way that I could better understand by telling the story of the man who got caught in a flood. He climbed to the roof of his house and prayed for God to save him. A boat came by to rescue him, but he refused to board, insisting that God would save him. After a while another boat came, which he also turned away. Then a helicopter came, but still he would not budge. Each time he insisted that God would save him. Finally, the water rose, and he drowned. When he got to heaven, he asked God, "Why didn't you save me?" God replied, "I sent you two boats and a helicopter."

So, I have decided to start this new chemo pill. I know that in the end, when God wants me to be healed, I will be healed. I am at a point now that I can say truthfully that if living with cancer for a while longer is going to do more for His kingdom than a healing, then I am okay with that. I have an unwavering peace about everything. I know God is healing me. Just because it didn't happen all at once doesn't mean it isn't happening.

I will start the chemo drug they are recommending, but that doesn't mean these last three weeks were wasted. God did so much healing in my spirit these past three weeks. I am still very excited and very much expecting Him to show up in big ways. In fact, He already has. My doctor pointed out just how far we have come. I am so blessed to be alive. From a medical standpoint, I should have died two years ago. The first time I sat on that exam table, I had an inoperable cancerous tumor the size of a football. At that time, I didn't have the privilege to consider "options." I was too afraid and desperate to take time and just draw near to God. When I look at where I was then and where I am now, it puts everything into perspective. Six tumors in my lungs that measure in millimeters are nothing compared to the dozens I have had before or the huge tumor in my liver that almost took my life. God HAS been healing me, and I trust Him to continue. I know He has done more in my spirit these past two years than He could have in a lifetime without cancer. I also know that He spoke healing to my heart three weeks ago when I decided to wait on Him. He knows better than I do what needs to happen for my healing to be whole and complete.

The story of Joseph has always been one of my favorite Bible stories, and it speaks to me more each day. Joseph did not understand why he was sold into slavery by his brothers or why Potiphar's wife accused him so that he ended up in jail. During those experiences, I do not doubt he knew in his heart that God had better plans for him. He knew God was speaking greatness to him, but he was sold into slavery and imprisoned. After Joseph became second-in-command over Egypt, I imagine he looked back and saw how God worked through his circumstances to fulfill His plan. I know God is speaking healing and a future into my heart. The song "You Know Better Than I" from the animated film *Joseph: King of Dreams* has become my theme song over the past two years.

Chemo will begin after I have a PET scan next week. Thankfully the chemo is in pill form and targeted to cancer cells, so I will not lose my hair and should not feel too sick. Right now, God has blessed me with amazing strength, and I feel great. I remember when I did not have the lung capacity to walk to class. Now, I am doing that AND exercising every day! Some good news from my scans is that my right lung has expanded almost back to its normal size! God is good.

I have been blessed to be in a Bible study with an AMAZING group of girls at college. We are doing something called "the love challenge." We broke down 1 Corinthians 4-7 and assigned one week to each attribute of love. This week was "love protects." I know that God has His arm around me, protecting me. Psalm 121:5 says, "The Lord watches over you—the Lord is your shade at your right hand." For the first time, I truly have no fear.

Second Corinthians 12:9 says that His power is "made perfect in weakness." It is okay.

Love and blessings,
Allie

CHAPTER SIXTEEN

A LEGACY OF FAITH

04/22/2012 Email to Allie Speck's Prayer Warriors
A lot has happened since the last update. Allie had the PET scan; the note from her doctor with the results said, "The final read on Allie's PET scan shows absolutely no disease in the liver and no new lung lesions or difference in existing ones."

This was great news! So, she started the new chemo pill, and her only side effects are headache and fatigue. Since she takes the pills at night, her sleep was so deep on Saturday that she overslept and was late for work. After working at Messiah until 4:00, she went to her second job and worked 5:00 to 9:00 p.m. She is amazing!

We pray that Allie can lead a normal life and still fight this cancer. She had a busy weekend and is preparing for finals next week.

On the 20th, we celebrated Andy's 16th birthday! We are proud of how he has handled this journey. His faith is as strong as his sister's, and they support each other in so many ways. It is a beautiful thing to witness.

Meanwhile, I am holding down the fort and directing all medical care. God knew what he was doing 28 years ago when He gave me the desire to be a nurse.

He knew that my family would need a nurse. I am thankful for the knowledge and skills I can provide to my family.

My devotion in *Jesus Calling* speaks to our crazy circumstances. It said when many things feel out of control and routines are not running smoothly, you feel insecure. Take refuge in the shelter of God's wings, where you are absolutely secure. When you are shaken out of your comfortable routines, hold onto Jesus.

04/27/2012 Email to Allie Speck's Prayer Warriors
Allie will be interviewed on the local news today to advertise an annual ice hockey competition between police and firefighters called the "Battle of the Badges." Each year they choose a charity to support, and this year they chose to help with Allie's medical expenses. I hope you appreciate how great Allie looks, considering she spent November to February in and out of the hospital and had four major surgeries. This may be the first time many of you are able to put a face with Allie's name.

05/01/2012 Email to Allie Speck's Prayer Warriors
Allie seems to be tolerating the oral chemo with only occasional headaches, slight nausea and fatigue. Taking the medication at night seems to give her a sound sleep. We pray it will fight the cancer while allowing her to live an almost normal life. We are so thankful.

05/10/2012 Email to Allie Speck's Prayer Warriors
Allie had a checkup at Hopkins today. It appears her liver is tolerating the chemo, and everyone thought she looked great. She has been able to finish her semester at Messiah and lead a pretty normal life. We feel prayers are being answered.

Allie leaves for Lancaster next week to start her internship with HOPE International. She is awaiting an appointment to have her port removed. The downside is that she will need to have blood drawn with a needle every two weeks.

In other big news, Andy passed his learner's permit! We have another driver in the house, and he is overjoyed. He recently attended his high school prom and looked so grown up. Allie took a ton of pictures. He did end up missing the entire baseball season and remains in therapy. He is taking a lifeguarding class with hopes to work at the local pool this summer. Thanks for your prayers.

We press on!! Allie and I will be sharing our testimony at two different mother/daughter banquets this month, and Allie will be speaking at another local church on May 20th. We are excited to tell others about the peace we have and how God is working through us to share Christ's love. We feel this is an important part of our journey.

Allie's testimony, May 20, 2012

(INTRODUCTION): I was asked to introduce Allie. We met this past fall. I signed up to be a small group Bible study leader at Messiah and was given a list of seven girls. When we first started meeting, we had a list of big stuff our group was going through, and I wondered how I would support them. But through those concerns, we got to know each other. From that flowed an opportunity for us to become roommates and for me to get to know Allie more. This is her story. It is HER story; do not elevate it on a platform. Learn from it and have better faith from it. So here is Allie Speck.

Good morning. It is such a blessing to be here. Your church is awesome. I would like to open in prayer. Father God, I thank You for this opportunity that You have given me to share my journey. I just pray for Your blessing over my words. Let them be acceptable in Your sight, and I ask that the glory be given to You and not to me. Bless each of us and protect us as we depart from this place. In Jesus's name, amen.

I'm not sure at what point you were introduced to my story, but I became sick my senior year of high school. As we began visiting doctors, I realized how serious my situation was. We saw a local liver surgeon who said he was 99 percent sure my tumor was cancerous and could not be removed. He gave me six months to a year to live. I was completely overwhelmed and said to God, "You put in my heart that You had a plan for me, and now it seems I am not even going to live long enough to fulfill any type of plan."

My mom prayed to God, "I am overwhelmed. I don't know where to go." God provided a miracle. I was seen by a liver surgeon at Johns Hopkins and scheduled for surgery for January 13th.

I was very confident that God was going to deliver me. This would be my testimony, and He would get all the glory. So, when I woke up from surgery and my mom told me he did not get it and it was cancer, I immediately thought it was a death sentence. But my mom said there was talk of treatment with chemo. It was a rare cancer. This did not fit into the plan I had, but I realize now it was God's plan, not mine.

I was terrified to get chemo. The hallucinations I experienced told me that chemo was just prolonging my death. I had prepared myself for physical side effects, but I was not prepared to be attacked mentally. I remember going home, falling on my knees and saying, "God, I can't do this." I had five treatments left, and I said, "I do not have the strength to do this." And it did not get any easier. There were several times that I truly thought I was dying. Each time got harder. I wasn't even trying to get better; I was just trying to stay alive. Trials are not just a test that we have to get through. They are a process of teaching, if we are willing to learn. It is not just holding on until it is over; it's learning to act in those moments, receive in those moments and give in those moments when you feel like you cannot give anymore.

It was at that point that I learned my tumor had shrunk enough to schedule another surgery. I remember going into the second surgery with a completely different mind-set. When I went into the first surgery, my thinking was God HAS to heal me because if He doesn't, who will do His will and save the world if I am no longer here? This time my thinking was, "If I should die during this surgery, I am okay with that because that would mean my death could do more for His kingdom than my life." When I woke up after surgery, I knew in my spirit that I had been healed. They removed all the tumors in my liver. I was cancer-free!

For a long time that was where my story ended. For eight months I was cancer-free. I felt healthy and went back to school. I signed up to travel to Kenya on a mission trip. I felt so compelled to share my testimony and was traveling to various churches and speaking. After those eight months, I started to not feel well again and called my mom. She said, "You have a scan in two weeks; you are probably just psyching yourself out. Don't worry."

When I went for my scans, they confirmed that my cancer was back. It was not only in my liver, but also in my lungs. I had no fear at that time because I thought, "Lord, You brought me through this once; YOU can bring me through again." I decided to embrace this opportunity as a time to learn, but, of course, I did not understand again. I said, "Lord, I thought we were done with this." But who am I to say when He is done and what He is using. So, I started chemo again, but this time I wanted to continue living. I wanted to go to school; I wanted to have a job; I wanted to see my friends. I didn't want to stay in the hospital. I didn't want to stay home. I wanted to keep living. I felt God put a call on my heart to live a normal life WITH cancer. I learned very quickly that God used just going to class, going to work and visiting my friends as a testimony. I had many people who came up to me at Messiah and say, "Thank you for being a living testimony." It was during that time that I realized that not only do I need to rely on God in desperate situations, but I also need to rely on Him day by day by day. Every morning when I woke up, I needed to say, "God, I'm tired. I'm sick. I need You to get me through today." Cancer taught me to have a desperation for God that I never had before. Before, I would get up and go through the whole day and not even think twice about how God was strengthening me. Now I don't wake up one morning without seeing how God is providing for me.

It was during that time I clung to the story of Joseph. It has always been one of my favorite Bible stories, and I never knew why until now. Joseph was given great visions by God; he knew in his spirit that he was destined for greatness. Yet he was born the next youngest of his brothers, and all of his older brothers despised him. He was not in any position of power or favor, yet he still continued to believe in God's promise. In answer to his belief, his brothers sold him into slavery. But Joseph continued to believe. He worked his way up in Potiphar's house as a servant. I don't doubt that Joseph thought, "Here is where I will get my favor." It was then that he was falsely accused by Potiphar's wife and thrown into jail for the rest of his life. We read the story knowing the ending, but Joseph didn't. I cannot imagine how he felt in that jail cell after God had planted all those great dreams in his heart. When you look back over his life, if he had not been the youngest, if he hadn't been despised by his brothers, if he hadn't been sold into slavery, if he hadn't been thrown into jail, he never would have been in a position to impact the thousands of people that he did. It was during his time in jail that he was given the opportunity to interpret Pharaoh's dreams. He became second-in-command over all of Egypt and brought them through a famine. Without those trials, Joseph might have lived just a normal life. When his brothers came to beg for food, he revealed, "I am your brother Joseph. What you meant for evil, God used for good." I know that is what God has done with my story: what Satan and the world intend for evil, God can use for good. There is nothing He cannot use, no place He cannot work in, and no area where His glory cannot shine. This is what my journey has taught me so far.

I am currently doing an internship with HOPE International. I was talking with some of the other interns last night, telling them that I would not be in this position if everything I went through had not happened. One of the interns wanted to share her testimony with me. She told me that she lived with her family in a village during a time of genocide. They were persecuted and driven out of the village. Her parents went to find a safe place, and she was left behind with her siblings. She was the youngest. While her parents were away, the rebel army attacked the village. She and her siblings hid in the church because her siblings said, "God will be a refuge for us." People came into the church and said, "Come with us; we have a better place for you to hide." They took them out of the church, betrayed them and handed them over to the army that was attacking the village. The villagers were rounded up and attacked with machetes, clubs, swords and knives. Because she was so small, the person in front of her was killed and fell on her. She lay there and watched her siblings and all of the people in the village be killed. The bodies were piled on top of her, and she lay there all day, thinking she was dead. Then she heard someone crying out to God, and she realized she was alive. She crawled out and ran away and hid in the bushes, but she was starving. She found someone and asked them to kill her so she would not starve to death, but that person said, "God wants you to be alive." That person hid her for three months until the persecution was over. She was the only survivor from her entire village.

I was so humbled by her testimony, which touched my heart. The one thing she said was Joseph's quote: "What they meant for evil, God used for good." She said, "I have forgiven the people who killed my family. Because Jesus has forgiven me, I can forgive." She said it took a long time, but she realized that God works in EVERYTHING. She said she lives her life every day to follow Christ because she knows that is the only reason she is alive.

I want to live like that. The only reason I am alive and the cancer did not take me is because God has something for me to do. I need to live my life every day, working toward whatever that purpose is for me. I want to follow God with that same desperation. I want to tell you that you need to follow Christ in that same way. Even if you don't have cancer, even if you never lived through genocide, even if you have never had a trying experience, I can guarantee you that God is sustaining you every day. He is keeping you alive, and He is doing it for a reason. It is *not to serve yourself; it is to serve others and to serve Him. I am so privileged to share this with you today.*

Thank you for this opportunity. I covet your prayers; I guarantee they are heard. We appreciate all the support you have given to me and my family, for God uses His church to support those who need it. Thank you for having me today.

(PASTOR): Thank you, Allie. You are a model for us of a legacy of faith as you trust the Lord. What are you facing today that Allie's testimony of God's faithfulness and trust in Him can sustain you? She's a model for us to follow. The model is faithfulness and trusting God in severe testing and trials. He is working to forge us into the people He wants us to be. Thank You, God! I am stunned by Allie's deep faith. Let faith arise in Jesus's name, amen.

05/31/2012 Email to Allie Speck's Prayer Warriors
We have exciting news to share. Allison is engaged! She and her fiancé love the Lord, and He will be at the center of their relationship, which is most important in any marriage. The engagement ring belonged to Allie's great-grandmother, and Allie has always said that someday she wanted it to be her engagement ring. The tentative plan is for a wedding in June 2013. This is a wonderfully happy time for all of us.

Life in the Speck household has been joyous. Allie is doing well on the oral chemo. She is working at HOPE International as an executive writing intern, and she absolutely loves it! This is her dream job, plus it earns her nine credits to complete her minor in Communications at Messiah. Two semesters should complete her English degree and allow her to graduate with her class. Life is good, and God has blessed us beyond what we deserve. We are keeping the faith and believing God is at work. We expect her scans in July to show improvement.

06/13/2012 Email to Allie Speck's Prayer Warriors
We have been busy making bridal appointments,

trying on dresses, looking for reception halls and enjoying the fun of planning a wedding. What an amazing time!

Andy passed his lifeguard certification and started his summer job at the local pool. He loves it and is a great role model for the younger kids! Summer is definitely here!

There has been a small setback. Allie had a sharp pain in her abdomen that resulted in a trip to the Emergency Room. They could not provide a reason for the pain. Today we are headed to Hopkins Oncology Clinic for a checkup. Pray that her pain resolves and that the chemo is shrinking the cancer.

Allie was asked to be the guest speaker at Relay for Life at her high school. As soon as she finishes speaking there, she will travel to Camp Yolijiwa to share her testimony with the kids at church camp. She is busy doing God's work. Pray for pain relief so she can be an effective witness, sharing what God has done for her.

06/17/2012 Email to Allie Speck's Prayer Warriors
Allie spoke at Relay for Life, then I drove her to the church camp, where she spoke to many youth. She kept her commitments despite the pain she was experiencing. I feel that because she did this, God rewarded her with pain relief. I believe that when the youth gathered around Allie and prayed, a healing power was released. The morning after these two speaking engagements was the first morning Allie awoke without pain. We are so thankful for heartfelt prayers.

Just like one of Allie's favorite verses, Romans 8:28, she stepped out in faith to share her testimony and God used it for good. So many young people came to Allie in tears at the camp, telling her how much her testimony meant to them. What a beautiful blessing!

06/22/2012 Email to Allie Speck's Prayer Warriors
Andy ruptured his eardrum diving into the pool.
Pray for healing, as he will be leaving next week with
our youth group for a Christian festival called Creation. Pray for safety, nice weather since they will
be sleeping in tents, and an amazing time of worship
with the Lord.

On short notice, Allison went to Hopkins today and
had her port removed in an outpatient procedure.
She is sore but doing well. We got home about 7:30
p.m. Her doctors feel the port is an infection risk. She
is not looking forward to being stuck for blood, especially since they had to stick her twice to get an IV for
the surgery today. Pray for her veins to show up when
they are needed! Needles are never fun, but we understand the long-term benefits of removing the port.

She is back at HOPE International in Lancaster and
doing well. She was very excited to learn that HOPE
is sending her to Creation with three other interns
who will operate a stand, educating people about
HOPE International's mission.

07/20/2012 Email to Allie Speck's Prayer Warriors
Following is the email from Allie's oncology doctor.
You will see that the PET scan Allie had yesterday
gave us disappointing news. We felt confident that
she was doing well on the oral chemo and moving
forward with life. What an amazing doctor Allie has,
as her faith has been a witness to us.

Zina,
The final read on Allie's PET scan is consistent with
progressive disease. There has been enlargement
of her existing lung lesions and new lesions seen in
both lungs. There are also two lymph nodes in her
chest that are enlarged and indicate spread of her
disease.

We think it is reasonable to consider an IV chemotherapy as well as an oral pill. This could slow the

progression of Allie's cancer. There has been no
demonstrated ability to cure it.

I can't imagine what you are going through as you
think about this news and what it may mean for the
immediate and long-term future. I want you to know
that we are going to keep fighting for Allie the best
way we know how. I am also very aware that "the
best way we know how" has earthly limits. I continue to believe that God has a plan for Allie, and that
is more powerful than ANY medicine, and we must
have complete faith in that.

Much love.

While on the way home from Hopkins, Allie and
I picked up her wedding dress. Sitting at a red
light, we saw a license plate that read RMNS 8 28
(Romans 8:28). We felt this was a sign that God will
continue to use this situation for good.

I remember praying long and hard about Allison's results and wishing I
had a better understanding of how this situation was going to help God's
kingdom. The Bible says in Proverbs 3:5 that we should not try to understand but have faith. And I guess true faith is genuinely trusting God
with the outcomes of life. I wanted to trust God with my whole heart,
but I just remember feeling like my heart was broken. I hoped that God
had an entirely different plan that I could not understand. And I realized
that treatment decisions needed to be completely up to Allison. It was
very difficult to listen to the medical recommendations that talked about
"slowing the progression of the disease" while trying to grasp the depth
of Allison's faith and trust in God to heal her if it be His will. I cannot
even put into words how torn my heart felt during this time. I do remember the oncology doctor saying that Allie was very dear to her and that
the journey she was on with our family had very little to do with earthly
medicine. Allie had taken her medical team on a deep faith journey that
changed many of their lives.

08/06/2012 Email to Allie Speck's Prayer Warriors
We were attending a friend's picnic in Duncannon
when a guy named Matt wandered into the back-
yard. He had a backpack and hiking stick and said

he was hiking the Appalachian Trail. He stopped
because he smelled food and saw the huge slip-and-
slide in the yard. He admitted thinking he could
possibly get food and bathe all in one stop. Then he
met Allie, and they spent the afternoon sharing their
stories with each other.

Matt is a "thru hiker" on the Appalachian Trail and
is hiking to raise money and awareness for children's cancer treatment. We believe his meeting
Allie was no coincidence. We ended up bringing him
home to spend the night at our house. Allie shared
her story with him while we washed his clothes. The
next day we gave him provisions and dropped him
off where we had picked him up so he could continue
his hike. What a gift from God!

08/16/2012 Email to Allie Speck's Prayer Warriors
Allie just returned from a week at Myrtle Beach,
refreshed and renewed. Many are asking when Allie
will start treatment, and I feel it is time to share where
we are in this journey. Allie has decided to wait on the
Lord and has chosen not to start chemotherapy.

We are seeking complete and total healing through
prayer. If we can trust man with Allie's future, why
can't we trust God? Do not misunderstand. Allie
would not be where she is today without her gifted
doctors. However, Allie feels a strong urge to wait
on God. She does not want to have scans at this time
so as to prevent the devil from placing doubt in her
mind. Allie feels good and is claiming complete healing. We believe in God's power to heal her, and we
will give Him all the glory. Allie has stopped the oral
chemo and starts her day thanking God for the healing He has already given to her. We appreciate your
prayers and hope you will join us in thanking God for
Allie's healing. Our God is powerful and capable, and
we will not set limits on Him.

"When Jesus had entered Capernaum, a centurion
came to him, asking for help. 'Lord,' he said, 'my

servant lies at home paralyzed, suffering terribly.'
Jesus said to him, 'Shall I come and heal him?' The
centurion replied, 'Lord, I do not deserve to have
you come under my roof. But just say the word,
and my servant will be healed. For I myself am a
man under authority, with soldiers under me. I tell
this one, "Go," and he goes; and that one, "Come,"
and he comes. I say to my servant, "Do this," and
he does it.' When Jesus heard this, he was amazed
and said to those following him, 'Truly I tell you,
I have not found anyone in Israel with such great
faith'" (Matthew 8:5–10).

In this scripture, the Roman officer was used to
being in control, but no amount of control could
heal his servant. Through faith, he handed control
over to Jesus.

We are choosing to do the same thing; we turn Allie
over to Him! God is and always has been in control.

CHAPTER SEVENTEEN
THE PLANS I HAVE FOR YOU

09/05/2012 Email to Allie Speck's Prayer Warriors
Allie is taking 18 credits at Messiah this semester, working two part-time jobs, and planning her wedding for next June! On Monday when I talked with her, she was headed to a Zumba® class at 10:00 p.m.! Her positive spirit and trust in God are allowing her to lead a normal life, and we are so thankful.

We recently learned that Allie's oncology doctor will be leaving Hopkins. We are very sad to see her leave, but we are thankful that God gave us the opportunity to meet her and share our faith journey with her; our connection has grown into a deep and lasting bond. She has promised to attend Allie's wedding and remain a part of Allie's life, even though she will no longer be Allie's doctor.

Here is a quote from her message telling us she was leaving:

There aren't many things that I am sure of in medicine, or in life, but I am completely certain that God put Allie and I together on this journey for very specific reasons. I am a better person and a better physician because of her, and I know that her influence will continue to help me inspire others to consider the total care of a patient from the biological, spiritual and emotional perspective. Allie has inspired every single person she has come into contact with at Johns Hopkins and beyond, and I know that God will continue to work His miracles through her every day.

09/22/2012 Email to Allie Speck's Prayer Warriors
Our belief is that Allie is healed. Some people have questioned our trust in God's plan, but we know that God is more than able. He is the Great Physician who formed Allie. We were in a place where man was trying to determine the next step in Allie's treatment. We are joining Allie in her belief that God knows just what she needs.

We have scheduled a closure visit with her oncology doctor. Allie wants to thank everyone for their care and share her decision to trust God's plan.

As Allie's mom, I have moments of doubt, and Satan whispers negative thoughts in my ear. But I have asked God for confirmation, and the scripture that keeps recurring is Mark 11:23: "Truly I tell you, if anyone says to this mountain, 'Go, throw yourself into the sea,' and does not doubt in their heart but believes that what they say will happen, it will be done for them."

Allie feels wonderful, and she and her fiancé are taking dancing lessons in preparation for the wedding. Wedding plans are full steam ahead, and life is good.

10/18/2012 Email to Allie Speck's Prayer Warriors
We had a good visit with the oncologist today. It was nice to spend time talking more about life and less about cancer. Allie has developed a cough, and she had a chest X-ray that shows persistent tumors in her lungs. However, they have not increased in size. The doctor told Allie that she has every reason to feel good about where she is and that God is allowing

her to feel well and do so many things despite the cancer. She called it a true miracle. She looks and feels healthy, and we know that is God's hand. We were told today that if Allison decides to choose a different path, plans can change in an instant.

Allison's Journal, October 23, 2012

"I know who goes before me.
I know who stands behind.
The God of angel armies
is always by my side."
(Lyrics from "Whom Shall I Fear")
Guess who is speaking in Messiah's chapel on Thursday. THIS GIRL! So blessed.

♥Allie

Allie's testimony, October 25, 2012

(INTRODUCTION): This semester the chaplain team at Messiah has been looking for stories that inspire us, encourage us and connect us. Through sharing our stories, we recognize that we serve an amazing God and that He works in our lives in a variety of ways. There was one story that left us speechless. A story where God was so evident, you could feel it. A story that could not go untold on campus. Allison Speck is one of the most amazing and faithful people you will ever meet. Please cherish this story.

Good morning! I want to apologize for my voice. I lost it yesterday and it has returned, but I sound like Joan Rivers. HAHA! Sorry!

I came to Messiah my freshman year, excited to get involved in mission work and most likely to overcommit my time as I am known to do. HAHA! I had not felt well during my senior year of high school, but various doctors could not find anything wrong. During finals week, I found a lump in my abdomen that ended up being a tumor the size of a football on my liver. I never imagined it could be cancer. But after seeing a local surgeon who painted a very grim picture and

gave me a six-month timeline, I realized that it was
more serious than I thought, and I heard the word
cancer for the first time.

So, there I was at 18 years old being told that I probably would not live to see 20. At the time, it didn't
really sink in. I believe God gracefully did not allow me
to understand the gravity of the situation. My mom
decided that we needed a second opinion, and that is
when I realized that no one wanted to take my case. It
seemed hopeless until, on Christmas Eve, my mom fell to
her knees and cried out to God.

Shortly after praying, my mom got a call from a friend
whose brother had connections at Johns Hopkins in
Baltimore, Maryland. To make a long story short, I had
an appointment with the top liver surgeon at Hopkins.
He gave me hope and offered to do surgery, explain-
ing that it was very risky and could be life-threatening.
I went into surgery in January believing that he would
remove the tumor, because there was a calling on my
heart to do wonderful things for God. I just didn't know
what it was I was going to do.

I came out of surgery and awoke to realize that not
only could the tumor not be removed, but it also was
cancerous. So, I went into surgery with a bad prognosis
and came out with a horrible one. I was told the cancer
was rare but treatable with chemotherapy. I didn't tell
anyone, but I was terrified of getting chemo.

My first chemo treatment was one of the most terrifying experiences of my life. I hallucinated, seeing and
hearing people who were not there. Some of the situations were funny, but most were frightening. There were
horrible voices that chanted over and over, "Chemo is
just prolonging your death. Why are you even trying?
Give up. You're going to die anyway."

I came home and began to experience the physical
side effects. Vomiting, weakness and generally just feeling horrible. I could not even walk without help. I went
to my bedroom, closed the door and fell on my knees. I
put my face in the carpet and cried out to God, saying,
"I cannot do this. You said You won't give us more than
we can handle, so You need to take this away because
I cannot handle it." If I had been writing my story, this

never would have happened. I wanted God to reach down and take it from me, NOW! After one treatment, I was done.

After that, things did not get easier. In fact, they got harder. Intense physical side effects, long stays in the hospital...my hair fell out, my fingernails fell off. I weighed less than 100 pounds at one point. But out of that intense treatment, there came a ray of hope. My tumor had shrunk, and the surgeon wanted to attempt surgery again.

So, in July, I had my second surgery, and in a span of 24 hours I became cancer-free. I was overjoyed! I praised God for delivering me, but the deliverance only lasted eight months. The cancer returned not only in my liver, but in my lungs too. In the medical world, I have a big word for "a very complicated cancer," and when this type of cancer spreads to your lungs, it is a death sentence. You cannot get rid of it. It is a lifetime cancer. I tried many things: multiple surgeries and procedures; different types of chemo. But nothing worked. This past summer I started an experimental chemo. I took it and prayed for healing. I said, "God, I know You have a good plan for me." Scans at the end of the summer showed that the chemo wasn't working; the cancer had spread. At that point, I felt God calling me to rely on Him completely. He said to my spirit, "Be still and know that I am God. Know that I have you. Know that I am writing your story." And in that moment, I decided to stop treatment, stop going to the doctors, stop trying to fix things. Because only God can fix this situation.

That is where I stand now. The last scan I had showed that the cancer had not progressed much further. In fact, it has stayed relatively the same, and I am believing God will keep it there. I believe He is even going to start to heal me. But I know that whatever happens, He is writing my story. And in the moment that I decided to stop treatment, I realized that I was completely handing my life over to God. I took my hands off and said, "You are the author and perfecter of my faith. You take my life and make it what it needs to be, and let it be for Your glory." And He has done exactly that. He has given me amazing opportunities to share His love. And if this had not happened to me, I would not be standing here before you speaking this morning.

So, in the end, what I have learned from my story is that God is good and you can trust Him—even if things are not going your way or just as YOU had planned. You should not trust God only when things are good because He's not just your God when it is okay. He is not just your God when it's convenient. He is the God of everything and of all time. He comes into every part of your story and works amazing things. So, in closing, I would like to leave you with a quote that I found a week ago that really speaks to what I have been through for the last three years. It is by Canon Battersby, and it is after he realized that he needed to trust God completely. He had this amazing revelation that he needed to hand his story over to God, and this is what he said:

"I thought of the sufficiency of Jesus and said, 'I will trust in Him.' I do not want to rest in emotions but rather just believe, and cling to Christ as my all...It is now eight years since I knew this blessing as my own. I cannot say that I have never for a moment ceased to trust the Lord to keep me. But I can say that so long as I have trusted Him, He has kept me. He has been faithful."

Allison's Journal, October 30, 2012

I spent today revising and rewriting my literary criticism midterm essay for World Literature. I suppose an unproductive two days must be followed by a productive one. I also had my first meeting tonight for my trip to Kenya. SO EXCITED!!!

My roommates and I finished a *Lord of the Rings* marathon this past weekend while surviving Hurricane Sandy. I can check that off of my bucket list.

"All you have to do is decide what to do with the time that is given to you" (Gandalf from *Lord of the Rings*).

♥Allie

11/01/2012 Email to Allie Speck's Prayer Warriors
Allison was asked to share her story in Chapel at Messiah last week. I could not attend, but I was told she got a standing ovation. The coordinator of chapel

said she has never seen a speaker get a standing ovation. Tom, my mom, my mother-in-law and my sister attended, as well as several friends from our church. One of Allie's friends texted me, saying, "Allie blows me away with her trust and faith in God!" Tom said there was a line of students waiting to talk to Allie after her testimony. Her Facebook page and Messiah mailbox are flooded with comments letting her know the impact her testimony made on those who attended. Allison was gifted from a young age to share her story, and we know this is a huge part of God's plan for her life. So blessed to be chosen to be her mom.

Allison's Journal, November 16, 2012

One more all-nighter to finish this theory paper, one media analysis paper and half of my one-act play to write tomorrow, then I am headed to...ROME! An amazing opportunity was dropped in my lap to visit a friend in Rome, and I said YES! I cannot even tell you how much I need this amazing vacation.

So many amazing things are happening: 17 hours until I leave for Rome, 47 days until my mission trip to Kenya, and 210 days until the wedding. AHHH!

I cannot help but think that at this time last year, I was in ICU after extensive lung surgery, and now I am traveling to Rome. O God, You are SO good to me! My cup overflows!

♥Allie

Allison's Journal, November 20, 2012

I am in Rome! Yesterday we visited the Sistine Chapel, the Colosseum and the Fontana di Trevi. Today we rented a moped and drove all around the Isle of Capri. AMAZING! I cannot believe I made it here. Tomorrow we are off to see Florence and Venice. Another adventure off my bucket list!

The friend we are visiting had good words of advice for us upon our arrival to Rome. He said, "Just make sure you can run faster than the person you hand your camera to." HAHA!

♥Allie

11/27/2012 Email to Allie Speck's Prayer Warriors
Allie just returned from a week in Italy and had
a fabulous time! She is feeling a bit jet-lagged and
trying to make up for lost time, but it was a trip of a
lifetime. We are so glad she had the opportunity to
go. She called us Thanksgiving Day from a gondola in
Venice. God is so good!

While Allie was in Rome, we took Andy and a friend
to the Ford Rouge Factory and Henry Ford Museum
in Michigan. He had a great time as well. Life is good.

Allie submitted her application to graduate in May
and found an apartment in Marysville, where she
and her fiancé will live after they are married. It
is a cozy old place with crooked floors and a retro
kitchen! She is busy planning room layouts. We are
all working together to paint, clean and prepare the
apartment. It is an exciting time!

12/07/2012 Email to Allie Speck's Prayer Warriors
Tonight, Allie looked so pretty as she attended a
Christmas party at college that she was too sick
to attend last year. God has been good, and we are
thankful.

She has an appointment at the clinic on campus next
week to get five vaccinations in preparation for her
trip to Kenya. At least these needlesticks will result
in the trip of a lifetime.

Allison's Journal, December 27, 2012

Hello, I just wanted to share that while packing for Kenya today, I pulled out my wedding dress and tried it on.
I paused to thank God a thousand times over for how
He has blessed me.
    I thought of Psalm 103:1–5: "Praise the Lord, my soul;
all my inmost being, praise his holy name. Praise the
Lord, my soul, and forget not all his benefits—who
forgives all your sins and heals all your diseases, who
redeems your life from the pit and crowns you with love

and compassion, who satisfies your desires with good
things so that your youth is renewed like the eagle's."

♥Allie

12/28/2012 Email to Allie Speck's Prayer Warriors
Today Allie turned 22! I am sitting here reflecting
that almost a year ago she was in the midst of major
surgeries, chest tubes and many emergency trips to
the ER for collapsed lungs, pneumonia and infection.
It was such a frustrating time in our lives. I look
back now and wonder how we made it through. Actually, I know how we made it through: with God's help.
But today we are on the other side of that dark time,
and we give praise.

On January 5th last year, Allison had lung surgery
and ended up in the hospital for 22 days. On January
3rd this year, she will leave for Kenya, and her trip
will total exactly 22 days! What a difference faith
and a year make.

Pray that Allie and her fellow classmates will be
blessed with traveling mercies and that they will
find the purpose for which God has sent them. She
is anticipating no bathrooms, snakes, spiders, bugs
and sleeping in a tent in a very remote village. This
is NOT my idea of a dream trip, but it certainly is for
our adventure-seeking daughter!

May your Christmas be filled with God sightings and
love. Hug your family tight, count your blessings and
seek miracles every day.

**01/13/2013 Email to Allie Speck's Prayer Warriors –
Prayers for Andy**
Andy had a car accident last night and is shaken up,
but he is okay. He was driving home in the rain, lost
control of his car, and hit a tree. He walked away with
just bruises and scratches. Looking at the car, we
KNOW God was watching over him. Today is my birthday and between his accident and Allison being in Kenya, I will be aging two years this year instead of one!

Allison's Journal, January 7, 2013

As I sat on the plane headed to Kenya, I thought about how faith works. It isn't something we create or grow; it is something we receive daily, hourly, every minute from God. He provides each of us our own measure of faith, but it is up to us whether we receive it or not. I can receive and believe or allow myself to doubt. I have learned that you cannot sit still in your faith because life is a current. If you are not moving toward God, then you are being pulled away from Him. I desperately want to be sold out for God, but there always seems to be this nagging shadow that I cannot get rid of. Maybe faith is being humble enough to admit my doubt and simply pray, "Lord, help my unbelief."

Two days ago, while walking through Nairobi, one of the girls fell into a ditch and got mud all down her side. There was a group of Kenyan men washing cars and one of them saw her fall. He went to her with his bucket, got on his knee and squeezed the sponge on his own foot to demonstrate his intention to clean off the mud. He began by washing her feet and proceeded to wash all the mud from her body as well. I snapped a picture and thought, "What a beautiful, humble act of love." It reminded me of Jesus washing the disciples' feet. He did not have to come and serve us, but He chose to. In the same way, this man had no obligation to wash her feet. He could have handed her the sponge, but he didn't. He knelt down in the dirt and washed her clean. That is grace, my friends.

Tonight is our last night in Nairobi. Our beds have cool mosquito nets over them. This will be our last night with running water and electricity for the next two weeks. Tomorrow we start our safari. Loving Kenya so far!

♥Allie

Allison's Journal, January 10, 2013

Today we visited the schoolhouse and handed out supplies to the children. As the children gathered around us, I saw many who were skinny with bloated bellies and I thought, "Why are we not giving them food to eat?

There has to be a way to get them more food." A part of me wants to return to this place and care for these children. I was surprised that my heart was not overflowing and that I was not getting fuzzy feelings toward the children. I thought my heart was not working, but then I realized that my love is bigger than that. When I look at these children, I don't just see them; I SEE them. I see their needs; I see their potential; I see so much. I want to teach them, discipline them, feed them and push them to be more than they realize they can be. I don't just want to hand them candy, make them smile and leave. I want to give them nutrition, knowledge and JESUS! I hope to do that on a return trip. I would love to adopt a child from here to raise him or her to know Jesus.

This afternoon we went on a hike up a mountain. It took an hour and a half to get to the top to enjoy the waterfalls and the pool. You would have been so proud of me. The hike was hard, and I thought about turning back. I was in tears at one point, but, as you know, I can be stubborn and sometimes that benefits me. So, no matter how much my body wanted to stop, I kept moving. It was so worth it! The pool and the waterfalls were beautiful. I hope this is one of many mountaintop experiences for me.

♥ Allie

Allison's Journal, January 11, 2013

Today we milked a camel and drank the milk. It tasted smoky because they sanitized the milk with fire. We shared stories around the campfire. Because we are on the equator, the sun sets at 7:00 p.m. and rises at 7:00 a.m. every day all year. We did some stargazing tonight and you cannot believe how many stars I saw with no pollution. AMAZING!

♥ Allie

Allison's Journal, January 21, 2013

I have been running a fever between 100 and 102 degrees with diarrhea and nausea for about four days. Our group leader took me to the hospital in Nairobi because I was delirious and severely dehydrated. They ran blood tests and gave me IV fluids. I feel SO much better. I have medicine to take, and I am back with the group. I was so sick, and all I wanted to do was to go home. While at the hospital, I saw a teenage girl sleeping on her mother's lap. It made me think about my mom and all the times she sat with me in the hospital. I thanked God that I was born in America into a loving family. We take so much for granted. America is clean, safe, medically advanced and educated. We have so many opportunities. Traveling to a place like this makes you realize just how blessed we are in America.

♥Allie

1/28/2013 – Message from Allie's oncology doctor about Allie's trip to Kenya

It must be WONDERFUL having Allie back in PA! I was just looking at some of her Facebook photos from Kenya. I am so incredibly proud and in awe of everything she has accomplished. What an amazing trip this must have been! God certainly had plans for Allie to bring her grace to another continent where people were in need of it.

I have been thinking a lot lately about Allie, about how most people live their entire lives never venturing out of their "comfort zone"—in love, in geography, in their thinking—and Allie is just so brave and fearless in so many ways. I believe that this power and fearlessness is part of the miracle that God has performed in her!

When I think of all the time that has passed between the last time we did any "earthly medical" therapy over the summer and everything that has transpired since...it is hard for me to explain, and I don't think it is my place to, but I believe it is nothing short of a healing miracle. As we said so many times, it was not the dramatic miracle of being cancer-free that we were originally praying for, but it was something even more transformative and wonderful that I have only begun to understand and probably never will. It seems to me that Allie has been in the best spiritual, emotional and physical health over the past nearly six months than since we started this journey together. And to think of all the things that are happening and continue to happen: college semesters, trips, working on her new house, planning the wedding...all I can say is that I am filled with overwhelming joy at it all!

Please give Allie a big hug from me and a WELCOME HOME! I do hope she writes about her travels in her gifted writing voice. So many people could learn from her experience in Kenya!

02/08/2013 Email to Allie Speck's Prayer Warriors
While in Kenya, Allie developed nausea and diarrhea, which has continued off and on since she has returned home. Allison is concerned that she may have contracted another bowel infection while in Kenya. She received treatment in Kenya, but her symptoms never completely resolved. We pray there is no infection. She is scheduled to have lung and liver scans in March, and we pray for the best possible news.

03/06/2013 Email to Allie Speck's Prayer Warriors
We received Allison's scan results; her lung lesions have grown slightly. She continues to have a strong sense that God wants her to wait and not begin treatment. She said it does not matter what the scans show; she believes she is healed. She has such strong faith and trust in our Lord. I wish my faith were stronger. I opened my devotional *Jesus Calling* today and the first sentence was, "Continue on this path with Me, enjoying My presence even in adversity." This is Jesus telling me to trust. I am doing my best to give Allie over to the One who made her and knows her better than I do.

**03/06/2013 Email to Allie Speck's Prayer Warriors –
Email from the oncology doctor**
Dear Zina,
I have so much I want to say but somehow can't find the words just yet. Your last sentence in your update

is extremely powerful as a mother and, I believe,
a miracle unto itself. Mary had to trust that the
Father's plan for Jesus was something bigger than
even her own love and vision as a mother. I have
thought about this many different ways, as a mother,
and I imagine that I will struggle to grasp it as long
as I am living an earthly life. But I have to imagine
that we must trust and continue.

To be frank, the fact that these lesions have grown
so slowly over the past year goes against anything
that I have learned or been trained in conventional
medicine. In addition, the fact that she has no symptoms except for an occasional cough and is otherwise
going about her life feeling healthy also goes against
what I have been told in training. But we know better! Something else is clearly determining how fast
these lesions grow. There is a powerful force making
sure that Allie has the time and the health for her
life to unfold exactly as God has planned it.

As a mother and friend, I see and feel your grief
too. But in your grief, I see the same grief of Mary...
before she truly understood that her Son would be
delivered from all suffering and change the course of
human history and give hope and love where there
was absolutely none from that time until the end of
time! And in that we all rejoice!

I completely support Allie's decision to not choose
treatment. I think she knows in her heart and deepest soul that there is something powerful at work
here, and I am so proud and in awe of her for following that. I am on this path with you forever, no
matter what happens!

With love.

03/13/2013 Email to Allie Speck's Prayer Warriors
We were told there is a new, small lesion in Allie's liver that is suspicious for cancer. Based on its size and
location, there has been no recommendation for sur-

gery or treatment. When I told Allie about the spot, she said, "Okay," and returned to the living room to continue planning her honeymoon to Hawaii. She has obviously not changed her mind about treatment.

As Allie's mom, I have had moments when I question if I should encourage her to seek treatment; yet, life without chemo and hospitals has become very comfortable. My mother's heart breaks when I think that perhaps her life may be shortened by this awful disease. Right now, I am doing my best to focus on the future and allow her to make the decisions she feels are best. Even Allie's oncology team said they have nothing to offer that is worth diverting Allie's attention from preparing for her wedding and honeymoon. Please pray for strength as we process this new information and rely on God to guide our path.

03/28/2013 Email to Allie Speck's Prayer Warriors
Today we learned that a 19-year-old young man whom Allie met through his cancer battle has died. Allie's post on Facebook said, "He inspired my fight as well as many others. He didn't just survive. HE LIVED!" God bless his family as they mourn.

CHAPTER EIGHTEEN
SURRENDER TO HIS WILL

04/06/2013 Email to Allie Speck's Prayer Warriors
Today we tried to surprise Allison with a beautiful
bridal shower, but, somehow, she knew. Oh well!
It was a beautiful day of love, and everyone there
gathered around Allie, laid hands on her and prayed.
Each person attending wrote their favorite memory
with Allison, and, as we read them aloud, she had to
identify the guest. What a joyous day of celebrating
the amazing woman Allison has become and praying
blessings onto the amazing wife she will be.

Allison's Journal, April 17, 2013

Three days until the weekend when we will have a
Hawk Rock campout to celebrate Andy's birthday.
Twenty-eight days until my last day for finals and 60
days until my wedding! So close, yet so far.

♥Allie

Allison's Journal, April 19, 2013

"Humble yourselves, therefore, under God's mighty
hand, that he may lift you up in due time. Cast all your
anxiety on him because he cares for you. Be alert and
of sober mind. Your enemy the devil prowls around like
a roaring lion looking for someone to devour. Resist him,
standing firm in the faith, because you know that the

family of believers throughout the world is undergoing the same kind of sufferings. And the God of all grace, who called you to his eternal glory in Christ, after you have suffered a little while, will himself restore you and make you strong, firm and steadfast. To him be the power for ever and ever. Amen" (1 Peter 5:6–11).

♥Allie

04/22/2013 – Note from Allie's doctor: "LOVED THE WEDDING INVITATION!"
I will do everything I can to be there to celebrate Allie's special day! I am just so proud of Allie for all the decisions she has made and all of her strength moving forward through what seems like insurmountable odds. As I think about the Good Shepherd sermons we all heard yesterday, it makes me appreciate all the more how we all belong to Him no matter what. In difficult times, we are reminded of the Cross, but with the Cross comes the Good News! Anyway, just wanted to let you know how happy I was to get the wedding invitation. See you soon!

Allison's Journal, April 25, 2013

"And this is my prayer in my battle
When triumph is still on its way
I am a conqueror and co-heir with Christ
So firm on His promise I'll stand.

"All of my life
In every season
You are still God
I have a reason to sing
I have a reason to worship."
(Lyrics from "Desert Song")

♥Allie

Allison's Journal, May 12, 2013

All I have to do is write this paper so I can finish another paper and study for my final on Monday so I can get down to planning this wedding. Sometimes I think life consists of things you need to get done so you can do other things that need done so you can get to the things you should be doing and on and on and on. And college is a big crazy whirlwind that you are thrown into and then all of a sudden it drops you into the real world. Oh well, thankful for a life full of endless opportunities. BRING IT ON!

♥Allie

Facebook post written by Allison for Mother's Day, May 12, 2013

It is 3 a.m., which means it is Mother's Day. I debated about writing this because I literally have so much to say that I could write forever, but thanks are in order. I need to tell you that my mom is amazing!

When a mother gives birth to a daughter, she naturally has dreams and aspirations for her. I would imagine the rest of the mother's life she spends her time readjusting and letting go of those dreams as she finds out that no child is quite what you expect. Let's admit it, I was a strange child and dreamed larger-than-life dreams. I would have terrified any parent. I had my mom's imagination and my dad's fearlessness. These traits propelled me into anything from climbing to the top branch of a tree just to smell the air to insisting I travel to a foreign country by myself at the age of 12 to bringing home countless stray dogs, cats and hitchhikers. I never got into trouble with the law, but I was difficult in much bigger ways—ways that made my parents learn how to let go and trust.

My parents raised me with deeply rooted values and introduced me to a relationship with Jesus Christ, and for that I am forever grateful. They taught me how to love others and how to give even when I could not afford it. They taught me how to be strong and how to stand my ground, but also how to let go.

Throughout my life, though, my mom has been very special to me. Looking back, I find it very fitting that she was captain of the cheerleading squad in high school, for she has been my biggest cheerleader in life. I spent my childhood and high school years taking for granted the amazing way she loved me. Then when college

and cancer happened simultaneously, I suddenly realized: my mom is a superhero.

I don't think I can make you understand what my
mom has done for me over the past four years of my
life. No amount of writing can make you understand the
MONTHS of sleeping on a cold windowsill of a hospital
room, the endless days of driving back and forth to
hospitals with no sleep, sitting anxiously in waiting rooms
for hours, going without food and sleep just to be at
my bedside when I awoke, hunting down doctors to
take my case and refusing to take "no" for an answer,
and let's not even try to measure the amount of vomit
she has cleaned up through chemo treatments. Even
on days when she was physically sick, on days she was
exhausted, on days she was down or scared, she was
ALWAYS there for me. Because of that, I slept soundly
at night. I awoke from surgery and had her smiling face
be the first thing I saw. I could reach across my bedrail
and find a hand waiting to hold mine. I could yell for her
and know that she would come. And even on my worst
nights when I was in pain or when chemo caused scary
confusion, when it made me forget my name and have
frightening hallucinations, when all I could remember
was "mom" and "Robert Frost," she would sit and read
his poetry to me until I fell asleep. No matter what happened, she was always there fighting for me, putting her
own life on hold to help me fight for mine.

My mom gave me life and my mom saved my life.
Even when I wanted to give up, even when my hope
wavered, she was there to remind me who I was.
Because of my mom, I am a fighter. Because of my
mom, I am a dreamer. Because of my mom, I am alive
and LIVING, not just surviving.

As a result, in seven days, I will walk across the stage
at Messiah's commencement ceremony and receive a
diploma that some doctors told me I would never see.
And a month after that, I will marry an amazing man at
a wedding that would never have come together without my mom's help, and I will start a new adventure.

My mom never stopped believing in me, and she
never gave up on the amazing places the Lord would
take me.

My earliest memories are smelling her perfume in the morning, sitting in the bathtub while she read to me, having her listen to me while I read her stories I had written myself, and falling asleep with her by my bed. I thank God for the amazing mother He gave to me. And I hope that I will grow into a woman who is as strong, loving and caring as she is. And even after writing all of this, I have not begun to say what I want to say to tell the world how much I appreciate my mother. Happy Mother's Day, Mom! I love you to infinity and beyond.

05/18/2013 Email to Allie Speck's Prayer Warriors
Today Allison graduated magna cum laude from Messiah College (now Messiah University) with a major in English and a minor in Communications. She did all of this in four years despite a cancer diagnosis that resulted in multiple surgeries, chemotherapy and too many hospital stays. Her determination to graduate with her class was accomplished today, and she graduated with honors. We are so incredibly proud! And in the words of Allison, who stopped treatment months ago: "I need hair so my cap fits for graduation!" Today she wore that cap with pride on top of a beautiful head of hair. Words cannot express our joy and excitement as Allison begins her life after college and looks toward a bright future.

Allie's testimony, June 4, 2013

(INTRODUCTION) Our guest speaker is Allie Speck, who just graduated from Messiah and is getting married in nine days. She has an amazing story, and we invited her to share that story tonight.

Let's pray. Father God, I thank You so much for this evening and for every person who has gathered here. I am excited for the things You have to say to them, and I pray that You would allow me to be a vessel for Your words. I pray that You will be glorified and not my story. Thank You for all that You have done for me. I am excited to see what else You have in store. Amen!

Every time I tell my story, it is a little bit different, and God leads me down a new path to share His message. As I was praying and preparing to share, He kept bringing up one aspect to me, and that is the difference between believing IN God and believing God. Believing IN God means we believe in who God is, that He exists and that He came and died on the cross for our sins. Believing God means we take seriously what He promises us. When we read His promises in His Word, when He speaks those promises to our hearts, when He speaks to us through other people, we genuinely believe Him and trust what He says.

I grew up believing God. I was raised in the church, I went to a Christian college, and I had a strong desire to serve God. I genuinely believed Him and believed in Him. I felt that He had good plans for my life, and then something very unexpected happened. A large tumor was found on my liver during my freshman year of college, and my life changed completely! I really did not think it was cancer or very serious until a local doctor told me that the tumor appeared to be cancer and that if they could not remove it, I would die in six months to a year. So there I was, at 18 years old being told that I would be lucky if I saw 19 and that I definitely wouldn't see 20. And that did not make sense to me because God had spoken good plans for my life. I trusted that He would take care of me and suddenly it seemed like He wasn't.

After the diagnosis, I expected God to deliver me because that was all that made sense. If God removed this tumor, I could continue doing what I wanted to do. But that was not what happened. After an unsuccessful surgery to remove the tumor, I was told the good news was that I could start chemotherapy. I don't know about you, but that wasn't exactly good news to me. I was petrified of treatment. I did not want things to change. I wanted to stay in my comfortable little bubble where God took care of me and did what I wanted. I wasn't angry; I just did not understand. "If God loves me and wants to do what is best for me, why is He letting me suffer?" I was led to Proverbs 3:5: "Trust in the Lord with all your heart and lean not on your own understanding." So I decided that I was not going to understand and I wasn't very happy about that because I'm a person who likes to have a plan and know what is going on. But I said, "Okay, God, fine. I'm not going to understand." I tried the best I could to trust God, but I am going to tell you that I really didn't trust Him, because I was still terrified. As I focused on Proverbs 3:5, I thought, "It doesn't matter what my mind says; God promises good things." I started chemo. Over the next six months, I lost all of my hair and about 40 pounds and had serious side effects from the treatment. I had hallucinations that frightened me and told me that I was going to die and that I was just prolonging my death.

I remember, after my first chemo treatment, being so mentally, spiritually and physically exhausted that I fell on my bedroom floor and said, "I am done!" One chemo treatment and I was done. The doctors were not encouraging. But I heard God say to me, "It doesn't matter what the doctors say. I say I've got you." Now when I say, "God spoke to me," I don't mean that He came down and spoke to me and things got miraculously wonderful. In fact, during most of that time, I couldn't feel God at all. I felt tired and I felt sick and I felt alone.

What God spoke to me is that it doesn't matter how I feel; He has me. At that point I was told that my tumor had shrunk enough to schedule another liver surgery. So I went into the second surgery with a completely different attitude. Initially I thought that if there was a loving God, He would take away my tumor, for that is what a loving God would do. But in preparing for the second surgery, I had a different outlook. I thought, "God, whatever You know is best for my life, that is what I want to happen." I woke up from surgery and knew immediately that the tumor was gone. So, previously, in the span of 12 hours I went from healthy to supposedly on my deathbed. And then in another span of 12 hours, I went from almost accepting death to being completely healed.

I spent eight months cancer-free and then relapsed. The cancer came back in my liver and spread to my lungs, and I went through the same feelings of not understanding. But this time I was angry, because it was like a cruel joke that God would deliver me and then send me right back into it. But God continued to speak to me, saying, "It doesn't matter what your circumstances are; I've got you," and God never gets tired of telling me that. So I started treatment again, including chemo and tons of lung surgeries with lots of complications. I barely came out of the lung surgeries alive, with several emergency surgeries and really bad experiences. And after all the treatment and surgeries, they did a scan and told me that the cancer had spread to new places and they didn't have any other chemo options for me. I could do experimental treatment, but that wasn't guaranteed to help me. It could slow down the cancer but wouldn't cure it.

So there I was in another situation where I said, "God, You told me that You had good plans for my life. I felt You speak them to my heart. You told me through Your Word that You will never leave me or forsake me. That You are with me always." It was then that I felt it was time to stop receiving chemo. I felt God speak to my heart, saying, "You need to be done with this and trust Me completely." That was terrifying. But the more I thought about it, the more I realized what an amazing opportunity it was: I get to literally trust God with my life. I get to hand the reins over to God and say, "Here; Your will be done, not mine." So that was what I did, and I felt God speak to me in my spirit, saying, "You don't need to worry. You don't need to fear death. You don't need to fear cancer. You just need to believe Me." God has shown me that it does not matter what my doubt says, what my confusion says, what my fear says, because God says over and over again that He has me. So I stopped chemo, and that is where I have been for about a year. Many of my symptoms have decreased, and a lot of my illness has seemed to disappear. Now, my scans aren't clear; in fact, my scans show tumor growth. But I believe that God has good plans for me no matter what the scans say, no matter what the doctors say, no matter what my logic says. I know what God has spoken to my heart.

Jesus says to me, "Didn't I promise you that I would be with you and that I will never leave you or forsake you?" God says, "I promised you something and I do *not break My promises." That is what God told me to speak about tonight. He has good plans for everyone, but maybe the victory isn't what we thought. Maybe the victory is peace in the storm instead of being taken out of the storm. Maybe the victory is in here [pointing to her heart]. Maybe the victory is when the storm and darkness come and we have no fear because we trust that God is with us.*

I guarantee that no matter what happens, God works all things for good. It says that in Romans 8:28. The question is, do you believe Him? When fear comes, do you question God and say, "I don't understand. Where are You? Why don't I feel You?" When doubt comes, do you say, "What are You doing?" When circumstances in life aren't what you thought they would be, what is your response? I am here tonight to tell you that your response can be, "It doesn't matter what my circumstances are, it doesn't matter what I feel, it doesn't matter what the world says...God promises not to leave or forsake me. He promises to be with me always. He promises that He will work everything for good." So tonight, if you have something you are fearing or something you are worried about, or if you have challenges in your life that you need to hand over to God, saying, "I believe that You have me and that You're not letting go," then I want you to pray with me now and hand those things over to God, saying, "Even when I feel afraid, even when I feel doubt, even when bad things happen, I will trust You because You know what is best."

Please bow your head. "Father God, I thank You that our circumstances don't change Your promises to us. We not only have the privilege of believing in You, but we also can trust You because You are good and You love us so much that You will never, ever leave or forsake us. I pray that You would speak that truth into each heart tonight." I ask everyone to pray with me, "Father God, I know You have got me. It does not matter how I feel. Lord, I feel afraid. Lord, I feel worried..." Whatever it is you feel, I want you to say, "God, I want You to take my feelings. In return I receive Your promise, and I will stand on that promise, trusting You with the outcome. Amen."

06/07/2013 Email to Allie Speck's Prayer Warriors
Allison continues to trust God with her health and
her future. She feels good, and wedding plans are full
steam ahead. One week from tomorrow, she will walk
down the aisle.

There have been many times that I sit back and
reflect on where our family has been and where we
are today, and I realize how many miracles God has
provided. Several doctors told Allie her case was
hopeless four years ago. One doctor gave her six
months to live in December of 2009. We were blessed to find a group of doctors whom God has worked
through to grant Allie "the hope and future" that
she claimed in her high school graduation scripture
choice, Jeremiah 29:11.

Life has been hectic lately with wedding plans, the
end of school for Andy, and college graduation for
Allie. During the stressful moments I remind myself
that, with God's help, we have overcome so many
hurdles. On June 15th, Allison will continue trusting the Lord as she walks down the aisle, beginning
a new journey. She is amazing, and her awesome
brother, Andy, will be right by her side, celebrating
with her. And we, the extremely proud parents, will
be celebrating life and peace and thanking God for
His blessings.

06/22/2013 Email to Allie Speck's Prayer Warriors
ALLISON IS MARRIED! It was an amazing day! Not
only gorgeous weather, but also God's Spirit of love
and joy was experienced throughout the day. If our
God is for us, then who can be against us? (Romans
8:31). Thank you for sharing in our extreme joy and
thanksgiving for God's healing miracle and love!

It was shortly after the wedding that Allie came to me and told me
she was having trouble breathing and had pain in her back. She requested scans and asked that I get them scheduled. I remember this moment
so well, and I thought it was just like Allie not to say anything about
being in pain or discomfort until the wedding was over. So, I contacted

Johns Hopkins, and scans were done. I always took Allie to Hopkins to review test results, but this time Allie told me that she wanted it to be her husband who took her. I realized then that my role had changed, and, although it was hard, I said that made perfect sense. They returned from the appointment, and Allison called me to say that the scans were "the same" and there were no changes. About a month later, with Allie's permission, I contacted the doctor and requested copies of her scan results that I kept for quick reference in case of an ER visit. I remember opening my email and reading the scans and being shocked. There was nothing status quo about these results. Her tumors had grown, some quite significantly. She had multiple tumors throughout her lungs and liver; the largest tumors measured three inches in size. I immediately emailed her oncologist and asked if he had reviewed these scans with Allison during her visit. This was his response:

> Hello, I believe that Allie knows the extent of her disease because she and I reviewed her scans together. We don't have anything curative to offer Allie. The best any treatment will be able to do is hold things at bay for a time. In a recent trial, 35 percent of patients receiving Allie's treatment had a six-month progression-free survival rate. All that we have to offer Allison right now is treatments that will hopefully slow down the progression of the tumors. My sincere hope is that we will accomplish better... perhaps shrink tumors...and do so in a way that does not compromise her ability to enjoy her life.

I was struck by the fact that Allison obviously was continuing to trust her Lord and Savior rather than believe the report of man—even to the point that she told us that her scans looked unchanged. I was scared but in awe of her amazing faith and strength to see beyond the scan results to all the joys that life had to offer. I never told her that I saw those scan results, and we never talked about them.

10/02/2013 Email to Allie Speck's Prayer Warriors
It has been quite a while since you have received an update. As Allie is a newly married young woman, I felt that it was not my place to send updates. Allie has had some changes and has made some decisions, and it is her place to explain. Below is an update written by Allie:

Hello, prayer warriors!

I would like to start by saying that it has been three and a half months since the wedding, and I am absolutely loving married life! We are settled into our apartment, and it's starting to feel like home. Thank you to everyone who supported our marriage through prayer. The Lord has been so good to us!

Secondly, we wanted to update you on what is happening medically so you can be in prayer. About a month ago I began having significant symptoms, including extreme shortness of breath, fatigue, night sweats and weight loss. I also started to have difficulty swallowing. The symptoms got so severe that they were interfering with my day-to-day life, and I chose not to ignore them.

After visiting Hopkins for a scan, I learned there was significant growth of the tumors in my lungs and liver. One tumor in particular is pressing against my esophagus, causing my swallowing issues. For the year and a half that I have been off treatment, I have had peace about it. Even my doctors were surprised by the slow growth of my tumors. Recently, the peace I had felt was removed and replaced with a need to DO something. This made no sense to me because, as far as I knew, there were no legitimate treatment options.

When I learned that the tumors had grown, I was also informed that there were some new treatment options available. The biggest one being "immunotherapy." It is a new way of treating cancer and is not chemo. I am signed up for the trial, but there is a waiting list. Meanwhile, I will begin a chemo pill that is new and promising. I will also be having a consult to begin radiation therapy to shrink the tumors in my lungs.

So, I am still fully trusting God and surrendering to His will. I know all healing comes from Him. Please pray with me that He works through this new medicine to bring about the healing. Please keep me and my husband in your prayers as we navigate doctor appointments, possible side effects and complications along with the new responsibilities of being married. God is our strength, and we know He will provide.

Allie

10/16/2013 Email to Allie Speck's Prayer Warriors
Your prayers are being answered! This past week, Allie looked amazing! She worked two eight-hour days and one ten-hour day! She went grocery shopping and even went to the gym. Today she received her tattoo markings for radiation and will begin treatment tomorrow at a facility near her job. This amazing young lady plans to get her radiation treatments over her lunch hour. This past Sunday, Allie shared her testimony with three different congregations. Completely amazing and inspiring!

We claim this scripture, Matthew 21:22: "If you believe, you will receive whatever you ask for in prayer." We know that Allie's amazing improvement is the result of answered prayers.

This past Saturday night, Andy was crowned Homecoming King at his high school, and Allie was there to cheer him on. It was a wonderful night for the Speck family!

Just to give you a little background history, in 2008 Allison was voted Susquenita High School's Homecoming Queen and in 1976 Tom was voted Susquenita's Homecoming King. Andy was told before the dance that he had big shoes to fill to keep up the family tradition, and he did not disappoint! As for me, I have earned the title of "Queen Mum," as I have given birth to royalty twice!

We thank God for the happiness this occasion brought to our family.

10/21/2013 Email to Allie Speck's Prayer Warriors
We are in need of strong prayers. About 2:00 this morning Allie began to have very sharp pain in her chest that did not resolve with pain medication. Her radiation treatment was canceled, and we took her to the ER. The doctor found nothing significantly wrong, but that does not explain her severe pain. They gave her medication and sent her home with pain pills. We pray this pain will disappear as suddenly as it appeared. Allie will not be able to work or drive while taking the pain medicine. We know that God hears all of our prayers, and, from a mother's heart, I am asking that you pray Allie's pain away, completely.

I wanted to share part of an email from one of Allie's nurses at Hopkins because it reminds us what an inspiration she is to others:

Allie is an amazing, strong, inspiring and beautiful young woman who has inspired me as well. I keep a picture of Allie and me on my desk at work, and there isn't a day that goes by that I'm not reminded of her courage and strength.

10/22/2013 Email to Allie Speck's Prayer Warriors
Your prayers are being answered, and we are overwhelmed at the responses we have received as we witness heaven's gates being flooded with requests for Allie and our family. Allie is not pain-free, but there is improvement. Her strength is amazing!

I was able to take her for radiation today. They gave her pain medication so she could tolerate lying flat for the treatment. She had soup for lunch and even stopped by work to get things to work from home. She was exhausted when we were done, but she did it.

I pray that Allie will have a restful, pain-free night and a better day tomorrow. We are blessed to be able

to communicate our needs and have them prayed for
by so many people.

Allison's Journal, October 26, 2013

Noticed a red square rash on my back and a matching
red square rash on my chest. It is a burn from my radiation treatment. I guess this is what being radioactive
looks like. Praying there is just as much damage being
done to the tumors.

♥Allie

11/12/2013 Email to Allie Speck's Prayer Warriors

It is time for an update. We have experienced a roller
coaster of emotions. As Allie's radiation treatments
progressed, so did her chest pain. On November 1st,
Allie received her 14th and final radiation treatment.
During the treatments, Allie went to the ER three
times for pain so intense that she could not eat or
drink. Each time Allie got some relief and was able to
go home.

On Sunday, Allie had so much pain that she was
unable to swallow her own saliva. We took her to the
ER, where she was admitted and had a procedure
to put a scope down her throat. The test showed a
bloody, raw section of esophagus that matched the
area being radiated. The doctor told us it was one of
the most severe cases of radiation burn he has ever
seen and was thankful that he did not perforate her
fragile esophagus with the scope.

Allie had a PICC line, which is basically a long-term
IV, placed in her right upper arm and started IV
nutrition that night. She will remain in the hospital,
receiving pain medication and nutrition, until she is
able to tolerate eating, drinking and taking pills.

As a result of her ongoing pain and the prescribed
pain medication, Allie has been unable to drive and
therefore unable to work. After missing two weeks of
work, she talked with her boss and agreed to write

a letter of resignation. Allie was sad that she had to give up her first job after college, but we feel confident that God has something else planned for her.

This cancer journey is overwhelming in so many ways. Pray for sustained trust in God, as we know that He is in control of all circumstances. We are trusting God with Allie's life and health, and we know that He has a "hope and a future" planned that we are unable to see with our earthly eyes.

11/21/2013 Email to Allie Speck's Prayer Warriors
Your prayers are needed! Allison spent a very long week in the hospital getting her pain under control and getting nutrition through her PICC line. She wants to be home doing what most of us take for granted...eating, talking and laughing with her husband.

She came home from the hospital late Monday evening but is struggling with nausea, pain and lack of energy. We are giving her IV fluids overnight, but she is very weak and feels sick most of the time.

She is frustrated with the duration of this setback. We ask you to pray for strength to continue this fight, peace in Allie's spirit, healing in her body and renewed energy.

Allison's Journal, November 24, 2013

Hold on. It WILL get better.
   Dear God, if today I lose my hope, please remind me that Your plans are better than my dream.

♥Allie

12/14/2013 Email to Allie Speck's Prayer Warriors
Allie remains on the home IV nutrition and still struggles to eat, battling both nausea and pain. There are good and bad days. We continue to have family spending days at the apartment to help her with meals and appointments, since she is still not able to drive.

Thanks for continuing to uphold Allie and our family in prayer. The struggle is unbearable sometimes, but God always lifts the burden when we let Him. Peace and love as we celebrate the true reason for the season...JESUS!

Facebook post written by Allison, December 17, 2013

WARNING: It is about to get real. I am laying myself bare before all of you because you need to know you are not alone. This week has been hell for me. My radiation burns seem like they still aren't healing, and, after two months of not eating, my body is breaking down. Even more, my spirit is breaking. I am not strong enough to do anything on my own. This week I descended into frustration, hopelessness and anxiety to where I could do nothing but cry.

I have held fast to the Lord for four years, through endless physical and spiritual trials, and somehow this recent trial has almost pulled me away from the God I love. Why do I tell you this? Because this week, when I fell in a heap, defeated, I let go of my pride and cried for help. Through the darkness came the most amazing people. My family, a dear friend and my husband. And when I was not strong enough, they fought back the darkness and carried me to Jesus.

I am not where I need to be. It will take time. But they will carry me until I can walk, and, with the power and promises of Christ, our Lord, and the Holy Spirit, I will not be destroyed. Today I am promising you this from the valley and someday, after I have suffered a little while, I will sing it from the mountain with a spirit so on fire, the devil will not quench it. God has already won! He hears me. He knows my voice. He does not disappoint. He is strong in my weakness. I will not be destroyed. I will not be destroyed. I am a daughter of the King. A sister to the living Christ. I will not be destroyed. AMEN and AMEN!

♥Allie

Allison's Journal, December 20, 2013

Today I had another scope of my throat to figure out why I am having trouble swallowing. Found out that my esophagus was almost completely blocked by scar tissue. The doctor was able to remove the tissue, and swallowing is so much easier. There are still some burns and a few raw areas, but my esophagus is healing and looks SO much better than it did a month ago. Thank You, Jesus!

♥Allie

12/29/2013 Email to Allie Speck's Prayer Warriors
On December 28th Allison turned 23! What a beautiful blessing! We are so proud of the strength, faith and courage she has demonstrated as she faced situations that most people cannot imagine. Love you, Allie!

We pray everyone had a blessed Christmas with family and friends. We diverted a potential Christmas disaster on 12/23. Andy stayed at the apartment with Allie and called me at work to say that Allie was not feeling well. I left work and found her pale, tired, sweating, feverish and very short of breath. Even though she did not want to go, I took her to the local hospital. She was admitted overnight and received blood. By morning she felt better and demanded to be discharged to enjoy Christmas Eve services. That is our girl! We celebrated our Savior's birth together, and it was an amazing family experience!

Wishing each of you a blessed New Year filled with God's promises. Love and thanks as we reflect on how much we have to be grateful for this past year. We are blessed. Trusting God and pressing on.

I remember thinking that prayer, oral chemo and trust in God were the best options for Allie. There were several times when she became overwhelmed by anxiety and fear. She would call and ask me to come to the apartment, sit with her and read scripture. I found myself fighting for her when it used to be the other way around. She had battled for more than four years, and she was weary. I gladly assumed the role of Allie's personal warrior, protector and spiritual guardian.

01/20/2014 Email to Allie Speck's Prayer Warriors
The holidays were rough. Allie and Tom were both
sick on Christmas Day. Allie improved with medicine, inhalers and rest. Tom ended up in the ER, but
he is improving. Please pray for both of them.

On New Year's Day, Allie was vomiting with terrible
pain in her stomach and back and had shortness of
breath. Allison asked us to pray for her. She fell into
a deep sleep, the vomiting stopped and the pain was
controlled with medication. We went to Hopkins the
next day, and testing determined it was a GI bug.

Sunday, I went to the altar at church and asked God
to confirm what He planned to do with Allie. Either
we were moving toward a healing or we were not,
and I needed to know. I asked for confirmation. It
was a scary request.

The next evening, I had an email from Hopkins
stating, "The radiologists thought that Allison's last
scan was actually stable to improved, compared
with September!" As I read this email, I cried as I
realized that God had answered my prayer for confirmation of the direction of our journey. This was
the first encouraging scan result Allie has had. I
thank God for hearing my prayer and answering it.

Allie continues to receive home IV therapy and has a
weekly nurse visit to change her PICC line dressing.
She is swallowing better and able to eat food. The
goal is to wean her off the IV feedings and back onto
real food. Her breathing is labored with exertion but
improved with inhalers. Her lungs have seen a lot of
trauma due to multiple surgeries and radiation, but
each day she seems a little stronger.

On January 10th, she required outpatient surgery
to remove an abscess from her breast. She breezed
through the surgery and was home that evening. The
area is still healing, and we thank God that there was
no sign of cancer.

The focus of my devotion in *Jesus Calling* said to
come to Jesus with positive expectations, knowing
that there is no limit to what He can accomplish.
We are not to be discouraged if prayers seem to be
unanswered. Time teaches us to wait upon Jesus and
trust Him in the dark. Instead of letting difficulties
draw us into worry, we need to view them as setting
the scene for God's glorious intervention.

We await that glorious intervention as we press on
and trust that God's plan is better than ours.

02/23/2014 Email to Allie Speck's Prayer Warriors
Allison has had a PICC line with IV nutrition since
November, when the radiation destroyed her esophagus. We have been weaning the feedings and giving
six small meals a day. Her weight is 104 pounds.
Some days are good, some days are not so good, and
some days are completely overwhelming.

She healed from her breast surgery and is scheduled for more outpatient surgery on March 3rd. She
will be getting a port placed and having two lumps
removed. The surgeon feels the lumps could be a
spread of her cancer.

Pray for strength, peace and comfort for Allie. This
has been a very long battle. She is tired and just
wants to feel normal. She misses everyday activities like driving her car, going out to eat, shopping
and going to the movies. We are asking God to
restore her completely.

Many days feel like we are at the bottom of the pit
looking up and the devil is telling us to give up. But
God has placed a promise in Allie's heart and spirit.
We will stand firm on our faith because only God can
provide a complete healing for Allie.

I remember how weak and short of breath Allie was right before the surgery to have a new port placed to start chemo, so I was shocked when she
called and asked if we wanted to meet her and her husband at the movies. I

cried tears of joy when we walked into the lobby of the movie theater and there she stood, dressed up and smiling, waiting for us to join them for an evening that everyone else often takes for granted. That is one of my favorite memories from what would become the last week of Allie's life.

03/06/2014 Email to Allie Speck's Prayer Warriors – Allison's Final Update
I never thought I would write this email. Allie's surgery was three days ago. She had a new port placed in her chest and two tumors removed. Due to complications, she had to return to surgery and was not discharged from the hospital until very late. She was starving and demanded that we have Red Lobster takeout waiting for her at the apartment. She only ate a little bit, but she savored it and thanked us for having it ready for her. As I said "good night" and "I love you," I did not know it would be the last time she would say it back to me.

The next day Tom stayed at the apartment with Allie. When I arrived after work, Allie was unresponsive. We called 911, and an ambulance took her to the ER. We arrived at the ER, and Allie seemed alert but very tired. The doctor said she was severely dehydrated and needed blood. I believed that she would be given fluids and blood and we would go home like we always did.

The ER doctor said her chest X-ray showed her lungs were full of tumors and asked how much oxygen she used at home. When we said she did not use oxygen, he was amazed. Her liver and kidney levels showed signs of organ failure, and when the doctor used the words *critical* and *ICU*, it got our attention. Allison was slipping in and out of consciousness, and we were being told she may not live the night.

The doctor entered the room to discuss what should be done if Allie's heart or breathing stopped. When the doctor said, "What is the plan?" Allie sat straight up on the stretcher, pulled off her oxygen mask, looked the doctor in the eye, and said, "God has a plan for me!" She laid back down, closed her eyes and did not speak again.

My friend took me home to get a change of clothes. When we returned to the hospital parking lot, she asked how to pray for Allie. For the first time, we prayed that God's WILL would be done; that He would either heal her on this earth or take her home, but I asked that He not let her suffer. Although I cried many tears, I had such peace when I handed Allie over to God completely.

She was admitted to the ICU about midnight. She did not respond, nor did she appear to be in discomfort. One by one, family members left the bedside. At around 3:00 a.m. on March 5th, Allie's husband and I held her hands as she drew her last breath on this earth and her first breath in heaven. Although we knew she was sick, we never expected her to leave us so quickly. What I can tell you is that after she drew her last breath, which was very peaceful, a smile appeared on her lips, and I knew that she was looking into the face of Jesus. Allie no longer struggles. She is now in the presence of her Lord and Savior.

We were blessed to have Allie as our daughter for 23 years. She changed many lives and lived a full and joyous life. While we will miss her terribly, she has completed her journey. Her life will be remembered as an amazing testimony of faith.

CHAPTER NINETEEN

A LIFE WELL LIVED

I remember meeting with the funeral director to discuss Allison's services. One of his questions was what clothing we would like her to wear. At that moment, I had a flashback to Allie's wedding day and remembered her telling me that she had never felt more beautiful than when she wore her wedding gown. She was so radiant and made an absolutely angelic bride. She stood at the altar and praised God with her hands lifted during the worship music. It was obvious to me that Allison should wear her wedding dress. I wept as I pictured Allison in heaven approaching the throne to meet Jesus in her wedding gown as she became part of the bride of Christ for all eternity.

Eulogy written by Allie's oncology doctor

> Although I cannot be here with all of you today, it makes my heart truly alive with joy to know that we are all bound by a common thread—that the beautiful and miraculous woman we are celebrating changed each of our lives forever. God brought us together through His lovely daughter Allie, and, through her, we have all become much closer to Him.
>
> Just like all of you, the day I met Allie, my life was changed forever. You see, I had returned to work after the birth of my first son, and I was struggling mightily to learn to do the kind of work that I do while also learning how to be a new mother and wife. One day when I was feeling particularly downtrodden, I realized God asked me to do this work, so I must ask Him to help me put things into perspective. So, after one particularly difficult

evening, I sat in my car in the parking garage at Johns Hopkins at 2 a.m. and asked Him to help me understand this role He had created for me. The next day, on a day when I was not supposed to be seeing patients, I was scheduled to see Allie following her liver biopsy. SHE was the answer to my prayers! And now, I understand why.

We are told, as oncologists, that we must draw boundaries between ourselves and our patients for the purposes of self-preservation. With Allie, all those rules went right out the window. How could they not? Allie was just about the easiest person to love. She wore her pain, her struggles, her triumphs and her beloved faith right there on her sleeve so that we could all experience it with her. When Allie walked into our clinic, darkness was immediately replaced by light. In the generous, loving manner she undoubtedly inherited from her mother, she made it her business to get to know our other patients, to become part of this new community, and to leave her indelible mark on it. And, as you well know, when Allie meant business, Allie meant business! Like a kindergarten teacher on the first day of school, Allie immediately got organized, getting to know everyone's names, disease stories, families—and found little ways she could ease their suffering with acts as simple as her beautiful smile. She particularly befriended a fiery little three-year-old redhead, who made it very clear that he did NOT appreciate coming into the clinic when "his Allie" was not there. Those two would sit and chat about life like two elders on the front porch. That was Allie—no matter how deep her suffering, she made it her business to bring light to others, and, in turn, lightened their loads.

As many of you know, there came a time in the natural history of Allie's disease when we did not have any therapy that, based on what I came to call "earthly medical evidence," would cure her. I didn't get too far into my shallow explanation of other treatments we could use to slow the progression of her disease when Allie made a profoundly courageous and faithful decision. She wished to stop all therapy and turn her health over to God's will. This was the resolution of many months of her struggling to reconcile her desire to rely on Him fully, but also accept that the medicine she received must be part of His plan.

Friends, what followed that decision defies any conventional medical explanation but is, in my mind, a miraculous testament to Allie's faith despite the fact that we are gathered here to commemorate her passing. After the decision to stop treatment, Allie spent a year in nearly perfect health, and in that year accomplished more, experienced more and brought hope and love to more people than most of us ever will in our lifetimes. She brought her light all the way to east Africa on a mission. She traveled with her family. She celebrated her graduation from Messiah with her dear friends, which, I can tell you from all the paper-writing sessions she persevered through during clinic while bags of chemotherapy were running through her veins, was a testament to her stunning tenacity and intellect. And, most importantly, she followed her heart, became engaged to and married the love of her life.

Since June 15, 2013, I have told every friend, nurse, medical student, resident physician, oncologist and patient I know about Allie's wedding. Seriously, half of my town knows how she designed, coordinated and handmade every detail! To me, her wedding was the single greatest representation of fearless and faithful love I have ever encountered. Allie's oncologist and my teacher, David Loeb, turned to me that day and said, "When people ask you why we do what we do and never lose hope, it is because of this day." I can feel nothing but joy that I will always remember the last time I saw her, beaming in that gorgeous dress, laughing like I'd never heard her laugh before, and dancing in her father's arms.

Several months after the wedding, Allie and I had a long conversation on the phone that, unbeknownst to me, would be our last. After some girl-talk about the wedding and honeymoon, we resumed a narrative we'd had for years about her struggle to reconcile her reliance on God and her desire to pursue additional treatment. It was the first time we really got to talking about death. We talked about the purpose of great suffering and of Christ's suffering.

After hearing her speak, as she did in so many of her
testimonials, I was reminded that every once in a while
God gives us someone like Allie, someone who lives
so fully—in health and in sickness, in fear and in love,
in darkness and in light—that they don't just touch the
lives of everyone around them; they also transform
them and give them purpose. Allie was God's gift to us.
And although her beauty, determination, courage and
unflappable devotion made us all feel better about ourselves and about this world, she never did belong to us.
She always belonged to Him.

Eulogy by Dr. Loeb

Dear friends,
   I have to start with an apology. I am so sorry I can't be
here to say these words myself, but my duties prevent it.
   It was an honor to be asked to say a few words about
Allie, just as it was an honor to know her and an honor
to care for her. I write these words with a heavy heart
because a brilliant light was extinguished far too early.
Allison was a remarkable young woman whom I will
never forget. It was an honor and a privilege to take
care of her, and I miss her warmth, her smile and, most
of all, her grace. There are many things I could say
about Allie, but many of them you already know. What I
would like to tell you about Allie, and about my relationship with her, is how much she taught me. Doctors often
say that we learn something from every patient we take
care of, but Allie's case was special. Certainly, I learned
about her particular cancer in young adults. Allie had a
very rare tumor, and whenever I take care of someone
with a rare disease, there is something to learn about
the cancer and about treating it. But in Allie's case,
what I learned is more important. I learned about living,
and I learned about hope.
   Allie knew her prognosis wasn't great from the very
beginning. Some of the treatments she was forced
to endure had terrible side effects, and she spent a
significant amount of time in the hospital and in pain.
In the past few months, she endured horrible pain
and had tremendous difficulty eating and drinking.

None of this kept Allie from hoping for the future and from living her life. When I met Allie, in January 2010, she was a freshman at Messiah, just on the brink of adulthood. Looking back on my notes from that first encounter, I am struck by two things I wrote: first, "Her long-term goals are to do missionary work abroad, either in Africa or in Southeast Asia," and second, "She has a long-term boyfriend of several years." From the beginning, Allison expressed hope that she would be able to do missionary work and hope that she would be married. Nothing that our treatment put her through dampened that hope, which she held onto so tightly. And nothing that we did kept her from not only having those hopes, but also achieving her goals. While undergoing treatments that would be difficult for anyone to endure, Allie graduated from Messiah, did missionary work in Africa, and in a ceremony I was honored to attend, got married. In short, she lived her life, and she let nothing extinguish her hope. Perhaps most importantly, she did these things with a quiet grace that I have rarely seen. Allie taught me never to let go of hope, never to stop living, and never to question why bad things have happened. The best way I can honor her, and I hope I can do this, is to never forget the lessons she taught me...to never give up hope, to never stop living and to accept what happens with grace and dignity. In short, I hope to never forget to live life the way Allison did.

Tribute from Allie's high school musical director dedicating the show to Allie

We dedicate this show and program in honor of Allison Speck, who was a student and long-time member of our theater programs during her time at Susquenita.

Allie was everything you needed to make a great show! She was hard-working no matter what part she played and had great respect for her directors and fellow cast members. Her short time on earth will never be forgotten. She showed us how to live life to the fullest and to never give up hope. We will miss her, but we will not forget her. We know that she will be at every rehearsal and show in spirit. See you when the next curtain opens, Allie.

A note from one of Allie's nurses at Hopkins

I am writing with tears in my eyes at the news of Allie's passing. I hope you know how much of an impact Allie's strength, courage and drive to conquer her dreams have made on me and my family. I try very hard not to get attached to patients, but Allie found her way into my heart and will always have a place there. She was one of my first patients, and she inspires me every day to be a better nurse and person. I have never met anyone like her, and I am honored to have known and cared for her. I have a heavy heart today, but whenever I see her picture sitting on my desk, I look up and know that heaven has gained an angel and that God has a purpose for everything. She is now without pain and at peace.

A note from one of Allie's college professors

I am heartbroken to hear of Allie's passing. She was so brave and so strong for so long that I think, even though your last message seemed dire, I never really thought this day would come. As you grieve, I hope you will find some consolation in the palpable reality that Allie, in her short life, did more for the kingdom than many of us will accomplish in a much greater span of years. That is to say, there are different measures of time, and while, by some measures, Allie's time here was short, by others, her time was full and rich and well-spent.

We planned two days for visitation prior to Allie's funeral service. I remember standing the first evening for over six and a half hours greeting friends, family and strangers. People stood in line for two to three hours to express their condolences. There were so many people who had never met Allie but knew of her journey through my emails or through social media. They came to tell us how her faith and trust in God influenced them and changed many lives. How incredible! The first night we greeted almost one thousand people. I was in awe and overwhelmed at the outpouring of love we witnessed.

An excerpt from an article by a local news reporter who attended Allison's funeral

Hundreds say final good-bye to Marysville woman, 23, who died from cancer

Allie Speck, 23, of Marysville, died early Wednesday morning after battling cancer in her liver and lungs since she was 18. She died with one hand clasping her husband's, and one clasping the hand of her mother, Zina Speck.

On Monday, more than 500 people attended her funeral service. It was all done in Allie's style, her mother said. The wildflowers were in tones of purple, yellow and orange. No roses, no carnations, Zina Speck told the funeral planners—the woman to whom they were paying tribute was far from standard.

Allie was a creative thinker with a passion for traveling; a faithful woman whose God was her one and only; and an adventurous, inspiring person who always seemed aware of the struggles of those around her. Allie fought a public battle with cancer, sharing her testimony on many occasions.

And while cancer was a large part of Allie's life and death, it's not her story.

What you have to understand about Allie is that she was a cancer patient, but she was much more than that. Her story is not about cancer, but about her faith, perseverance and strength.

More than 1,500 people lined up Sunday and Monday to pay their respect to Allie's family, say good-bye, and share their memories. Some waited for three hours in line. Many people who were there, Zina Speck said, had never met Allie, but were inspired by her story—they'd seen her Facebook page or heard her speak at a church or youth group. They were impressed by her selflessness, which was apparent from a very young age.

A letter was found in the Speck house this week that Allie had written to Santa when she was a child:

I don't want much for Christmas, I just want snow. I figured if you can make reindeer fly, you can make it snow. I wanted a bracelet but I don't want anything on it because I want to start a charm bracelet, so I wondered if you could take all my presents and give them to the homeless and the poor and the kids who don't have any toys so they can have a Merry Christmas. They need them more than I do. Oh, and by the way, the kids in the orphanage in Russia don't have any boots, so they can't play in the snow, so I wondered if you could give them some boots. Thanks. Love, Allison Speck

Zina Speck had one message for those who attended Allie's funeral: "Do not mourn her. Rejoice that you knew her."

Last December, when Allie was going through some intense radiation, Tom had a conversation with an old friend. The man's wife asked Tom if he believed angels walk among us. He said he did, and the friend's wife then took it a step further.

"Well Tom, listening to you talking, it sounds to me like your daughter was an angel and she was put here for a reason," the woman said.

"When she said that," Tom said, "it just floored me that she could be right."

Pastor James Parker echoed those thoughts Monday. "I always told her she danced with angels," he said. "Sometimes we entertain angels and we're unaware. I am certainly wondering."

Their angel died with one hand in her husband's, the other in her mother's. They say a smile appeared on her lips after she took her last breath. Zina Speck believes her daughter was looking into the face of Jesus.

The same sentiment was heard during a eulogy written by one of Allie's doctors and read Monday at her funeral by her mother.

"Allie was God's gift to us," Zina Speck read. "She never really did belong to us. She always belonged to Him."

An email from one of Allie's nurses

I met you and Allie about two and a half years ago when she came to the hospital where I work. First of all, she was my all-time favorite patient ever, and I will always remember meeting her. I remember how we talked for a long time about missions and how important they were to both of us. I remember her saying that she really wanted to go to Africa but was unable to go at that time. I'm glad she ended up going! I remember hearing all about her story and her faith. I have been receiving your email updates for the past two and a half years, so I feel like I know you and your family. I was upset over her passing, but I wanted you to know that your daughter inspired me. I have been on three mission trips to Guatemala and hope to do more. I want you to know that Allie touched so many lives...even people that you don't even realize. I am grateful to have met her.

An email from a doctor at Hopkins who never met Allie

Your beautiful daughter and your family are an inspiration. She was an incredible girl and is a reminder to me why I became a physician. She touched many people, even those she did not meet. I am truly sorry for your loss.

06/10/2014 Email to Allie Speck's Prayer Warriors
June 5th was three months that Allison has been gone from our life. I have learned so much in those three months. We have learned that we are stronger than we imagined. I learned that Andy spent almost five years being the most amazing, giving and understanding young man we could have possibly asked for. He deserves every ounce of praise and is a fantastic baseball player, loving brother and amazing son. I have learned that support, love and understanding do not always come from the people you expect. Sometimes it comes from people you barely know, people you just met, or people you may never see again.

Andy will graduate on June 6th and attend Messiah College in the fall. Allison is smiling because she wanted him to go to Messiah. She felt he needed the spiritual support and sense of Christian community that is felt there. Andy has an amazing opportunity to travel to Lima, Peru, and will visit Machu Picchu. Allie would love this sense of adventure and travel. He has promised to write her name all over Lima and Machu Picchu. I have assured him that Allie is with him wherever he goes.

Allie and her illness introduced me to her amazing group of friends who truly get what it means to love as God loves us. I learned that God's love isn't found in a church pew or even in people who call themselves Christians; it is found in people who sacrificed time to provide care and support to our family during our grief and loss. Unexpected friends, in some of the most unlikely circumstances. Amazing!

My final thought is to thank everyone who keeps Allie's spirit alive every day. I have read that one of people's biggest fears is to be forgotten when they die. Allison was incredibly giving and caring. She left a legacy of love, faith and friendship. She will never be forgotten;...she lives on through the lives she touched and changed.

Be kind to one another, never take a true friend for granted, grab hold of life's amazing opportunities, and trust God when you face life's obstacles. Blessings to all who have shown us love. We are truly grateful.

11/15/2014 Email to Allie Speck's Prayer Warriors – Allie and God are watching
I am writing to you today to share a beautiful blessing!

November 5th was eight months since Allie went to be with her Lord. I try to ensure the day of her passing is not filled with sadness but hope. My personal mission is to continue sharing Allie's journey and faith. I know God's plan is better; notice I did not say easier.

I asked God to let me know that Allie can see how we are honoring her life and keeping her faith and spirit alive. I wanted a message confirming that she knows her life story will not be forgotten and that she made such a huge difference in many lives.

As I was driving to work and listening to the local Christian radio station Word FM at 88.1 in Harrisburg, what do I hear? ALLIE'S VOICE! This is what I heard:

Hi! My name is Allie, and three years ago I was diagnosed with cancer, and my mom has been amazing! She has stood by me through everything.

(RADIO ANNOUNCER): THERE IS HOPE, GRACE AND A MOMENT DESIGNED BY GOD, JUST FOR YOU.

She cut back her work hours so she could come and stay with me at the hospital. She gave up such a huge portion of her life, and I can honestly say that if it was not for her, I would not be alive. She is such an amazing woman of God and such a prayer warrior. Not only was she there for me, she also was on her knees for me. I thank God every single day that He blessed me with such an amazing mom.

It was unbelievable! I was stunned to hear Allie talking about how much she appreciated and loved me. I was overwhelmed...and not because she never told me these things. She told me almost EVERY day. She knew I gave up things to be with her, and I would not change one minute of the time I spent with her. But to hear her voice after eight months, knowing I had asked God to let her come through... WOW! We serve an amazing God who can do far more than we could ever ask (Ephesians 3:20). I have no doubt that Allie had a hand in orchestrating my "God sighting." Anyone who knows Allie knows that she had a flare for the dramatic. So, for her to talk to me through my radio...I should have expected nothing less from my girl!

At work I emailed the radio station and explained hearing Allie's voice and the fact that she went to be with the Lord in March. I asked if I could receive copies of Allie's message. This was the reply:

It is absolutely an honor to send you both Allie's original call and the produced version that played this morning. She left that message for us in May of 2013. I had it created into the Listener Story just two months ago.

I'm imagining God patiently waiting this morning for the right moment to present you the gift of hearing her voice. He designed the timing just for you!
I'm weeping over the obvious hand of God at work today. Your story has blessed us.
Thank you for being such a great mom to Allie and for your example to all of us. Today you have the gift of her voice...someday you'll see her again.

I know without a doubt that Allie is watching and God is directing my path. I will continue to help others, trust God and share our journey with anyone who needs encouragement. Allie rests with her Lord, and the message she recorded in May of 2013 was sent to me in God's perfect timing. We have an indescribable God who hears us, loves us and wants us to trust Him. I hope that this story encourages you to believe that God CAN work for good in ALL things, even our heartbreak and sorrow.

To God be the glory for allowing Allie to leave me a message of encouragement and love that I can listen to EVERY day!

I love you, Allie! You carried your cross with dignity and grace, and I am so proud of the legacy you have left. I am so very proud to be your mom and Andy's mom. I am beyond blessed. ♥

CHAPTER TWENTY
GRIEF

03/06/2015 Email to Allie Speck's Prayer Warriors
It is unimaginable that Allison has been gone for an
entire year! My heart aches as I miss my beautiful
daughter every day. She can NEVER be replaced,
and the hole in my heart can NEVER be filled with
anything that feels like Allie. But as I looked through
her writings, I found this poem Allie wrote on February 28, 2013, about grief, which begins with a quote
from C. S. Lewis:

Grief feels a lot like fear, in that
with a flip of a switch it seems,
we are suddenly leagues under crushing black,
waiting to wake from a dream.

With our eyes turned down and hearts turned in,
we can be quick to forget
That there still sings on in a world gone dim
a bird which darkness has not abashed yet.

In that melody that pierces through
all clouds, all dark and all pain,
is a feel of what souls know to be true:
all will be gathered home once again.

And across the cold mountains and barren moors
rings softly and strong, this tune:

that there IS a stable and there IS a door
and the one gone before made it through.

How well Allie describes the feelings of grief and
loss! She uses words like *crushing*, *black* and *fear*.
She describes my loss with the perfect words and
images. And yet, she reminds me of the bird singing
a melody of hope that is muted by our suffering, yet
sings on. The bird sings of the same hope that Jesus
provides to all who have died, because He is the One
who went before and made it through.

What peace to know Allie walks with her Lord in
a place with no pain where she can sing and worship God forever! It is so selfish of me to want her
back on this earth. She endured so much pain and
so many trials here, and yet her faith was strong
and certain. I am so proud of the legacy she has left
that has strengthened my faith and encouraged our
family to help others even as we journey through
our own sorrow.

Thank you to all who have loved us, supported us and
sent us cards, messages, hugs and love. To all of you,
I share a quote I found written by Allie. She wrote, "I
hope that when I die, people are so thankful for my
life that they won't be too distressed about my death."
I could not be more thankful for your life! Therefore,
I will do my best to not be distressed today but to celebrate the amazing woman of God you were and the
example you set for the world to see.

I will love you forever.

Until we can be together again,
Mom

CHAPTER TWENTY-ONE
UNTIL WE MEET AGAIN

When a local newspaper reporter was interviewing Allison in 2012, she answered a question this way: "Cancer isn't a death sentence; it is simply a calling to live with more vivacity." What a perfect summation of Allie's life. She lived vibrantly, and her life inspired all those who knew of her to have faith and trust in God in all circumstances. As I prayed and sought God's guidance, I was led to the final chapter of this book. It seems fitting that Allison wrote the first chapter of this book while she was in college, and as I sought God's direction, she provided the last chapter as well in yet another miraculous way.

I have struggled with going through Allison's personal items in her bedroom; I have spent many days lost in memories as I sorted through her dressers and closets. Her bedside stand held lots of diaries, songs written on scraps of paper, passports, postcards of places she had visited, pictures and various keepsakes. I had been through her bedside stand several times, always deciding to keep certain sentimental items and part with others. Some days I could spend hours lost in her memories and sometimes I had to leave her bedroom after a few minutes due to overwhelming emotions.

One day in the midst of the 2021 pandemic, I spent a Saturday in Allie's bedroom, and as I opened the drawer of that bedside stand, like I had done several times before, I found an envelope that I had never seen. The envelope was sealed, and on the outside of the envelope, in Allie's handwriting, it said, "Only open on 07/08/2008," with a heart drawn after the date. Before I share the contents of the letter in the envelope, I need to remind you that Allison was diagnosed with cancer in 2010, so this was written two years before she became sick. All I can say is that Allie was, is, and always will be my inspiration, and her life changed mine and the lives of so many others. Enclosed in that envelope were Allison's words of encouragement for me and for you.

Please honor her life by reading the words that she wrote and consider what she is asking you to do as a challenge to live your life vibrantly for Christ, no matter what trials you face.

> If you are reading this, it means I didn't make it back. It means I left, and, instead of returning to my mortal home, I have returned to my immortal home with my Savior. If you have found this note, I want you to know that I am in a beautiful place and that I will be waiting for you there. I am there with all the ones who have gone before. Picture it. Spending eternity with the One who created you! I want you to know that when your time comes, I am going to do my best to meet you, but do not lose faith. Do not let your relationship with our Lord suffer. This was not a curse or a punishment. It was a blessing and an honor. The Lord has found the grace and mercy to accept me, the mess that I am, into His kingdom. My service on earth is done, but YOURS is not. So, my only wish for you is that you will pray, find your calling and then pray and listen and fulfill that calling with all of your heart.
>
> I am not going to tell you not to be sad or not to cry. I am not going to tell you to be strong. In the Bible, it tells us that there is a time to grieve, and this is one of those times. It is always sad when someone leaves, but I do not want you to dwell on my parting. Remember me, but as a hope, a promise, that there will always be better things to come.
>
> To my family: Words can never describe how much I love you, and it makes me cry to think of leaving you here. You will never know how much you mean to me.
>
> Mom and Dad: THANK YOU for everything you have done. For putting up with a scatterbrained, big dreaming and tempered daughter. Thank you for showing me how to love by expressing and sharing your love. I will never be able to put into words how much I love you both.
>
> Andy: You are an AMAZING boy! Different from the others, and that is GOOD. Don't be afraid to be a little different. Read my journals and diaries when you get a little older. They may teach you some things. Know that God has a plan for YOU! A wonderful plan! Always read

your Bible and pray and learn to listen to Him and not to the world. I love you SO much.

I promise to give kisses to Pappy and Grandpa. Everyone, I WILL SEE YOU AGAIN. This is not an end or a goodbye. It is the beginning of a wonderful life that we will all share one day.

I have completed my journey, but yours is still unfolding. Walk through life boldly, with the assurance that the Lord walks with you. Love wholeheartedly, knowing that you are God's hands and feet. You are the glimpses of heaven others get to see. Laugh hard, knowing each one may be your last, and smile often, but do not be afraid to cry. No one is perfect, so don't pretend to be. Remember that you do not truly live until you live FOR HIM.

Until we meet again,
♥Allie

PHOTOS

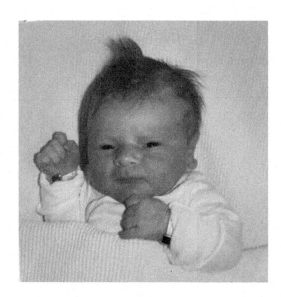

Allison Margaret Speck, born December 28, 1990, weighing 9 pounds, 6 ounces.

1995 Christmas photo, age five.

At home, age seventeen.

On a high school trip to Paris,
summer 2009.

Freshman year at
Messiah College.

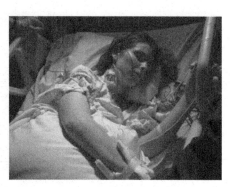

In ICU after her cancer diagnosis, January 2010.

Andy, Zina, Allison and Tom—
SPECK STRONG!

Allison fighting to
Live Strong.

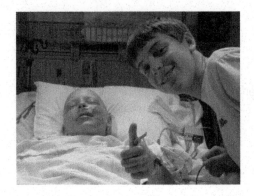

Andy with Allison after the surgery that made her cancer-free!

At home—Carl is gone, and Allie is cancer-free!

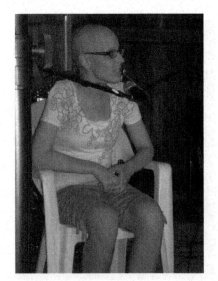

Sharing her testimony.

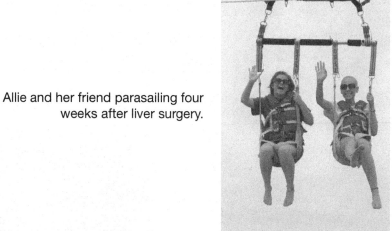

Allie and her friend parasailing four
weeks after liver surgery.

Allie and Andy enjoying time together
at home and being silly.

Allison with her brother, Andy.

Allison and Andy at the softball
fundraiser—TEAM SPECK!

In the Florida Everglades
with Messiah College
group—January 2011.

Snorkeling in Florida with
her Messiah biology class.

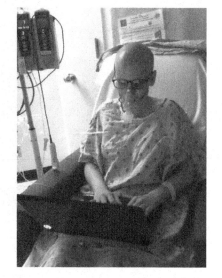

Getting a respiratory treatment
and writing a college paper.
Always hopeful.

At Johns Hopkins receiving
chemo, longing to be outside.

Kenya—Allie
showing the
amazed children
their pictures on
her camera.

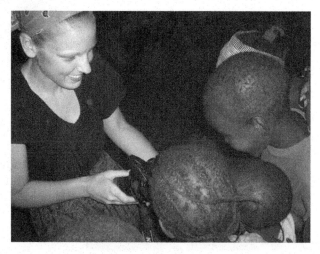

Tom, Allison and Zina
on Allie's wedding day.

A beautiful bride,
June 15, 2013.

Allison, Zina, Andy and
Tom—the last family
picture together at Zina's
50th birthday party,
January 2014.

REFERENCES

Chapter Two
A devotion written by Allison
Michael Tait quote, "Martyr Sayings and Quotes," Wise Sayings, accessed December 2, 2022, https://www.wisesayings.com/martyr-quotes/.

Chapter Six
Allison's Journal, March 8, 2010
Anne Frank, *The Diary of a Young Girl* (New York, New York: Bantam Books, 1993), 171.

Allison's Journal, March 14, 2010
David Campbell, artist, "Better Than I," written by John Bucchino, in *Joseph: King of Dreams,* animated film, 2000, lyrics © EmiApril Music, Inc., Cairon's Land Music Publishing, Dwa Songs.

Chapter Seven
03/25/2010
Kelly McFadden, "God of Miracles," HomeWord Devotional, March 25, 2010, https://www.lightsource.com/devotionals/homeword-with-jim-burns/home-word-mar-25-2010-11627965.html.

04/21/2010
Joel Olsteen, *Your Best Life No*w (New York, New York: Warner Faith, an imprint of Time Warner BookGroup, 2004), 23.

05/06/2010
Corrie ten Boom quote, "Uplifting Corrie ten Boom Quotes," Everyday Power, accessed December 2, 2022, https://everydaypower.com/corrie-ten-boom-quotes/.

Chapter Eight
06/01/2010
Max Lucado, *Grace for the Moment* (Nashville, Tennessee: J. Countryman, a division of Thomas Nelson, Inc., 2000), 174.
06/03/2010
Joyce Meyer, *Be Anxious for Nothin*g (New York, New York: FaithWords, a division of Hachette Book Group USA, 2007), 58.

06/19/2010
Jim Burns, *Addicted to Go*d (Ventura, California: Regal Books, 1999), 16-17.

Chapter Nine
06/29/2010
Joyce Meyer, *New Day, New You* (New York, New York: FaithWords, a division of Hachette Book Group USA, 2007), 181.

Chapter Ten
07/10/2010
Joyce Meyer, *Be Healed in Jesus' Name* (Fenton, Missouri: Life in the Word, Inc., 2000), 59.

07/14/2010
Joyce Meyer, *New Day, New You* (New York, New York: FaithWords, a division of Hachette Book Group USA, 2007), 196.

07/19/2010
Meyer, *New Day, New You,* 200.

07/27/2010
Meyer, *New Day, New You,* 209.

08/09/2010
Allan Seager, "The Window – A Short Story," Woodward English, accessed December 15, 2022, https://www.woodwardenglish.com/the-window-short-story-with-vocabulary/.

08/22/2010
Meyer, *New Day, New You,* 233.

Chapter Eleven
Allison's letter to another young woman, October 2010
Mary Tyler Moore quote, BrainyQuote®, accessed March 3, 2023, https://www.brainyquote.com/quotes/mary_tyler_moore_131899.

11/19/2010
Joyce Meyer, *New Day, New You* (New York, New York: FaithWords, a division of Hachette Book Group USA, 2007), 323.

Ralph Abernathy quote, Brainy Quote®, accessed February 17, 2023, https://www.brainyquote.com/quotes/ralph_abernathy_143902.

12/17/2010
Meyer, *New Day, New You,* 346.

Chapter Twelve
03/27/2011
Bruce Wilkinson, *You Were Born for This* (Colorado Springs, Colorado: Multnomah Books, 2009), 98-100.

Chapter Thirteen
04/02/2011
Matt Redman, artist, "Blessed Be Your Name," *Where Angels Fear to Tread* album, 2002, lyrics © Thank You Music Ltd.

05/08/2011
Chris Tomlin, artist, "Faithful," *And If Our God Is for Us* album, 2010, lyrics © Sweater Weather Music, Worshiptogether.com Songs, Sixsteps Music, Worship Together Music, Sixsteps Songs, Vamos Publishing.

06/02/2011
Jentezen Franklin, *Right People, Right Place, Right Plan* (New Kensington, Pennsylvania: Whitaker House, 2007),75.

07/07/2011
Joyce Meyer, *Never Give Up!* (New York, New York: FaithWords, a division of Hachette Book GroupUSA, 2008), viii-x.

07/18/2011
Franklin, *Right People, Right Place, Right Plan*, 115.

Chapter Fourteen
09/25/2011
Matthew West, artist, "Strong Enough," *The Story of Your Life* album, 2010, lyrics ©Songs Of Southside Independent Music Publishing, Songs For Delaney, Atlas Holdings, Highly Combustible Music, Atlas Music Publishing LLC Ii, One77 Songs, Get Ur Seek On, Anthem Highly Combustible Music.

10/23/2011
Sarah Young, "Jesus Calling: October 14," *Jesus Calling Daily Devotional*, accessed December 30, 2022, https://www.jesuscallingdailydevotional.com/2019/08/jesus-calling-october-14th.html.

11/20/2011
Sarah Young, *Jesus Calling* (Nashville, Tennessee: Thomas Nelson, 2004), 356.

Chapter Fifteen
01/07/2012
Sarah Young, *Jesus Calling* (Nashville, Tennessee: Thomas Nelson, 2004), 8.

01/09/2012
Young, *Jesus Calling*, 11.

02/03/2012
Young, *Jesus Calling*, 36.

03/23/2012
Robert Lowry, "Nothing But the Blood of Jesus," hymn, 1876, public domain.

03/29/2012
Young, *Jesus Calling*, 85.

Chapter Sixteen
04/22/2012
Sarah Young, *Jesus Calling* (Nashville, Tennessee: Thomas Nelson, 2004), 110.

Chapter Seventeen
Allison's Journal, October 23, 2012
Chris Tomlin, artist, "Whom Shall I Fear (God of Angel Armies)," *Burning Light*s album, 2013, lyrics © Capitol Christian Music Group, Capitol CMG Publishing.

Allison's testimony, October 25, 2012
Canon Battersby quote, "Andrew Murray: Note D. – Chapter X: Canon Battersby," Blue Letter Bible, accessed December 30, 2023, https://www.blueletterbible.org/ Comm/murray_andrew/two/two_note_d.cfm.

Allison's Journal, October 30, 2012
Gandalf quote, "Lord of the Rings: The Fellowship of the Rings Quotes to Live By," The Pop Culture Studio, accessed December 30, 2023, https://thepopculture-studio.com/2016/12/31/soapbox-10-lord-of-the-rings-the-fellowship-of-the-ring-quotes-to-live-by/.

03/06/2013
Sarah Young, *Jesus Calling* (Nashville, Tennessee: Thomas Nelson, 2004), 69.

Chapter Eighteen
Allison's Journal, April 25, 2013
Hillsong Worship, artist, "Desert Song," written by Brooke Ligetwood, *This Is Our God* album, 2008, lyrics © Hillsong Music.

01/20/2014
Sarah Young, *Jesus Calling* (Nashville, Tennessee: Thomas Nelson, 2004),7.

Chapter Nineteen
An excerpt from an article
Anna Orso, "Hundreds say final good-bye to Marysville woman, 23, who died from cancer," *Patriot-News*, March 10, 2014,https://www.pennlive.com/mid-state/2014/03/hundreds_say_final_goodbye_to.html.

11/15/2014
Meg Geissinger, "Listener Story," November 5, 2014, radio broadcast, Word FM at 88.1 in Harrisburg, Pennsylvania, FourRivers Community Broadcasting Corp., Harleysville, Pennsylvania.

Chapter Twenty
03/06/2015
C.S. Lewis quote, *A Grief Observed*, "Quotable Quotes," Goodreads, accessed March 1, 2023, https://www.goodreads.com/quotes/649744-no-one-ever-told-me-that-grief-felt-so-like.

ACKNOWLEDGMENT

I need to express my appreciation for the support, love and encouragement that Sandy Martz demonstrated throughout the nine years it has taken to create this story of Allie's faith journey.

On Saturday, November 22, 2014, Sandy came to my home for coffee. I was eight months into grieving the loss of my daughter, Allison. What Sandy did not know is that I had been praying and asking God for guidance to write a book about Allison's journey to share with the world. I had a strong desire to share Allie's testimony but no idea where to begin. During the visit, Sandy shared the following email message that she had received from a woman in her church.

Sandy,
Every morning I spend time reading and studying the Word, and today I felt God urging me to tell you that I had a vision of you helping Zina share Allie's story. You helped Zina compile Allie's work into a publishable book/CD/DVD. Perhaps excerpts of her messages and then Zina's hindsight on how her story is still at work. I am moved by Allison's intro-spection into God's Word, and the way she rejoiced even in what most would consider the darkest hours. Zina's last email message seemed to leave me feeling like she was trying to find a way to continue Allie's work here on earth. Not sure if God has ever laid this on your heart, but for whatever reason, it seems crystal clear to me this morning. You, Zina and Allie's message.

Sandy's email reply:
Oh my, how God works. This idea has been running around in my head and heart for quite a while...maybe a year. Zina expressed a desire to do a Bible study with me, but perhaps what God wants us to do is write one!

In December of 2014, Sandy and I began working together to create the book you now hold in your hands. After our first meeting, as we were deciding how to get started, Sandy sent me this summary of ideas, which showed me how perfect she was to be my helper:

> What is faith? Who is Jesus? What does Scripture say? How do I confess and forgive? Why do I need to pray? Am I called? How does grace work? What is my purpose? These questions have been asked for many years. For Allison Speck, the answer is simple and obvious: LOVE. It will be important to capture the spirit of Allie—love, openness, adventure, joy—no matter what we do.

As the book developed, Sandy constantly provided support, as seen in this message dated 06/25/2017:

> I can only imagine how difficult this journey is for you. You are so brave to open up your soul to the pain. Again, I see how Allie is her mother's daughter! Know that I am praying for you...that this journey will somehow bring you comfort and peace and that it will be the message you want the world to hear.

This has been a nine-year project, and without Sandy's encouragement, this book would not have been possible. I was reminded of her constant encouragement as I read this message from January of 2021 as she organized the email updates into chapters:

> Happy New Year! I will upload these emails and get reorganized and have chapters 9-11 to you soon. It is an honor to be a part of this...I have grown so much in my faith by being part of Allie's journey and yours. Thank you, my friend!

In January of 2022, with the book in a semifinished state, I met Marsha Blessing with Orison Publishers, Inc. Sandy sent me this email about two weeks before our first meeting with Marsha to discuss having the book published.

> You are a very strong lady with a huge heart. It is my prayer that this book journey has been a way for

you to grieve and remember your beautiful daughter.
Her story is God's story, and it is important to share.

And the rest, as they say, is history. I thank God for Sandy's gifts that
assisted me to create Allison's faith story. God knew I needed Sandy for this
project and brought us together. There were months when I was so overwhelmed by emotion that I didn't touch the book. Sandy was always there
when I was ready to pick it back up and start again. Without her patience and
encouragement, this book would not exist. I cannot express how important it
was that God chose Sandy to be my teammate. She is a beautiful soul whose
love of Jesus and Allie shine through in this book.

Sandy, your gifts and your friendship have been a blessing that is worth
more than words can express. I am forever grateful for your faith, your will-
ingness to heed God's call, and your amazing support.